A GUIDE TO
CO-TEACHING

SECOND EDITION

A GUIDE TO CO-TEACHING

Practical Tips for Facilitating Student Learning

SECOND EDITION

RICHARD A. VILLA
JACQUELINE S. THOUSAND
ANN I. NEVIN

A Joint Publication

CORWIN PRESS
A SAGE Company
Thousand Oaks, CA 91320

Council for
Exceptional
Children

For information:

Corwin Press
A SAGE Company
2455 Teller Road
Thousand Oaks, California 91320
www.corwinpress.com

SAGE Ltd.
1 Oliver's Yard
55 City Road
London EC1Y 1SP
United Kingdom

SAGE India Pvt. Ltd.
B 1/I 1 Mohan Cooperative Industrial Area
Mathura Road, New Delhi 110 044
India

SAGE Asia-Pacific Pte. Ltd.
33 Pekin Street #02-01
Far East Square
Singapore 048763

Printed in the United States of America.

Library of Congress Cataloging-in-Publication Data

Villa, Richard A., 1952–
A Guide to co-teaching : practical tips for facilitating student learning / by Richard A. Villa, Jacqueline S. Thousand, Ann I. Nevin. — 2nd ed.
    p. cm.
"A joint publication with the Council for Exceptional Children."
Includes bibliographical references and index.
ISBN 978-1-4129-6058-8 (cloth)
ISBN 978-1-4129-6059-5 (pbk.)
    1. Teaching teams. I. Thousand, Jacqueline S., 1950– II. Nevin, Ann. III. Council for Exceptional Children. IV. Title.

LB1029.T4V55 2008
371.14'8—dc22   2007036517

This book is printed on acid-free paper.

08 09 10 11 12 10 9 8 7 6 5 4 3 2 1

Acquisitions Editor:	Allyson P. Sharp
Editorial Assistant:	David Andrew Gray
Production Editors:	Cassandra Margaret Seibel, Eric Garner
Copy Editor:	Sarah J. Duffy
Typesetter:	C&M Digitals (P) Ltd.
Proofreader:	Charlotte J. Waisner
Indexer:	Ellen Slavitz
Cover Designer:	Michael Dubowe

Contents

Acknowledgments

Corwin Press gratefully acknowledges the contributions of the following individuals:

Diane Baumstark
National Board Certified Teacher
Detroit Public Schools
Detroit, MI

Laura Cumbee
Student Support Teacher
South Central Middle School
Emerson, GA

Jill England
Inclusive Educational Consultant
  (Private)
Ypsilanti, MI

Kathleen M. Falcetta
National Board Certified Teacher
Granville Elementary School
Granville, NY

Mary A. Falvey
Professor
California State University,
  Los Angeles
Los Angeles, CA

Leigh Ann Finley
National Board Certified Teacher
Rosa Parks Elementary School
Lexington, KY

Douglas Fisher
Associate Professor
San Diego State University
San Diego, CA

Nancy K. French
Executive Director, Research
  Professor
The PAR²A Center
University of Colorado, Denver
Denver, CO

Debi Gartland
Professor of Special Education
Towson University
Towson, MD

Jeanine M. Heil
National Board Certified Teacher
State Professional Development
  Coordinator
New Jersey Department of
  Education
Trenton, NJ

Tonia Illig
Special Education Teacher
Tuscarora Elementary School
Addison, NY

Janine Jellander
Assistant Principal
Agoura High School
Agoura Hills, CA

Marguerite Lawler-Rohner
Art Teacher
2004 Maine Teacher of the Year
Cape Elizabeth Middle School
Cape Elizabeth, ME

About the Authors

Ezral Anthony Wallace

Richard A. Villa, EdD, is president of Bayridge Consortium, Inc., in San Diego, California. His primary field of expertise is the development of administrative and instructional support systems for educating all students within general education settings. Dr. Villa is recognized as an educational leader with the commitment and the conceptual, technical, and interpersonal skills to inspire and work collaboratively with others in order to implement current and emerging exemplary educational practices. This has resulted in the inclusion of children with intensive cognitive, physical, and emotional challenges as full members of the general education community in the school districts where he has worked and with which he has consulted. Dr. Villa has been a classroom teacher, special education administrator, pupil personnel services director, and director of instructional services. He has presented at international, national, and state educational conferences and has provided technical assistance to departments of education in the United States, Canada, Vietnam, and Honduras and to university personnel, public school systems, and parent and advocacy organizations. He has authored nine books and more than 100 articles and book chapters. Dr. Villa is known for his enthusiastic, humorous style of presenting.

Jacqueline S. Thousand, PhD, is a professor in the College of Education at California State University, San Marcos, where she teaches special and general education professional preparation and master's-level courses and works with local school districts on school reform initiatives. Before moving to California, she taught at the University of Vermont, where she directed inclusion facilitator and early childhood–special education graduate and postgraduate professional preparation programs and coordinated federal grants, all concerned with the inclusion of students with disabilities in local schools. Dr. Thousand is a nationally known teacher, author, systems change consultant, and disability rights advocate. She has authored numerous books, research articles, and chapters on issues related to differentiated instruction and universal design, collaborative teaming and teaching, creative problem solving, cooperative group learning, organizational change, inclusive education, and positive behavioral supports. She is actively involved in international teacher education endeavors and serves on the editorial boards of several national and international journals.

Ann I. Nevin, PhD, professor emeritus at Arizona State University and a visiting professor at Florida International University, is a scholar and teacher educator who graduated magna cum laude from the University of Minnesota with a PhD in educational psychology. Her doctoral research focused on how teachers and administrators can integrate students with special learning needs. She also earned advanced degrees in special education and educational administration and has participated in the development of innovative teacher education programs since the 1970s. She is an author of books, research articles, and numerous chapters, and her advocacy, research, and teaching include more than 35 years of working with a diverse array of people to help students with disabilities succeed. As Dr. Nevin explains, "I believe that the purpose of education is to empower others." In recognition of her lifetime achievements, Dr. Nevin received the 2007 Landis M. Stetler Award from the Florida Council for Exceptional Children for individuals who have made a significant contribution to the education of children and youth with exceptionalities.

Letter to the Reader

Do you remember when you first knew that you were meant to be a teacher? Ann Nevin remembers being a first grader in a one-room schoolhouse on Troy Road in Schenectady, New York, when the teacher asked her to explain to an older classmate how to do a math problem. Richard Villa reflected daily on the teaching methods used by the nuns during his second-grade year, thinking that if his teachers taught in different ways, more of his classmates would be successful. Jacqueline Thousand similarly recalls playing teacher with her younger brother, who had to endure, from the time Jacqueline was in kindergarten, hours of her replicating what her teacher had done that day in school. We have in common the fact that we all fell in love with teaching at an early age, but we also share the fact that our sole model of teaching was the *lone arranger* model until well into our careers as educators.

Fortunately, we have learned a great deal about co-teaching through our co-teaching experiences with one another and with many other educators over the years. The most important thing that we have learned is that we greatly prefer co-teaching to teaching alone. Why? There are at least three reasons: IQ, CQ, and EQ. Our IQs (intelligence quotients) improve exponentially with a co-teaching partner's knowledge added to the experience, whereas our CQs (creativity quotients) increase because of the synergy that comes with problem solving with another person. Our EQs (emotional quotients) also increase because of the interpersonal interactions that we have with our co-teaching partners. We also have noticed an increased appreciation and valuing of people who have different knowledge bases, opinions, practices, and beliefs. We wrote this book so that you, too, might enjoy more fun, more creativity, more productivity, and more effective outcomes for your students. Each chapter is the result of our co-teaching with each other and collaborating to write this book. Aside from our own personal experiences, there are many other reasons to prefer co-teaching and argue for the use of co-teaching arrangements in all schools. We hope you can add your own reasons as you explore better ways to teach.

New to This Edition

New to the second edition of *A Guide to Co-Teaching: Practical Tips for Facilitating Student Learning* are the following:

- a new chapter on the role of paraprofessionals as co-teachers (Chapter 8)
- updated references throughout the book based on the current collaborative and co-teaching research
- an expanded discussion on Response to Intervention (RTI)
- additional lesson plans in the Resources section
- more detailed descriptions regarding the four approaches to co-teaching reflecting best-practice, teaching in a co-teaching environment, and observing co-taught classes
- an expanded Resources section

A multimedia kit for *A Guide to Co-Teaching: Practical Tips for Facilitating Student Learning* (second edition, ISBN: 978-1-4129-5484-6) will also be available. This interactive resource will include the following:

- a DVD with workshop, classroom implementation, and resource materials presented with an easy-to-navigate menu
- a VHS tape with matching video content
- a detailed Facilitator's Guide connecting core content of the book and video/DVD with extended workshop activities and discussion questions
- a paperback edition of *A Guide to Co-Teaching: Practical Tips for Facilitating Student Learning* (second edition)

PART I

Introduction to Co-Teaching

The first part of this second edition of *A Guide to Co-Teaching*: *Practical Tips for Facilitating Student Learning* comprises three chapters. Chapter 1 introduces you to the basics of co-teaching. It describes what co-teaching is and is not and presents the key elements to co-teaching. Chapter 2 examines the historical origins of and the legal support for co-teaching. It shares the research and documented benefits of co-teaching for students and teachers. Chapter 3 provides an overview of the four approaches to co-teaching—supportive, parallel, complementary, and team teaching. It also introduces three co-teaching teams that are revisited throughout Part II of the book to illustrate the four approaches.

What Is Co-Teaching?

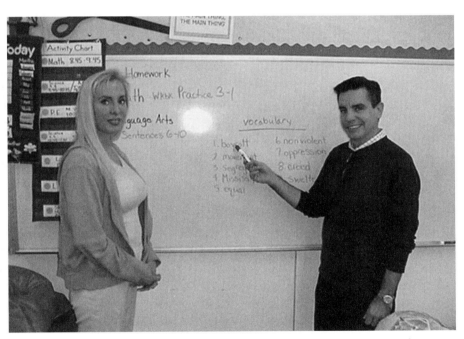

Susan Cushman

Topics Included in This Chapter:

- What co-teaching is not
- What is co-teaching?
- The elements of co-teaching
- Importance of systemic supports

We just found out that we are expected to co-teach. What is co-teaching? What is it not? What elements or variables need to be in place so that we know we are really co-teaching? Is there a process that will help us successfully co-teach? The answers to these questions are discussed in this chapter.

■ WHAT CO-TEACHING IS NOT

Although the concept of co-teaching is not new in education, there are many teaching arrangements that have been promoted in the history of American education that may look like co-teaching. If you are a person who learns from nonexemplars, then the following discussion may be helpful.

Using your own experience as a guide, can you think of nonexemplars for what co-teaching is not? We can think of several from our experience.

Co-teaching is not one person teaching one subject followed by another who teaches a different subject. Many teachers are familiar with this structure if their students travel in groups within a departmentalized administrative framework. In this case, however, the teachers often do not have time to plan or evaluate instruction. Instead, they are responsible for covering the subject matter individually within their curriculum areas (e.g., science), and then the math teachers who are then replaced by the language arts teachers and so on.

Co-teaching is not one person teaching one subject while another person prepares instructional materials at the photocopier in the teachers' workroom or corrects papers in the teachers' lounge. This is a familiar arrangement for those teachers who have the luxury of working with a paraprofessional, a parent, or a community volunteer in the classroom.

Co-teaching is also not occurring when one teacher conducts a lesson and others stand or sit by and watch. This often happens when there are observers or volunteers who come into the classroom with no specific function or assignment.

Co-teaching is not happening when the ideas of one person prevail for what is to be taught or how it will be taught. This type of structure often occurs when a group of would-be co-teachers defer to the eldest, to the person with the most presumed authority, or to the person with the most convincing voice.

Finally, co-teaching is not simply the assignment of someone to act as a tutor. For example, the early schoolmistresses and schoolmasters in one-room schoolhouses were known to use older students to help teach younger students. It is not known to what extent the older student had input in the selection of the lesson, design, and delivery of the lesson, and so on. Many of those student helpers went on to normal schools to become teachers themselves. In this case, the student was an assistant teacher often assigned to teach individuals or groups of pupils while the schoolmistress taught another individual or group.

Instead, the twenty-first-century notion of co-teaching places it within the context of some of the most innovative practices in education. The reassignment of existing personnel to co-teaching teams results in a knowledge and skill exchange among team members and higher teacher-to-student ratios, outcomes that benefit more students than the individual student in need of intensive instructional support. Skrtic (1991) considers this a dynamic structure in which complex work is more likely to be accomplished and novel instruction is are more likely to be crafted to meet individual student needs.

WHAT IS CO-TEACHING? ◼

Co-teaching is two or more people sharing responsibility for teaching some or all of the students assigned to a classroom. It involves the distribution of responsibility among people for planning, instruction, and evaluation for a classroom of students. Another way of saying this is that co-teaching is a fun way for students to learn from two or more people who may have different ways of thinking or teaching. Some people say that co-teaching is a creative way to connect with and support others to help all children learn. Others say that co-teaching is a way to make schools more effective. Co-teaching can be likened to a marriage. Partners must establish trust, develop and work on communication, share the chores, celebrate, work together creatively to overcome the inevitable challenges and problems, and anticipate conflict and handle it in a constructive way.

THE ELEMENTS OF CO-TEACHING ◼

Our definition represents an integration of our firsthand experiences with other school-based teams that actively support students in heterogeneous learning environments (Villa and Thousand 2004) and our reading of the literature on cooperative group learning (Johnson and Johnson 1999), collaboration and consultation (Fishbaugh 1997; Friend and Cook 2002; Hourcade and Bauwens 2002; Idol, Nevin, and Paolucci-Whitcomb 1999), and cooperation (Brandt 1987). Enhancing the initial definition presented in the previous paragraph, a co-teaching team may be defined as two or more people who agree to do the following:

1. Coordinate their work to achieve at least one *common, publicly agreed-on goal*

2. Share a *belief system* that supports the idea that each of the co-teaching team members has unique and needed expertise

3. Demonstrate *parity* by alternatively engaging in the dual roles of teacher and learner, expert and novice, giver and recipient of knowledge or skills

4. Use a *distributed functions theory of leadership* in which the task and relationship functions of the traditional lone teacher are distributed among all co-teaching team members

5. Use a *cooperative process* that includes face-to-face interaction, positive interdependence, interpersonal skills, monitoring co-teacher progress, and individual accountability

Each of these factors is explained in more detail in the following sections.

Common, Publicly Agreed-On Goal

Many co-teachers begin with an agreement to achieve one instructional event, such as a school play, as a team. Their successes then lead them to agree to co-teach instructional thematic units for a six-week period of time, perhaps culminating in a schoolwide celebration. Over time, they see that their unique expertise, skills, and resources are needed for more extensive periods of time, thus leading to more formal co-teaching assignments.

Shared Belief System

Co-teachers agree that not only do they teach more effectively, but their students also learn more effectively. The presence of two or more people with different knowledge, skills, and resources allows the co-teachers to learn from each other. Often individuals decide to become co-teachers as a result of taking inservice courses in specific instructional methods such as cooperative group learning or differentiated instruction. Having a shared language to discuss teaching and learning is both an outcome and a necessary component of co-teaching.

Parity

Parity occurs when co-teachers perceive that their unique contributions and their presence on the team are valued. Treating each member of the co-teaching team with respect is a key to achieving parity. Co-teaching members develop the ability to exchange their ideas and concerns freely, regardless of differences in knowledge, skills, attitudes, or position. Soliciting opinions and being sensitive to the suggestions offered by each co-teacher is especially important when there is a perception of unequal status because of position, training, or experience. Parity between a teacher and a paraprofessional, for example, could be demonstrated when the paraprofessional uses his or her unique knowledge to enhance a lesson developed with the teacher. Reciprocally, the teacher is in an expert role when the paraprofessional imitates a teaching-learning procedure that the teacher has demonstrated. The outcome is that each member of the co-teaching team gives and takes direction for the co-teaching lesson so that the students can achieve the desired benefits.

Distributed Functions Theory of Leadership

Nancy Keller, an experienced co-teacher from Winooski, Vermont, states that as a member of a co-teaching team, "I do everything a normal teacher would do except that now there are two or more people doing it" (personal communication). What is important about this statement is the implicit recognition that co-teachers must agree to redistribute their classroom leadership and decision-making responsibilities among themselves. This phenomenon of role redistribution in which the functions of the traditional lone leader or lone teacher are divided among members of a team is known as the *distributed functions theory of leadership* (Johnson and Johnson 1999). There are functions or jobs that occur before, during, and after each lesson; co-teachers must decide how they will distribute these jobs from one lesson to the next. Some responsibilities must occur daily, others weekly or periodically, and still others once or twice a year. Teachers decide how the content will be presented—for example, one person may teach while the other(s) facilitates follow-up activities, or all members may share in the teaching of the lesson, with clear directions for when and how the teaching will occur. Another decision involves identifying the teacher who communicates with parents and administrators. Some co-teachers decide that co-teaching team members will rotate that responsibility. Still another decision involves describing how co-teaching team members will arrange to share their expertise; some decide to observe one another and practice peer coaching. Remember, when co-teachers make these decisions, they will experience more success if they use the cooperative process described in the next section.

Cooperative Process

There are five elements that facilitate cooperative processes: face-to-face interactions, positive interdependence, interpersonal skills, monitoring co-teacher progress, and individual accountability. Each of the five elements is now defined in more detail.

Face-to-Face Interactions

Face-to-face interaction is an important element for co-teachers as they make several important decisions. Co-teachers need to decide when and how often they will meet as well as how much time meetings will take during school hours. They need to decide when others (e.g., parents, specialists, paraprofessionals, psychologists) should be involved. They also need to develop a system for communicating information when formal meetings are not scheduled (e.g., a communication log book at the teachers' desk, Post-it notes on the bulletin board of the classroom). Face-to-face interactions are necessary for co-teachers to make these and other critical decisions.

Positive Interdependence

Positive interdependence is the heart of co-teaching. It involves the recognition that no one person can effectively respond to the diverse psychological and educational needs of the heterogeneous groups of students found in typical twenty-first-century classrooms. Co-teachers create the feeling that they are equally responsible for the learning of all students to whom they are now assigned and that they can best carry out their responsibilities by pooling their diverse knowledge, skills, and material resources. To establish positive interdependence, co-teachers can establish a common goal, create rewards for their success, and divide the labor of the delivery of instruction.

Interpersonal Skills

Interpersonal skills include the verbal and nonverbal components of trust, trust building, conflict management, and creative problem solving. Such social interaction skills are needed for achieving the distribution of leadership functions and for ensuring that no child is ignored. Individual co-teachers will find that they are functioning at different interpersonal skill levels, depending on their previous training, personality styles, and communication preferences. Effective co-teacher partnerships encourage each member to improve his or her social skills by giving feedback and encouragement to each other.

Monitoring Co-Teacher Progress

Monitoring refers to the process of frequently debriefing about the successes and challenges of co-teaching lessons. Co-teachers check in with each other to determine whether (1) the students are achieving the lesson's learning goals, (2) the co-teachers are using good communication skills with each other, and (3) the learning activities need to be adjusted. Methods of monitoring can range from very simple to more complex. For example, some co-teachers use a checklist on which they each literally check off their agreed-on responsibilities. Some co-teachers set up a brief, 15-minute meeting each day while their students are at recess to discuss the three aspects of monitoring (goals, communication skills, adjusting the activities). Co-teaching team members also can take turns sharing accomplishments, reporting on what each one contributed to the success of the lesson, and making suggestions about what might need to be changed to improve the lesson.

Individual Accountability

Individual accountability is the engine of co-teaching. It is clear that co-teaching is effective based on the actual delivery of skills and knowledge by each co-teacher. Individual accountability is a form of acknowledging the importance of the actions from each co-teacher. Individual accountability in co-teaching involves taking time to assess the individual performance of each partner for one or more of four purposes. One purpose is to increase partners' perceptions of their contributions to the co-teaching endeavor. A second purpose is to provide partners with recognition for their contributions. Yet another is to determine whether any adjustments need to be made in any of the partners' co-teaching roles and actions. A final purpose is to identify when one or more of the partners may need assistance (e.g., some modeling or coaching, access to additional resources or supports) to increase effectiveness in the performance of assigned roles and responsibilities.

You will see how the five elements of the cooperative process operate in varying degrees for each of four approaches to co-teaching—supportive, parallel, complementary, team teaching—that are defined in Chapter 3 and illustrated in Chapters 4 through 7.

■ IMPORTANCE OF SYSTEMIC SUPPORTS

Administrative support is another reason for the successful and beneficial outcomes of co-teaching. Beneficial outcomes increase when the school principal or assistant principal works with the faculty to provide systematic professional development, establish coaching and mentoring opportunities for learning new ways of working together, and arrange master schedules so that co-teachers can teach and plan together. An important aspect of administrative support is realizing that new roles and responsibilities emerge as a result of changing the way that teachers, paraprofessionals, related services personnel, and students work together. Parts II and III of this book illustrate the new roles and relationships that co-teaching affords adults and students. In Part IV, you learn about professional development and logistical and administrative supports that promote systematic development of co-teaching (Chapter 10). Chapters 11 and 12 of Part IV offer guidelines for meshing planning with co-teaching activities and tips for communicating and managing conflict so that you thrive rather than merely survive with your co-teachers. In the Epilogue, you meet two middle level teachers who show how they developed a shared voice through their individual and shared professional development activities. We hope you can agree that, although systemic support is important and valued, your individual action is even more important—you know that you can take action even in the absence of systemic supports. We are always inspired by Margaret Mead (an American anthropologist) who writes, "Never doubt that a small group of thoughtful, committed people can change the world; indeed it's the only thing that ever has." We hope you count yourself as one of those people.

2

Why Co-Teach?

What History, Law, and Research Say

Erin Jarry

Topics Included in This Chapter:

- What are the origins of co-teaching?
- How does federal law support co-teaching?
- What are the benefits of co-teaching?
- What accounts for the benefits of co-teaching?
- Summary

Why do we devote the second chapter of this book to the tracing of the historical origins, the legal rationale, and the documented benefits of co-teaching? As you begin to co-teach, there will be those who ask you to explain or defend your co-teaching practice. This chapter offers you critical information to support your practice of co-teaching and your beliefs and experiences about the benefits of co-teaching. It is also an interesting account for those of you who enjoy knowing the historical context and the rationale for what you do.

■ WHAT ARE THE ORIGINS OF CO-TEACHING?

Do you wonder where the idea of co-teaching originated? The history and evolution of co-teaching in U.S. schools can be traced back to the 1960s, when it was popularized as an example of progressive education. In the 1970s, co-teaching was advanced by legislated school reforms and the need to modify instruction for a more diverse student population. By the 1990s, studies of the effectiveness of school-based collaborative activities, with co-teaching as one example, appeared in the research and practice literature. School personnel began to trust that co-teaching led to results that were valued by students, their teachers, parents, the larger community, and boards of education. For example, in an early synthesis of collaborative consultation research, the emerging data for preschool through high school levels indicated that students with disabilities at all grade levels could be educated effectively in general education environments, making both academic and social gains, when teachers, support personnel, and families collaborated (Villa et al. 1996). Another comprehensive study by Walther-Thomas (1997) evaluated co-teaching models in 23 schools across eight school districts. Outcomes included improved academic and social skills of low-achieving students, improved attitudes and self-concepts reported by students with disabilities, and more positive peer relationships. Students perceived that these improvements were the result of more teacher time and attention. The co-teachers themselves (general and special education teachers) reported professional growth, personal support, and an enhanced sense of community within the general education classrooms. The most frequently mentioned drawback was the lack of staff development to learn how to be more effective co-teachers. They might have benefited from a book like this!

■ HOW DOES FEDERAL LAW SUPPORT CO-TEACHING?

Federal legislative changes, such as those required by the Individuals with Disabilities Education Improvement Act (IDEIA) of 2004 (Pub. L. No. 108-446) and the No Child Left Behind Act of 2001 (NCLB; Pub. L. No. 107-110), have focused attention on students with increasingly diverse learning characteristics achieving high academic performance in general education. To illustrate the recent increase in student diversity, data from the U.S. Department of Education (2006) indicates that the proportion of students with disabilities with primary placements in general education increased from 33% in 1992 to 48.9% in 2006. These proportions can be expected to increase given national trends over the past three decades and IDEIA's requirement to include students with disabilities as full participants in rigorous academic and general education curriculum and assessment. Changing legal requirements and student demographics combine to point to the need for increased collaborative planning and teaching among school personnel who are attempting to comply with legal mandates. Co-teaching is one cost-efficient, legally available supplementary aid and service that can be brought to general education to serve the needs of students with (and without) disabilities through IDEIA.

The stated goal of NCLB is "to close the achievement gap with accountability, flexibility, and choice, so that no child is left behind" (U.S. Department of Education 2007). Like IDEIA, NCLB's requirements for high standards and student performance are intended to foster conditions that lead to better instruction and learning, equality of opportunity to learn, and excellence in performance for all children. The specific conditions fostered by this comprehensive act are (1) the preparation, training, and recruitment of high-quality teachers; (2) language instruction for students with limited English proficiency and children of migrant workers; (3) schools equipped for the twenty-first century; (4) informed parental choice; (5) innovative and research-based instructional programs, particularly in literacy; and (6) accountability for educational outcomes.

A promising NCLB requirement is for all teachers to meet the standards that would certify them as highly qualified. According to NCLB, all teachers must demonstrate subject matter competence in every subject area they teach. Historically, special educators and teachers of students who are learning English often were responsible for teaching the core academic subjects (i.e., language arts, social studies, science, mathematics) to students with special needs or students learning English in separate classrooms. With the advent of NCLB and the 2004 IDEIA clarifications about the *highly qualified* requirements for special educators, it is now established that special educators must have an academic major or advanced degree and pass a competency exam or be deemed competent based on a *high objective uniform state standard of evaluation* (HOUSSE) in each academic subject they teach. In other words, for special educators to continue to teach core academic subjects only to children with disabilities, they now must obtain or demonstrate a rigorous background in each core academic subject taught.

The conference report accompanying the IDEIA amendments (H. Rep. No. 108-77) also clarify that special educators could be considered highly qualified with their state credential or license without the additional subject matter requirements described in the last paragraph if their instruction was consultative in nature and included adjustments to the learning environment, modifications of instructional methods, and curricular adaptations. What this means is that a special educator co-teaching with a general educator can simultaneously address the *highly qualified* dilemma (i.e., by having the general educator be the highly qualified content teacher for students) and achieve the desired

IDEIA outcome of increasing the time that students eligible for special education spend in general education core content area classes. Creating co-teaching partnerships between highly qualified general educators, who have demonstrated subject area expertise, and special educators, who have complementary expertise in specialized content and strategies for adjusting curriculum, instruction, and the learning environment, also increases the probability of implementing the research-based curricular and instructional approaches required by NCLB and the general education early intervention—Response to Intervention (RTI)—approaches forwarded by IDEIA. It should be noted here that experts have identified co-teaching as an important service-delivery approach for improving the conversational and instructional skills of students learning English (Bahamonde and Friend 1999; Mahoney 1997).

The inclusion of students with language and learning differences and their teachers in general education through co-teaching arrangements, combined with the practices required by NCLB and supported by the early intervention thrust of IDEIA, should actually help teachers in today's standards-based classrooms. All students need their teachers to learn and use the most effective teaching strategies, educational materials, and lesson formats currently known. Teachers can accomplish this by exchanging such information and expertise through their co-teaching partnerships.

In summary, at the heart of IDEIA and NCLB is the goal of increasing the achievement for all students—students with and without disabilities, students learning English, students who are considered disadvantaged. Legal trends, then, reinforce the notion that teachers and other school personnel (e.g., special educators, related services personnel such as speech and language therapists, teachers of students learning English, gifted and talented education educators) can no longer be most effective as isolated professionals.

■ WHAT ARE THE BENEFITS OF CO-TEACHING?

What are the documented benefits of co-teaching for teachers, students, and schools? Schwab Learning (2003) studied the impact of collaborative partnerships and co-teaching. At 16 California schools, staff members and parents made a commitment that (1) every child would learn and be successful and (2) every teacher would be responsible for every learner. Teachers, administrators, and support staff creatively arranged for every student to receive blended services from Title I teachers, reading specialists, special educators, paraprofessionals, and so on. Results included decreased referrals to intensive special education services, increased overall student achievement, fewer disruptive problems, less paperwork, increased number of students qualified for gifted and talented education, and decreased referrals for behavioral problems. In addition, teachers reported being happier and not feeling so isolated. New research on the impact of co-teaching and inclusion for students in secondary schools indicates similar results (e.g., Villa et al. 2005).

Studies that document the impact of placement—where a student with disabilities is educated—are important because co-teaching is one method of providing an inclusive educational placement. Blackorby et al. (2005) reported on a comprehensive study of 11,000 students in the United States, which showed that students with disabilities who spend more time in general education classrooms are absent less, perform closer to grade level than their peers in pullout settings, and have higher achievement test scores. Although students with disabilities were found to perform overall more poorly than their same-grade peers without disabilities, overall, the study confirmed that students with disabilities in general education settings academically outperformed their peers who were educated in segregated settings when standards-based assessments were used.

What does the research say about students with a variety of instructional needs in co-teaching classrooms? Co-teaching is effective for students with a variety of instructional needs, including English language learners (Mahoney 1997), those with hearing impairment (Compton et al. 1998; Luckner 1999), those with learning disabilities (Rice and Zigmond 2000; Trent 1998; Welch 2000), high-risk students in a social studies class (Dieker 1998), and students in a language remediation class (Miller, Valasky, and Molloy 1998). To illustrate, Welch showed that students with disabilities and their classmates all made academic gains in reading and spelling on curriculum-based assessments in the co-taught classrooms. Likewise, Caywood and Fordyce (2006) found that when general and special education co-teachers incorporated assistive technology into a restructured curriculum, peer assistance, one-on-one tutorials, cooperative group learning, activity-based instruction with supports through co-teaching, and systematic paraprofessional instruction in differentiated instruction so as to decrease student dependence on paraprofessionals (see Chapter 8), students with autism were successfully included in the co-taught high school language arts classrooms. Mahoney found that in addition to meeting educational needs, "for special education students, being part of the large class meant making new friends" (p. 59).

How is impact measured? According to research published since the first edition of this book, prevalent measures have included teacher grades and student scores on standardized achievement tests in math and reading (e.g., Garrigan and Thousand 2005; Magiera et al. 2005). As pointed out in a comprehensive critique of the literature on collaborative teaching (Thousand, Villa, and Nevin 2007), some researchers have examined the impact of co-teaching on the participating teachers through classroom observations and text analysis of teachers' verbatim responses to questionnaires, surveys, and interviews (e.g., Cramer and Nevin 2006; Magiera et al. 2005; Salazar and Nevin 2005; Santamaria and Thousand 2004). Rarely have researchers or practitioners analyzed the impact of co-teaching on other variables. However, in an earlier study by Vaughn et al. (1998), measures were developed to account for friendships, self-concept, and peer acceptance. Other researchers have documented the actions taken by general and special educators as they implement co-teaching (e.g., Garrigan and Thousand 2005; Magiera et al. 2005). The lack of agreement about what constitutes meaningful impact in co-teaching research may explain some discrepancies in results (e.g., Zigmond 2004). Research results could be improved and be more helpful to teachers if multiple measures were used to examine not only student achievement, but also student social, self-esteem, and friendship development as well as co-teacher's development of instructional competence, confidence, and self-efficacy (Thousand et al. 2007).

■ WHAT ACCOUNTS FOR THE BENEFITS OF CO-TEACHING?

Modeling of Collaborative Skills and Increased Teacher Responsiveness

What can account for positive results such as those described here? First, co-teaching allows students to experience and imitate the cooperative and collaborative skills that teachers show when they co-teach. All students benefit when their teachers share ideas, work cooperatively, and contribute to one another's learning. There is a growing research base to support this claim. As previously suggested, with multiple instructors, there is increased flexibility in grouping and scheduling, thus making it possible for students to experience less wait time for teacher attention and increased time on task, an important factor documented to increase achievement.

Two Heads Are Better Than One

Second, co-teaching provides a greater opportunity to capitalize on the unique, diverse, and specialized knowledge, skills, and instructional approaches of the co-teachers (Bauwens, Hourcade, and Friend 1989; Hourcade and Bauwens 2002). For example, when content area teachers co-teach with education specialists such as special educators, reading specialists, or teachers of English learners, they meld their differing expertise. Stated otherwise, the expertise of the *masters of content*—the content area teachers—are blended with and supported by the expertise of the *masters of access*—the specialists in differentiating instruction. The result is a broader range of students having access to the core curriculum. Further, the higher teacher-to-student ratio that results allows for more immediate and accurate diagnoses of student needs and more active student participation in a variety of learning situations. Students and their teachers say they have more fun and feel better about the work they do while in co-taught classrooms, and principals and superintendents appreciate the increased community spirit at schools where co-teaching prevails.

Opportunities to Use Research-Based Interventions

Third, teachers who co-teach often find that they can structure their classes to more effective use research-proven strategies required of both NCLB and the early intervention proposals of IDEIA. For example, Miller et al. (1998) described how a co-teacher team (a special educator, a general educator, and two paraprofessionals) integrated whole- and small-group instruction, peer teaching, and small cooperative learning groups to provide language remediation activities within the general education curriculum. More recent research shows that differentiated instruction can be employed through co-teaching in classrooms with a wide variety of individual student differences and in multi-cultural and urban elementary, middle, and high schools (see, e.g., Cramer et al. 2006; Garrigan and Thousand 2005; Salazar and Nevin 2005).

Increased Capacity to Problem Solve and Individualize Learning

Fourth, co-teaching and other collaborative activities are vehicles for inventing solutions that traditional bureaucratic school structures have failed to conceptualize. Because team structures bring together people with diverse backgrounds and interests, their shared knowledge and skills often generate novel methods to individualize learning (Nevin et al. 1990; Skrtic 1987). In fact, collaborative co-teaching arrangements can be found in model schools where all students (including students with severe disabilities) are educated in general education classrooms in their neighborhood schools (Villa and Thousand 2004). In interviews with 95 peer collaborators and 96 others who were not collaborating, Pugach and Johnson (1995) found that those in the peer-collaboration group had reduced referral rates to special services, increased confidence in handling classroom problems, increased positive attitudes toward the classroom, and more tolerance toward children with cognitive deficits. Powerful outcomes such as these encourage administrators, advocates, and even state departments of education (Arguelles, Hughes, and Schumm 2000) to adopt cooperative models such as co-teaching for the effective education of students with disabilities.

Empowerment of Co-Teaching Partners

Fifth, teachers view co-teaching as a way to become more empowered. There is evidence to suggest that teachers feel empowered when they can make decisions collaboratively (Duke, Showers, and Imber 1980). They report increases in their skills (Thousand, Nevin, and Fox 1987), and they experience increased higher-level thinking and generate more novel solutions (Thousand et al. 1995). Other valued outcomes include increased attendance and participation at team meetings, persistence in working on difficult tasks, and attainment of the overall team goals (Johnson and Johnson 1997).

Teacher satisfaction in co-teaching arrangements also has been linked to basic needs satisfaction. Glasser (1999) proposed that people choose to do what they do because it satisfies one or more of the five basic human needs: survival, power over or control of one's life, freedom and choice, a sense of belonging, and fun. Specifically, each teacher's potential for survival and power in educating a diverse student body creates opportunities for regular exchange of needed resources, expertise, technical assistance, and professional growth through reciprocal experiences. In co-teaching, teachers experience a sense of belonging and freedom from isolation by having others with whom to share the responsibility for accomplishing the challenging tasks of teaching in classrooms of diverse students. It is fun to problem solve creatively and to engage in stimulating adult dialogue and social interactions.

Based on interviews of co-teachers that we have conducted over the past two decades, co-teaching can help educators meet these five basic needs. For example, teachers report that co-teaching helps meet the need for survival and power because it promotes perspective taking, increases student–teacher direct contact time, and increases the number of students who get the help they need. Co-teaching helps meet the need for freedom and choice because it can facilitate a shared responsibility for all children, provide opportunities to work with a variety of students, and reduce the amount of direct support needed from administrators. Co-teaching helps meet the need for belonging because it can alleviate isolation, motivate a commitment to others, increase social support, and allow for integration of specialists' expertise into the classroom. Co-teaching helps meet the need for fun by enabling creativity, providing someone to laugh and talk with, creating a positive learning environment, and improving staff morale.

■ SUMMARY

In summary, co-teaching may offer the following beneficial outcomes:

1. Students develop better attitudes about themselves, academic improvement, and social skills.

2. Teacher-to-student ratio is increased, leading to better teaching and learning conditions.

3. Teachers are able to use research-proven teaching strategies effectively.

4. A greater sense of community is fostered in the classroom.

5. Co-teachers report professional growth, personal support, and enhanced motivation.

6. Increased job satisfaction can be experienced because needs for survival, power, freedom and choice, a sense of belonging, and fun are met.

Co-teaching provides a vehicle for teachers and students to move from feelings of isolation and alienation to feelings of community and collaboration. In other words, the lone arranger model of teaching is replaced with a co-teacher model. We hope you agree that the effort required by co-teaching is worth it because it results in happier and more successful children as well as more competent and confident faculty.

3

The Day-to-Day Workings of Co-Teaching Teams

Erin Jarry

Topics Included in This Chapter:

- What does co-teaching look like? Four approaches
- Who co-teaches?
- Meet three co-teaching teams
- Roles and responsibilities of co-teaching partners
- Issues to resolve in planning co-teaching lessons
- How do we know that we truly are co-teaching?

What does co-teaching look like? Are there different approaches to co-teaching that we can use? Who co-teaches? Give us an example of an elementary, middle level, and high school co-teaching team. How do we start? What are our roles and responsibilities when we co-teach? What are the roles and responsibilities of our partners? What are some of the issues that we will inevitably encounter? How does the co-teaching team resolve these issues? The answers to these questions are addressed in this chapter and elaborated upon in subsequent chapters.

■ WHAT DOES CO-TEACHING LOOK LIKE? FOUR APPROACHES

Co-teaching has many faces. In a national survey, teachers experienced in meeting the needs of students in a diverse classroom reported that they used four predominant approaches to co-teaching—supportive, parallel, complementary, and team teaching (National Center for Educational Restructuring and Inclusion 1995).

Supportive Co-Teaching

Supportive co-teaching is when one teacher takes the lead instructional role and the other(s) rotates among the students to provide support. The co-teacher(s) taking the supportive role watches or listens as students work together, stepping in to provide one-to-one tutorial assistance when necessary, while the other co-teacher continues to direct the lesson. This is one of the two co-teaching approaches often favored by teachers who are new to co-teaching.

Parallel Co-Teaching

Parallel co-teaching is when two or more people work with different groups of students in different sections of the classroom. Co-teachers may rotate among the groups, and sometimes there may be one group of students that works without a co-teacher for at least part of the time. Teachers new to co-teaching often choose to begin with this approach.

Complementary Co-Teaching

Complementary co-teaching is when co-teachers do something to enhance the instruction provided by the other co-teacher(s). For example, one co-teacher might paraphrase the other's statements or model note-taking skills on a transparency. Sometimes, one of the complementary teaching partners preteaches the small-group social skill roles required for successful cooperative group learning and then monitors as students practice the roles during the lesson taught by the other co-teacher. As co-teachers gain confidence, complementary teaching and team teaching approaches are added to their repertoire.

Team Teaching

Team teaching is when two or more people do what the traditional teacher has always done—plan, teach, assess, and assume responsibility for all of the students in the classroom. Team teachers share the leadership and the responsibilities. Co-teachers who team teach divide the lessons in ways that allow the students to experience each teacher's strengths and expertise. For example, for a lesson on inventions in science, one co-teacher whose interest is history will explain the impact on society. The other co-teacher, whose strengths are more focused on the mechanisms involved, explains how the particular inventions work.

The key to successful team teaching is that co-teachers simultaneously deliver the lessons. Both teachers are comfortable alternately taking the lead and being the supporter. The bottom line and test of a successful team-teaching partnership is that the students view each teacher as knowledgeable and credible.

Under what circumstances can you envision using each of the four co-teaching approaches? Remember that no one approach is better than another, and when deciding which to use, the goal always is to improve the educational outcomes of your students through the selected co-teaching approach. Each approach has value, and each approach has cautions associated with its use. In subsequent chapters of this book, we explain each of the four co-teaching approaches in detail. Many people who are beginning to co-teach start with supportive and parallel co-teaching because these approaches involve less structured coordination with members of the co-teaching team. Gradually, as co-teaching skills and relationships strengthen, co-teachers venture into complementary and team-teaching co-teaching, which require more time, coordination, and trust.

WHO CO-TEACHES? ■

Practically anyone who has an instructional role in a school can co-teach: classroom teachers, paraprofessionals, special and bilingual educators, content specialists such as reading teachers, support personnel such as speech and language therapists and school psychologists, volunteers, and students themselves. Returning to the marriage analogy introduced in Chapter 1, in our international and multicultural world, there are marriages in which partners may be very different or quite similar with regard to the culture, life history, or language that they bring to the marriage.

Which couples might have the more difficult time communicating? We have asked this question numerous times. The majority of people who respond suggest that people who come from different backgrounds or different cultures might have a more difficult time communicating, at least initially. Co-teachers with different content-area expertise, training backgrounds, or teaching experiences—essentially people who come from different cultures and speak different professional languages—may have a more difficult time communicating, at least initially.

As an old saying goes, however, although we get together on the basis of our similarity, we grow because of our differences. As in a successful marriage, once partners figure out and understand each other's perspectives, they are no longer just two individuals, but a union that is fundamentally different from each person alone. Furthermore, because of their differing perspectives, experiences, and skills, they create a synergy that is greater than either of their individual strengths.

Meet Three Co-Teaching Teams

How we co-teach is best explained by examples. In the following vignettes you meet teachers who use the four co-teaching approaches explained in this book. Later, we peek into their classrooms to see how they implement supportive, parallel, complementary, and team-teaching approaches to co-teaching. Table 3.1 introduces you to the teachers at a glance, showing their names, their co-teaching partner(s), and the curriculum areas for which they are responsible.

Table 3.1 Meet the Co-Teaching Team Members

Meet the Partners	Co-Teaching Role(s)	Curriculum Area(s)
Elementary		
Ms. Gilpatrick	First-grade classroom teacher	All core areas
Ms. Hernandez	Paraprofessional	
Ms. Nugent	Speech and language therapist	
Middle Level		
Mr. Silva	Science and math teacher	Science, math, language arts, and social studies
Ms. Spaulding	Special educator	
Ms. Kurtz	Language arts and social studies teacher	
Ms. Olvina	Paraprofessional	
High School		
Mr. Woo	Social studies teacher	Social studies
Mr. Viana	Special educator	

An Elementary Co-Teaching Team

Ms. Gilpatrick is a veteran teacher of 27 years who currently teaches first grade but over the course of her career has taught all of the elementary grades, K through 6, and has had up to 40 students in a class. Currently, she has 24 students in her first-grade classroom, four of whom are eligible for special education and three of whom are new to the United States and are learning English. Three additional students are eligible for Title I supplemental support in literacy. One student is eligible for district Gifted and Talented Education (GATE) services.

Ms. Nugent is the school's speech and language therapist who has a strong interest in the language and literacy development of young learners and emerging readers. She is new to the school district but has seven years of previous experience in elementary school settings. As part of her interview, she was told that the school would be experimenting with a new model of collaboration and co-teaching and that, if she took the job, she would be expected to work closely with the general education teachers and other support personnel. She agreed that this was something she was interested in doing, although it would be a new experience for her. Ms. Nugent has traditionally pulled students out of the classroom to work individually and in small groups for speech and language services.

One of the students eligible for special education has autism and has a part-time paraprofessional, Ms. Hernandez, who spends three hours a day in the classroom during the literacy and mathematics blocks. Ms. Hernandez is a recent high school graduate and is attending the university part time in the evenings. She hopes one day to be a teacher.

A new school year is approaching. The staff had been alerted in the previous year that there were changes on the horizon. They received an article describing the benefits of in-class student supports and the effectiveness of co-teaching arrangements. At the annual district inservice and planning week that precedes the new term, details of the new plan unfold. Teachers, none of whom have had training or experience co-teaching, are introduced to the concept of differentiated instruction for all students. They are told that the district is committed to the education of students of varying learning styles and abilities in general education classrooms, with supports being provided by special education, Title I, bilingual, and GATE personnel.

Ms. Gilpatrick and Ms. Nugent are paired as a teaching team, along with the paraprofessional, Ms. Hernandez. As already noted, neither of the professional educators have had prior experience in collaborative teaching. They admit to one another and Ms. Hernandez that they are looking forward to the year with trepidation. The two teachers have many questions. How will they work with one another on a day-to-day basis? What will the role of the paraprofessional be with the student with autism, other students in the classroom, and the teachers? How will the people who provide extra instruction coordinate their activities (e.g., programs for Title I, bilingual, and GATE)? What administrative support, training, and planning time will be provided?

Ms. Hernandez, too, has questions. What will be her responsibilities in the classroom, and to whom should she report? She learns that at this point, no time has been scheduled into her school day or week to meet with the professional educators to learn how to do her job. She wonders how she will ask questions or give suggestions and ideas. Although she believes she has a lot to contribute, she feels timid about expressing her concerns because she is young and not yet a certified teacher.

A Middle Level Co-Teaching Team

Mr. Silva is a seventh- and eighth-grade science and mathematics teacher who is bilingual in Spanish and English. He is starting his third year of teaching at the same new, relatively large suburban middle school at which he taught his first two years. Mr. Silva teaches five periods—three periods of science and two periods of mathematics.

In Mr. Silva's first year of teaching, Ms. Olvina, a paraprofessional, was assigned to work with him in one of his science and one of his math classes to support the learning of

(Continued)

(Continued)

several students with special needs. In his second year, Ms. Spaulding, a special educator who was hired at the same time as Mr. Silva, co-taught with him for one science class, and Ms. Olvina continued to provide support to students in one of Mr. Silva's other science classes and in one math class. This was Ms. Spaulding's first co-teaching experience. Although she would have preferred to teach language arts and social studies, her content-area strengths, she enjoyed getting to know more about the science curriculum and Mr. Silva's hands-on activities and cooperative learning lessons. Mr. Silva thought that their first co-teaching experience worked relatively well. His big concern was that Ms. Spaulding was often pulled away from their classroom to attend emergency special education–related meetings with the principal, parents, students, and other teachers.

This year, the school has been restructured into transdisciplinary teams, each of which will be jointly responsible for the education of a common group of students. The restructuring is the next step in the district's ongoing journey to de-track students in all of the content areas and to integrate the curriculum and faculty in heterogeneous family-like clusters through 90-minute block-scheduling arrangements. Mr. Silva, Ms. Spaulding, Ms. Olvina, and a language arts and social studies teacher, Ms. Kurtz, have been clustered together as a teaching team. They must organize themselves and their instruction to ensure that the educational needs of all the students under their charge are met. As in all of the clusters, the students are heterogeneously grouped. The class size averages 26, with the natural proportion of students with varying characteristics and needs (e.g., students eligible for GATE services, Title 1, and English language learning support). A slightly disproportionate number of students are eligible for special education in this cluster (i.e., 17% compared with the district average of 13%), which has allowed for a full-time special educator and paraprofessional to be assigned to this team.

To support faculty and staff with the transformation to transdisciplinary teams, the central office has purchased several sets of videotapes and books regarding differentiated instruction, collaborative learning, and co-teaching; these are available in a professional development library that has been set up at each school in the district. In addition, the district's inservice training events are focused expressly on developing teachers' co-teaching skills. Release time and substitutes have been provided so that every team can visit and talk with teachers at other middle schools and high schools who already have some experience with co-teaching and integrated-curriculum teaching arrangements.

A High School Co-Teaching Team

Mr. Woo is a high school social studies teacher who has been teaching for 12 years. He is very concerned with covering the curriculum and addressing state and district social studies curriculum standards. His U.S. history class is a required course for high school graduation, and, although some might consider the content dry or boring, he works hard to develop instruction that will activate student interest. For example, he uses various active learning techniques, such as partner and cooperative group learning, role-plays, and debates, and takes the class on field trips to governmental meetings, including state board of education and county and state legislative meetings. He strongly believes in service learning, a district graduation requirement, so he incorporates into the course syllabus and grading criteria multiple ways in which students can show what they know through community involvement.

Mr. Woo is known throughout the school for his high expectations of every student in his class. Although students consider his course one of the toughest, they routinely report liking it more than most of those they take.

Mr. Viana is a special educator who has been working with students in the eleventh and twelfth grades for 15 years. For the first time, he has been assigned to co-teach, and it happens to be with Mr. Woo. Mr. Viana previously taught students with disabilities in a resource room. Students came to his resource room from their general education classrooms, and he focused on teaching study skills, providing homework support, modifying tests, and remediating deficits. As a high school student, he attended the school where he currently teaches, and he has lived in this community all of his life; he is a varsity track coach and is popular with the students and their parents, as well as with the faculty.

Mr. Woo is open to having another person, such as Mr. Viana, work as a co-teacher in his classroom. He is unsure of how to use this extra adult, however, because his students are so accustomed to supporting one another through the cooperative group learning and other active learning methods that he routinely employs. Mr. Woo is especially committed to student empowerment and worries that the special educator might attempt to hover, provide too much support, or prematurely intervene with unnecessary support in the students' group work or, conversely, that Mr. Viana might have nothing to do.

Mr. Viana is somewhat intimidated by Mr. Woo's reputation and his expertise in both content and instructional methodology. Like Mr. Woo, Mr. Viana is unsure of what his role will or should be in Mr. Woo's government classes.

ROLES AND RESPONSIBILITIES OF CO-TEACHING PARTNERS

There are many actions that co-teachers, including the co-teachers in the three teams just described, take before teaching, during teaching, and then after the lessons are taught. For example, before the lesson begins, co-teachers identify the resources and talents each member brings to the lesson, discuss the content areas that will be co-taught, analyze the students' needs in the class, and decide how student outcomes will be assessed. They often make upfront decisions, such as deciding which member of the co-teaching team will explain their arrangements to administrators and parents.

During teaching, effective co-teachers explain each teaching-team member's role to the students, dynamically communicate with each other to check perceptions, ask questions, reinforce each other, provide feedback, monitor student and teacher performance and compare with goals, and ask if progress is adequate or if improvements are needed. Co-teaching teams can also arrange for a mentor or coach to observe their co-taught lessons and provide feedback to improve instructional outcomes.

After the lesson, effective co-teachers continue to communicate with and coach each other as they collaboratively plan lessons and activities. They might decide to contact parents to support classroom activities, structure a skills-oriented lesson for students whom they have identified as needing extra instruction, or set up a new learning center to respond to students' interests. We believe that celebrating accomplishments, especially the small steps along the way, is an action to include after every lesson.

Some co-teacher actions must take place on a daily basis; others are necessary periodically or only once or twice a year. Examples of daily activities include giving feedback on homework and in-class assignments, recording student progress, and collecting necessary materials for each lesson. An activity that co-teachers should make sure is accomplished each week might be, for example, communicating with administrators and parents. Those activities that occur only periodically include completing formal progress reports, conducting parent-teacher meetings, and structuring teaching assignments for the next year to include co-teaching.

■ ISSUES TO RESOLVE IN PLANNING CO-TEACHING LESSONS

As the previous discussion of actions that co-teachers take before, during, and after co-teaching suggests, there are numerous organizational, logistical, instructional, and communication issues related to role clarification that must be jointly agreed to by members of co-teaching teams. Table 3.2 highlights some of the questions that members of each team must answer for themselves. The sooner that co-teachers have the conversation about these questions, the better. Friend (2008) suggests that *pet peeves* is an important issue that should be discussed right up front. Returning to the marriage analogy, co-teachers might consider this set of conversations and agreements as their prenuptial agreement. It should be noted that answers to the questions change as team members have more experience with one another and with co-teaching. We therefore encourage co-teaching teams to periodically revisit and discuss the items in Table 3.2.

Co-teachers have found it helpful to decide on the actions for which they individually prefer to have input, primary responsibility, secondary responsibility, or equal responsibility. Table 3.3 offers an example of a decision-making matrix that one co-teaching team created to help its members resolve their issues of how to distribute their roles and responsibilities. The matrix is not meant to be an exhaustive list of all of the responsibilities that a co-teaching team might take on, but rather a sampling of role-clarification decisions teachers frequently identify as important. Note that this team created a key that the co-teachers use to indicate the degree to which each team member would take responsibility for a task (i.e., P = primary responsibility, S = secondary responsibility, E = equal responsibility, I = input in the decision making).

You will notice that Table 3.3 includes a subset of the issues that appear in Table 3.2, ones that this particular co-teaching team considered most important to attend to and track on a periodic basis. We encourage readers who are co-teachers or who become co-teachers to dip into the items in Table 3.2 to create their own version of Table 3.3.

Table 3.2   Co-Teaching Issues for Discussion and Planning

Time for Planning

- How much time will we need?
- Where will we find the time that we need?
- How will we use our time together?
- What records can we keep to facilitate our planning?

Instruction

- What content will we include?
- Who will plan for what content?
- How will we share teaching responsibility?
- Who will adapt the curriculum and instructional and assessment procedures for select students?
- What are our strengths in the areas of curriculum, instruction, and assessment?
- What unique talents, interests, life experiences, and cultural heritage(s) does each of us contribute to the instructional process?
- How will the content be presented—will one person teach and the other(s) arrange and facilitate follow-up activities, or will all members share in the teaching of the lesson?
- How will we arrange to share our expertise? How can we arrange to observe one another and practice peer coaching?
- Will we rotate responsibilities?
- How will we assess the effectiveness of our instruction?

Student Behavior

- If we could each have only three class rules, what would those be?
- Who will decide on the disciplinary procedures?
- Who will carry out the disciplinary procedures and deliver the consequences?
- How will we be consistent in dealing with behavior?
- How will we proactively address behavior?

Communication

- What ground rules do we want to establish to govern our communication during planning and while teaching?
- What types and frequency of communication do we each like to have with parents?
- How will we explain this collaborative teaching arrangement to the parents?
- Who will communicate with parents? Will there be shared responsibility for communication with parents of students with identified special education and other specialized needs, or will particular members of the co-teaching team have this responsibility?

(Continued)

Table 3.2 (Continued)

- What types and frequency of communication do we each like to have with students?
- Who will communicate with students?
- How will we ensure regular communication with one another?
- Who will communicate with administrators?

Evaluation

- How will we monitor students' progress?
- How will we assess and grade students' performances?
- Who will evaluate which group of students—do team members collaborate in evaluating all students' performances, or is each team member primarily responsible for evaluating a subset of students?

Logistics

- How will we explain our co-teaching arrangement to the students and convey that we are equals in the classroom?
- How will we refer to each other in front of the students?
- How will teacher space be shared?
- How will the room be arranged?
- Who will complete the paperwork for students identified as eligible for special education?
- How will the decision be made to expand or contract team membership?
- How will a balance of decision-making power be maintained among co-teachers?

■ HOW DO WE KNOW THAT WE TRULY ARE CO-TEACHING?

The issues and responsibilities of co-teachers described in this chapter, as well as the research on collaborative teaming, reveal multiple dimensions of effective co-teaching. To highlight these dimensions, at the end of this book we offer (as Resource M) the Are We Really Co-Teachers? self-assessment, which co-teachers can use to track the progress of their co-teaching relationship. If you wish to preview this tool and use it as an advance organizer of information to come, please do so. You will find an example of its use in Table 11.3 in Chapter 11. If you do not use it as an advanced organizer, know that it provides a nice synthesis of the information you will have read up through Chapter 11. Finally, if you are interested in more details about the research and rationale for co-teaching on which this assessment is based, be sure to revisit Chapter 2.

Table 3.3   Sample Co-Teaching Roles and Responsibilities Matrix

Directions: Insert P, S, E, or I to designate level of responsibility. Plan to revise based on changes in co-teacher skills and/or student needs.				
	Person Responsible			
Responsibilities	*Name*	*Name*	*Name*	*Name*
Develop units, projects, lessons				
Create advance organizers (e.g., concept map, lecture guide)				
Monitor and assess student progress				
Assign grades				
Schedule/facilitate team meetings				
Assign responsibilities to paraprofessionals				
Train paraprofessionals				
Supervise paraprofessionals				
Recruit and train peer tutors				
Facilitate peer support and friendship				
Communicate with administrators				
Communicate with related service providers (e.g., speech)				
Communicate with parents				
Developing Individual Education Programs (IEPs)				
Other:				

CODE KEY: P = Primary responsibility

S = Secondary responsibility

E = Equal responsibility

I = Input in the decision making

PART II

The Four Approaches to Co-Teaching

In Part II the elementary, middle level, and high school co-teaching teams introduced in Chapter 3 are followed as they use each of the four co-teaching approaches. Chapter 4 describes and provides examples of *supportive* co-teaching and features vignettes of each of the three teams implementing the supportive approach across various curriculum areas. The chapter ends by analyzing how the cooperative process—face-to-face interaction, positive interdependence, interpersonal skills, monitoring, and accountability—was used by each of the three teams and by answering frequently asked questions about supportive co-teaching. Chapter 5 follows the same format as Chapter 4, but focuses on *parallel* co-teaching, highlighting seven variations of parallel co-teaching. Chapter 6 is devoted to *complementary* co-teaching, and Chapter 7 to the *team-teaching* co-teaching approach.

As you read about each of the four co-teaching approaches in the following chapters, you may find it helpful to use the advance organizer presented in Figure II.1 to compare and contrast what you are learning about the approaches. Can you detect the key features (i.e., differences) of each? What are some cautions for using each of the approaches? Also, as you read the chapters, you may discern that there are some common features or similarities across the four approaches that can be noted in the top section of Figure II.1. If using an advance organizer helps you organize information and solidify your learning, enjoy using this learning tool as you study the following chapters.

Figure II.I Similarities and Differences of Supportive, Parallel, Complementary, and Team-Teaching Approaches

Similarities Among the *Four Co-Teaching Approaches*		

Supportive Differences	*Parallel Differences*	*Complementary Differences*	*Team-Teaching Differences*
Supportive Cautions	*Parallel Cautions*	*Complementary Cautions*	*Team-Teaching Cautions*

The Supportive Co-Teaching Approach

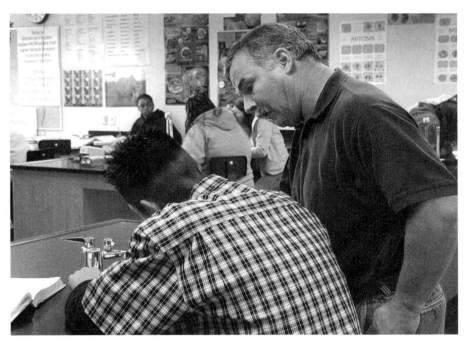

Jacqueline S. Thousand

Topics Included in This Chapter:

- Vignettes: Supportive co-teaching
- Analyzing the cooperative process in the supportive co-teaching vignettes
- Frequently asked questions

With supportive co-teaching, one teacher is assigned primary responsibility for designing and delivering a lesson, and the other member(s) of the team provides support to some or all of the students in the class. Basically, one teacher leads and the other supports. Said another way, one teacher functions as the sage on the stage, and the other functions as the guide on the side. It should be noted that who is in the lead and who is supporting does not need to remain the same throughout the lesson. For example, a general education classroom teacher may take primary responsibility for teaching a lesson, while a supporting co-teacher (e.g., special educator, speech and language therapist, paraprofessional, teacher of students who are learning English) circulates among the students monitoring academic and social progress, promoting peer interactions, or providing task assistance when needed. Supportive co-teaching between a special and a general educator also might involve the supporting special educator reviewing a test-taking strategy with a student prior to a test, giving specific feedback to a student about his or her use of social skills in the general education classroom, or teaching a student how to use an augmentative communication system that is being used with classmates in the classroom. Still another example might involve co-teaching with someone who is expert in teaching students who are learning English. While the classroom teacher models a written language pattern orally and in writing (e.g., on an overhead projector, on a whiteboard, on easel paper), the co-teacher circulates around the classroom to check for the English language learners' understanding of the pattern and the associated writing assignment.

■ VIGNETTES: SUPPORTIVE CO-TEACHING

If you peek into the classrooms of the co-teaching teams described in Chapter 3, you might see and hear the activities summarized in Table 4.1.

The following vignettes illustrate how supportive teaching might play out in elementary, middle level, and high school classrooms as co-teachers conduct standards-based lessons.

An Elementary Co-Teaching Team

During math, Ms. Gilpatrick (the classroom teacher) and Ms. Hernandez (the paraprofessional) are in the classroom. Ms. Gilpatrick begins by leading a large-group activity in which she checks students' understanding of number recognition for the numbers 0 through 9 with whole-class choral response and by calling on individual students. Following this activity, Ms. Gilpatrick checks for understanding of the concept of more because this is a vocabulary term used when describing the addition process (e.g., What does 2 oranges plus 1 more orange equal?). She then models several examples of single-digit addition, using real objects to match written numbers to show the concept as well as the operation of addition.

Students' desks are arranged so that every student has a partner. The co-teachers distribute to each pair a small container of colored, interconnecting blocks, which the students can use to solve several addition problems that have been written on the board. Each student also has a number line taped to the top of his or her desk. Students have had previous instruction and practice on how to use the number line and blocks to arrive at a total. After a short period, partner pairs are called up to the front of the room to show how they arrived at their solution. There are colored number lines and translucent two-dimensional blocks on the overhead that the students can use as they give their answer to show the thinking processes by which they arrived at their conclusion. The other students in the class also have attempted to solve the problem and have previously written the answers on their individual whiteboards, which they hold up after each pair's demonstration.

Once students have completed the guided practice, they are given a choice of three pages that contain problems they are to solve independent of the teacher's instruction: one with four problems, one with six, and one with ten. All pairs are to complete a minimum of eight problems, but any pair can do all three teacher-designed worksheets for additional practice. Students are instructed to be prepared to explain how they arrived at each answer to the teacher, the paraprofessional, another classmate, or the entire class.

Ms. Hernandez and Ms. Gilpatrick have had no time to plan. Ms. Hernandez arrives just as Ms. Gilpatrick finishes modeling the activity for the large-group instruction. Ms. Hernandez walks around checking students as they use the manipulatives and write their answers on the whiteboards. She continues to circulate around the room, providing support as needed during the time that partners complete the worksheets. She ensures that students with special needs, those who receive tutorials from the Title I aides, and those who are learning English can follow the instructions and perform the addition procedures. She pays particular attention to Elisa, the student with autism, but observes her from a distance rather than sitting by her and thus fostering codependence. In addition to asking questions of other partner pairs, Ms. Hernandez periodically asks Elisa or her partner to show how she arrived at the answer to one of the problems.

A Middle Level Co-Teaching Team

Mr. Silva (the science and math teacher) wants students to compare and contrast animals that reside in various environments (e.g., ocean, desert, mountain) and learn about environmental damage or threats to each of these ecosystems. Working in groups (i.e., five groups of four and two groups of three), students are asked to create two visual representations: one will depict the similarities and differences between the environments, and the other will represent some of the environmental concerns for each of the three ecosystems.

At this time, Ms. Spaulding (the special educator) is in the science class with Mr. Silva, and Ms. Olvina (the paraprofessional) is with Ms. Kurtz in her language arts class. Mr. Silva and Ms. Spaulding previously collaborated and assigned students to heterogeneous groups, avoiding best friends and worst enemies in the groups and assuring diversity across gender, race, language, and ability. Some students use Venn diagrams, others create tables, others draw or cut out pictures or use other materials to represent the ecosystems graphically. Mr. Silva teaches, checks understanding, monitors group interactions, and answers students' questions. Ms. Spaulding quietly observes various students to help Mr. Silva plan for future modifications, roles within groups, and future grouping suggestions. Ms. Spaulding also

(Continued)

(Continued)

collects data on students' level of participation in their groups and demonstration of social skills (e.g., turn taking).

After the lesson, Mr. Silva and Ms. Spaulding meet briefly to discuss what occurred in this lesson. They take turns describing what went well, what they would change the next time they teach this unit, and to what extent they fulfilled their agreed-on tasks. They also take time to outline their plan for the next unit of study (specifically, group composition, content modifications, social skills to teach and monitor). They agree to share their results and plans with the other members of the middle level teaching team, Ms. Olvina and Ms. Kurtz.

A High School Co-Teaching Team

During a common planning period the week before they are scheduled to co-teach five classes, Mr. Woo (the social studies teacher) and Mr. Viana (the special educator) met to address several issues. They used the matrix shown in Table 3.3 (in Chapter 3) to help determine the appropriate goals and activities for each of the classes, clarified Mr. Viana's responsibilities, and decided how to group students for the various learning activities. Based on his knowledge of students' strengths and needs, Mr. Viana suggested which students should work together, indicating specific roles within the cooperative learning groups that some learners might take (e.g., a student who is not reading at grade level could function as a timekeeper). Mr. Woo explained that if students have questions, he wanted Mr. Viana to encourage them to ask one another to solve the problem before asking an adult for help. Mr. Woo identified four of the eight groups he wanted Mr. Viana to monitor for academic work, role performance, and use of social skills.

On the following Monday, Mr. Woo and Mr. Viana check in with each other briefly before the class begins. Mr. Woo begins the lesson by introducing the activities, explaining the academic and social (i.e., reaching consensus, listening, equal participation) objectives, and telling the students that they will have a common goal. He describes the individual roles (e.g., timekeeper, recorder) within the groups, notes that each student will be held accountable, and outlines the criteria for success. The class is divided into thirds. Each third is further divided into groups of three.

The co-teachers make an on-the-spot adjustment for one group by assigning a fourth member because Mr. Viana believes one student in that particular group will benefit from additional peer support and modeling. Each third of the class is to learn and be prepared to teach about one of the three branches of government (i.e., legislative, judicial, and executive). Students within each "expert group" will become experts on their branch of government through a variety of means, such as textbooks, news magazines, and other printed materials; Internet sites; videos; and interviews. In two days' time, after students have become experts in their areas, Mr. Woo will reconfigure the groups to include an expert with knowledge of each of the three branches of government. This will allow students to jigsaw their information, teach one another, and then apply their collective knowledge to determine the role of each branch of government when given a set of scenarios (e.g., declaring war, how a bill becomes a law, raising taxes, determining guilt, sentencing, the possibility of pardoning those who violate the law).

Mr. Viana passes out the task instructions, a list of resources, and some materials to each of the expert groups. As students get organized to begin studying their respective branch of government, Mr. Woo and Mr. Viana move among the groups to monitor student understanding of the assignment, role performance, and use of small-group social skills. Mr. Woo monitors the time and gives the class a five-minute warning that the period is almost over so that groups can wrap up.

Table 4.1   The Many Faces of Co-Teaching: Co-Teaching Teams' Use of Supportive Co-Teaching

Meet the Co-Teachers	Co-Teacher Roles	Curriculum Area(s)	Teaching Learning Strategies	Planning Method
Elementary				
Ms. Gilpatrick, classroom teacher	Leads the lesson	Mathematics	Manipulative and number line, partner learning	On-the-spot planning
Ms. Hernandez, paraprofessional	Circulates to check understanding and task completion			
Middle Level				
Mr. Silva, science and math teacher	Leads the lesson	Science	Cooperative group learning, multiage grouping	Reflective guided planning
Ms. Spaulding, special educator	Observes to plan for future groupings			
High School				
Mr. Woo, social studies teacher	Leads the lesson	Social studies	Cooperative group learning (jigsaw with expert groups), authentic assessment, computer technology	Preplanning
Mr. Viana, special educator	Suggests student group membership, encourages students to use problem-solving methods, passes out papers, and, along with the teacher, monitors the group interactions			

■ ANALYZING THE COOPERATIVE PROCESS IN THE SUPPORTIVE CO-TEACHING VIGNETTES

The cooperative process differed when supportive co-teaching was applied at three levels—elementary, middle level, and high school. The five elements of the cooperative process are face-to-face interaction, positive interdependence, interpersonal skills, monitoring, and accountability.

All three supportive co-teaching vignettes show that the co-teachers were face-to-face during the teaching of the lesson, while both the middle level and high school supportive co-teaching teams also had face-to-face time after the lesson. The high school supportive co-teaching team met before, during, and after the lesson. Positive interdependence is evident in all three vignettes; each supportive co-teaching team had a division of labor (although the elementary team had an unspecified agreement). Interpersonal communication skills were evident in the high school supportive co-teaching vignette, especially when Mr. Woo communicated how he wanted Mr. Viana to interact with the students. Monitoring occurred on the spot for all three supportive co-teaching teams. Both the middle level and high school co-teachers included a debriefing time to discuss what went well, what needed to be done differently, and what would be done next time. Accountability was implied in the vignettes, with the high school co-teachers being more articulate about how they held each other accountable for the tasks they agreed to achieve.

We advocate that supportive co-teachers incorporate as many elements of the cooperative process as possible. This happens when co-teachers experience frequent face-to-face interactions, realize that they are positively interdependent, make opportunities to practice their social interpersonal skills, monitor how well they work together, and hold each other accountable for the tasks they set for each other. The research is clear that when all five elements are present, the quality of the co-teaching relationship improves. And when the quality of the co-teaching relationship improves, the outcomes in terms of student achievement are positively affected.

FREQUENTLY ASKED QUESTIONS

We have interviewed many co-teachers, students, parents, administrators, and advocates on the use of co-teaching arrangements in the classroom. The following questions are those asked most frequently when people first learn about the supportive co-teaching approach.

1. I am concerned about co-teaching with a paraprofessional who is not well trained to work with students with special needs. Isn't it a problem that people with the least amount of preparation are assigned to support children who have the most intensive needs?

Systems must be in place to ensure that paraprofessionals receive the training, supervision, and coaching necessary to meet the needs of children with special needs in an inclusive setting. There are several ways to address a lack of training. For example, the paraprofessional and his or her co-teacher could visit a paraprofessional who has received training to work with students with special needs. Or the special educator for the school could visit the co-teaching team to show both co-teachers strategies and techniques to use with not only the students who have special needs but also other students who are at risk for school failure. The paraprofessional could participate in training programs specially designed to differentiate instruction, such as the one developed by Doyle (2002). The paraprofessional could then share the new skills with the co-teacher. The job definition for the paraprofessional must include guidelines for training and support in differentiated instructional techniques. Roles and responsibilities as well as suggestions for co-teaching with a paraprofessional are further discussed in Chapter 8.

2. What is the most difficult problem to overcome when working with a paraprofessional and a classroom teacher using the supportive co-teaching approach?

No matter whether it is a classroom teacher, a special educator, or a paraprofessional who is playing the supportive role, the supportive co-teacher must not become "Velcro-ed" to individual students. He or she should not function as a hovercraft vehicle blocking a student's interactions with other students. Hovering can stigmatize the student. It also runs the risk of stigmatizing a co-teaching team member who works predominantly with one student. Students from preschool through high school explain that if a teacher is glued to a particular student, the teacher becomes a barrier to other children's desire to interact socially with that child. Not only that, students often raise this question: "If the special teacher helps me, will people think that I'm a special education student?" (Villa and Thousand 2002, 304). An important component of successful supportive co-teaching is ensuring that students perceive each member of the co-teaching team (special educator, regular educator, or paraprofessional) as their teacher.

We hope you agree that the vignettes featured in this chapter show how the supportive co-teaching teams organized their interaction so that students perceived each of the co-teachers as their teacher. Administratively, to avoid stigmatization further, the job definition for paraprofessionals hired to work with individual children with special needs can include responsibilities for all the children in the classroom.

3. Does supportive co-teaching always occur inside the classroom?

We suggest that the place co-teachers should work most often is the classroom where all the children meet. Occasionally, however, co-teachers may work for a short period with an individual child or a group of children outside the classroom, in the library, or in the computer lab. If you choose to use this approach, we advise that, to avoid stigmatization of students or instructional personnel, the same students or member of the co-teaching team should not always be the ones leaving the general education classroom.

(Continued)

(Continued)

4. I'm a professional special educator who has just been assigned to work as a co-teacher with a general educator. How do I avoid acting in a subsidiary role by just walking around and helping the students?

Are you worried that you'll go into a classroom and just drift around, working with one or two students, waiting and watching the flow of the classroom teacher's lesson? This indicates your concern that all of the skills you've acquired will not necessarily be used. One way to address this concern is for co-teachers to learn to use the other approaches to co-teaching described in subsequent chapters of this book. Then you and your co-teacher can agree to a goal that will help your relationship capitalize on all four approaches instead of relying on only one. The benefits of the increased awareness that all educators bring to their co-teaching partnerships far outweigh the temporary discomfort that occurs when a team is just beginning to use the supportive co-teaching approach. It is not uncommon for special educators and support personnel to discover, when they enter a general education classroom, that it is a very different world from the one-on-one or small-group instruction typically found in resource rooms or self-contained classrooms. With a supportive co-teaching arrangement, both co-teachers have the chance to become familiar with each other's curriculum and teaching techniques. The goal is to nurture and enrich the relationship so that both co-teachers can experience an evolution of their skills. Remember that this involves taking time to talk, establish trust, and communicate. When you expand your co-teaching repertoire beyond just the supportive approach, you can avoid the resentment that some special educators have toward classroom teachers for not using their expertise. Similarly, when classroom teachers expand their repertoires, they can avoid the resentment that some classroom teachers have when they feel they are left with the majority of the responsibility for planning, teaching, and assessing the learners in the classroom.

The Parallel
Co-Teaching
Approach

Erin Jarry

Topics Included in This Chapter:

- Vignettes: Parallel co-teaching
- Analyzing the cooperative process in the parallel co-teaching vignettes
- Frequently asked questions

Parallel co-teaching is when co-teachers instruct different groups of students at the same time in the classroom. A benefit of parallel co-teaching is that it decreases the student-to-teacher ratio, allowing for increased individualization to meet students' needs. Parallel co-teachers may teach the same or different content. They may split the class evenly among themselves, or one person may work with the majority of the students while another works with a small subgroup of the class. One variation on parallel co-teaching, often referred to as *station teaching*, involves one group of students working with one co-teacher, another group working with a classroom support person (e.g., special educator, paraprofessional), perhaps a third group working with yet another support person, and a fourth group working independently. Over the course of one or several class periods, students rotate among all of the stations and their respective co-teachers. In summary, parallel co-teaching has many faces. Table 5.1 briefly describes several variations of parallel co-teaching.

■ VIGNETTES: PARALLEL CO-TEACHING

Let's once again peek into the classrooms of our elementary, middle level, and high school teams as they teach standards-based lessons. Table 5.2 summarizes the variations of parallel co-teaching and the diverse instructional methods used by these teams.

Table 5.1   Examples of Parallel Co-Teaching Structures With Co-Teachers Teaching the Same or Different Content

---

Split Class. Each co-teacher is responsible for a particular group of students, monitoring understanding of a lesson, providing guided instruction, or reteaching the group, if necessary.

Station Teaching or Learning Centers. Each co-teacher is responsible for assembling, guiding, and monitoring one or more learning centers or stations.

Co-Teachers Rotate. The co-teachers rotate among two or more groups of students, with each co-teacher teaching a different component of the lesson. This is similar to station teaching or learning centers, except that in this case the teachers rotate from group to group rather than having groups of students rotate from station to station.

Cooperative Group Monitoring. Each co-teacher takes responsibility for monitoring and providing feedback and assistance to a given number of cooperative groups of students.

Experiment or Lab Monitoring. Each co-teacher monitors and assists a given number of laboratory groups, providing guided instruction to groups that require additional support.

Learning Style Focus. One co-teacher works with a group of students using primarily visual strategies, another co-teacher works with a group using primarily auditory strategies, and yet another may work with a group using kinesthetic strategies.

Supplementary Instruction. One co-teacher works with the rest of the class on a concept or assignment, skill, or learning strategy. The other co-teacher (a) provides extra guidance on the concept or assignment to students who are self-identified or teacher-identified as needing extra assistance, (b) instructs students to apply or generalize the skill to a relevant community environment, (c) provides a targeted group of students with guided practice in how to apply the learning strategy to the content being addressed, or (d) provides enrichment activities.

Table 5.2 The Many Faces of Co-Teaching: Co-Teaching Teams' Use of Parallel Co-Teaching

Meet the Co-Teachers	Co-Teacher Roles	Curriculum Area(s)	Teaching Learning Strategies	Planning Method
Elementary				
Ms. Gilpatrick, classroom teacher	Station teaching—the three co-teachers each guide one station	Literacy	Station teaching	Preplanning and postinstruction debriefing
Ms. Hernandez, paraprofessional	One independent station		Visual and kinesthetic demonstration	On-the-spot briefing of paraprofessional
Ms. Nugent, speech and language therapist			Modeling and guided practice	
			Motivation through friendly compete *with the teacher* competition and choice in practice options	
Middle Level				
Mr. Silva, science and math teacher	Split class	Interdisciplinary, thematic unit integrating language arts, math, science, and social studies	Interdisciplinary, thematic instruction	Preplanning
Ms. Spaulding, special educator	Same content		Differentiation of materials	
Ms. Kurtz, language arts and social studies teacher	Alternating instructors		Frequent monitoring and adjusting	
Ms. Olvina, paraprofessional				
High School				
Mr. Woo, social studies teacher	Large- and small-group split class	Social studies test preparation	Individualized and differentiated direct instruction	On-the-spot division of labor
Mr. Viana, special educator	Different content	Assistance in planning for a major homework assignment	Guided assistance	Individual planning
			Self-correction	Check-in prior to lesson delivery

An Elementary Co-Teaching Team

Ms. Gilpatrick (the classroom teacher) and Ms. Nugent (the speech and language therapist) now meet weekly to plan. They are trying out parallel co-teaching, in which each works with different groups of children at the same time. In preparing to introduce the class to compound words, they created materials the week before.

Ms. Hernandez (the paraprofessional assigned part time to their classroom) arrives. Ms. Nugent briefs her while Ms. Gilpatrick takes attendance, collects the milk money, and gives the daily announcements. Ms. Nugent quickly explains the goals of the week and how Ms. Hernandez will support students at the station to which she has been assigned, as well as how each of the other three stations will work.

To introduce compound words, Ms. Gilpatrick and Ms. Nugent stand at the front of the room, each holding a large piece of construction paper with a word written on it (Ms. Gilpatrick has the word cup; Ms. Nugent has the word cake). Ms. Gilpatrick has students identify the word she is holding with a choral response. Ms. Nugent does the same for her word. Next the two teachers move together to form a single compound word (cupcake). Ms. Gilpatrick and Ms. Nugent ask the students, through choral response, to identify each of the words they are holding up on construction paper and then to identify the compound word formed when they are joined. The two teachers repeat this modeling for an additional six compound words. Next, Ms. Gilpatrick assigns students to one of four stations through which all students will rotate over the course of the morning.

Ms. Hernandez is at the first station. She has several identical piles of simple words (written on flash cards) that can be combined to make compound words. Ms. Hernandez pairs the students, gives each pair one pile of words, and instructs students to sit together on the neighboring rug area to create from their flash cards as many compound words as they can in five minutes. She first models two examples using her pile of words. Then she sets a timer and challenges pairs to beat her in creating compound words that make sense by recording their words on a teacher-made word chart with 10 entry spaces per side. As the students work, Ms. Hernandez closely observes and reinforces their creation of compound words; intervenes with a question, if a word is not a "real" word; and provides guided support to any pairs who need it. The student with autism is strategically paired with a classmate who is especially skilled at imitating the teachers' models and guiding classmates to complete the task. Ms. Hernandez gives extra attention to this partnership to ensure that they are able to create words, but she does not intervene unless it is clear that they need support.

When the timer goes off, pairs share their words. Ms. Hernandez writes them on chart paper, putting check marks next to compound words that more than one group created. Students initial the chart while she congratulates them on beating her in the number and creativity of their words. If there is time, the students are given some new flash cards with additional words to work with to add even more compound words to their list.

With each new group, Ms. Hernandez provides the same instructions so that the groups will be motivated to compete with the teacher. The station proves highly motivating to the students. In the afternoon, Ms. Gilpatrick shares the composite list of words with the whole class (Ms. Hernandez is now working with another teacher) so that students can celebrate their competence in creating compound words.

Ms. Nugent is at the second station. She and the students are seated around a kidney-shaped table, with Ms. Nugent on one side and the students sitting in a semicircle on the other side, allowing Ms. Nugent to observe and interact easily with all students in the group. Each student is given a piece of paper that contains a word bank from which to combine words to make a compound word that makes sense in one of several sentences also written on the page. Ms. Nugent has the students rotate reading each of the sentences prior to looking at the word bank so that they understand the context of the activity. She then models a couple examples with a different word bank and different sentences on the large whiteboard behind her that is in full view of all students in her group. Moving to papers she handed out, she ensures that students complete the exercise by providing guided practice until she observes that each student can work independently. She has a second and third practice page ready for students who move more quickly so that they can practice independently.

Ms. Nugent keeps data on each of the groups that rotate through her station, noting the level of support each student needs. She shares these data with Ms. Gilpatrick at their next planning meeting.

Ms. Gilpatrick is seated at the third station on a carpeted area with a large whiteboard, a dozen erasable markers, paper, and several big books, each of which includes compound words. On the left and right sides of the whiteboard, she has listed several words that can be combined to make compound words. She models how to connect words on the left and right to create words that make sense and has individual students come forward to model connecting a few more. She then forms pairs and has each pair select and scan one big book, underlining with erasable markers all of the compound words they can find. She debriefs by having pairs show and tell their compound words to other group members. Next, she gives each student a piece of paper with the two ends of the paper folded inward to create a kind of door; when opened, the door reveals the inside of the paper. She has created samples with a single word on each flap, and together the two words form a compound word; when the flaps are opened, the two separate words appear inside, melded into the single compound word. Ms. Gilpatrick guides students through the process of creating this visual representation for the first word that each pair found in their big books. She then challenges the students to go through and create opening doors for the remaining words in their big books until the time is up. Students leave with their compound-word creations to take home and share with their parents.

At the fourth station, set up as an independent practice station, students work in pairs at one of five classroom computers to create sentences that include compound words the students formulated at previous stations. The first students at this station have not yet been to another station, so they are given a list of words they can combine and use in a sentence. Each pair is to create at least three sentences, each with a different compound word. Pairs earn bonus points that can be traded for free time on Friday if they create more than three correct sentences with compound words. At this station, students also practice their technology skills by pulling up the program they are to use to compose the sentences, putting their names at the top of the document, spell-checking the document, saving the document to the desktop, printing the document, and placing it into the teacher inbox. This procedure for producing work at the computer has been rehearsed as a classroom routine. This fourth station allows students to demonstrate independence while doing a meaningful and relevant language arts task.

(Continued)

(Continued)

Students at the fourth station know they are free to go to any of the adults in the room for assistance after they have consulted their peers who are working at other computers. The co-teachers in this class want students to rely on their peers to help them problem solve their own issues, and this task provides a natural opportunity for them to do so.

All students rotate through all four stations. The task at each station takes approximately 15 minutes. At this point in the year, students are quite capable of actively engaging for this period of time, with teacher support and intervention as needed.

A Middle Level Co-Teaching Team

The middle school has embarked on a journey to develop transdisciplinary teaming and curriculum integration. This team—Mr. Silva (the math and science teacher), Ms. Spaulding (the special educator), Ms. Kurtz (the language arts and social studies teacher), and Ms. Olvina (the paraprofessional assigned to the team)—has arranged with the principal to have a common preparation period that leads into to their lunchtime. This allows them to meet to discuss curriculum, teaming, and specific student issues. The team's first endeavor is to create an integrated unit of study about the historical tension between progress and preservation, with a focus on global environmental issues. The team members are excited; they all see ways in which math, science, and literature can tie into this social studies–based theme.

During the unit, students will read literature that deals with environmental issues. For instance, Rachel Carson's (2002) classic, Silent Spring, *will bridge language arts and science. In language arts, students will examine the persuasive literary elements in the text. In science, students will read for information, identifying the negative impact of pesticides on the food chain and the lives of birds and other wildlife.*

Language arts and social studies are integrated through a series of lessons that develop students' skills in debating and delivering persuasive speeches regarding the positive and negative impact of progress on the health, quality of life, economic situation, and other aspects of various societies. In this way, Ms. Kurtz addresses key middle level language arts standards related to speaking and reasoning, and key social studies objectives regarding reasoning and environmental issues in international settings as well as the United States. Ms. Kurtz is comfortable giving Ms. Olvina more than a behind-the-scenes role, so while Ms. Kurtz works with half of the groups who are developing persuasive speeches and debates, Ms. Olvina works with the other half. They rotate between groups from one day to the next, so that the classroom teacher can monitor all students and all students see that both Ms. Olvina and Ms. Kurtz have expertise and can be of assistance.

Mr. Silva and Ms. Spaulding are enjoying the chance to connect science and math with literature and social studies creatively through the theme of progress versus preservation. For math, they have planned for students to do calculations; produce charts, graphs, and tables; and make projections based on current data regarding the destruction of various rainforests, smog levels in major cities worldwide, the effects of smog and other contaminants on life expectancies, and the human and financial costs of these and other forms of progress. Mr. Silva will introduce a unit on probability and have students apply what they are learning to science by having them forecast possible destruction-versus-preservation scenarios locally, nationally, and internationally. The co-teaching team has asked the librarian to bookmark a diverse array of Internet sites on the classroom and library computers so that students can begin to collect data.

For science, the team decided to connect the scientific and social roles of organizations and agencies such as the United Nations, the Environmental Protection Agency, and the U.S. Department of Agriculture, as well as other government entities and the courts. Although this is traditionally thought of as social studies content, Ms. Kurtz agreed to plan with Mr. Silva and Ms. Spaulding to ensure that the content was included as part of the science lessons. Mr. Silva and Ms. Spaulding also are taking the lead on introducing Silent Spring, *using it as scientific evidence of environmental damage. Together they generated a series of questions on the progress-versus-preservation theme for students to consider as they read the book.*

To differentiate instruction, they set up their lessons so that students can read the book in a variety of ways. In addition to the original printed format, audiotapes of the book read by students from a previous year's class are available to those who learn more easily through auditory versus visual means, find the text beyond their reading decoding or comprehension skill levels, or enjoy and learn best from having two forms of content input (e.g., auditory and visual). The book is also available on classroom and library computers in a rewritten, simplified format and in larger print (accessed from the Braille Institute's library for a student with visual impairments who was in this class two years earlier). It is available in a Spanish translation so that students who are primarily Spanish speakers may read both books simultaneously, thus ensuring access to the content of the book and development of English comprehension for those learning English. For other students who are studying Spanish as a second or third language, the simultaneous reading of English and Spanish text promotes their Spanish literacy development. All of these materials and accommodations are made available to every student in the class.

In terms of co-teaching, Mr. Silva and Ms. Spaulding have decided that they can best provide students in this lesson with individualized support by dividing the class in half, with each teacher taking 13 of the 26 students. They have learned that this is a form of parallel co-teaching. They think that parallel co-teaching really suits how they will use Silent Spring.

In setting up parallel co-teaching, Mr. Silva first introduces Silent Spring *to the entire class and tells the students the questions they are to answer. He then explains that each teacher will work with half of the class so that everyone gets attention from one of the teachers. He further explains that both groups will be working on the same goals and will have a variety of resources for accessing the content of the book (as described previously). He then divides the class. Both his group and Ms. Spaulding's are heterogeneous in terms of students' gender, reading level, and eligibility for special services (e.g., special education, gifted and talented education). The only deliberate clustering of students is done to ensure that the two students who are learning English and who speak Spanish as their primary language are with Mr. Silva because he is a proficient Spanish speaker and is certified as a bilingual teacher. He wants to make sure that he can check the students' understanding of content; differentiate materials and scaffold the instruction, if needed; and provide the option for the students to produce their work in Spanish rather than or in addition to English if they desire. These two students are new to the class and district and are still being assessed for their level of proficiency in English.*

(Continued)

(Continued)

In both Mr. Silva's and Ms. Spaulding's groups, students are seated in desks in a semi-circle arrangement facing their teacher's desk. The two instructors alternate between giving short task instructions and rotating among the 13 students to check for student engagement, answer questions, pose questions, and provide positive feedback for work engagement. They also pair students for reciprocal reading at various intervals and assemble students into triads and quads to discuss questions jointly and speculate on responses before they formulate their individual answers. This parallel co-teaching arrangement allows each teacher to monitor easily and readily a smaller number of students; flexibly group and regroup students to maintain their interest and create synergy and higher-level thinking through conversation; gather diagnostic information about students' interests, motivational factors, and literacy skills; and individualize accommodations for students as needed (e.g., use of audiotapes with a tape recorder and headset for students to scaffold instruction in their reading of the book).

A High School Co-Teaching Team

Leading up to the time that this lesson was developed, Mr. Woo (the social studies teacher) and Mr. Viana (the special educator) had taken advantage of the fact that there are two educators in the classroom in order to designate Fridays as a day to experiment with dividing the class between the two instructors. From week to week, they reconstitute the membership of their respective groups so that there is no stigma of any sort attached to working with one or the other of the educators. They both agreed that it was important to keep group membership flexible, based on the content and the purpose of a lesson and students' background knowledge and strengths. They have divided the class before this lesson, usually when certain groups of students needed some reteaching or an enrichment exercise. They have also divided the class based on the learning styles of students, with one teacher working primarily with visual learners and the other primarily with auditory learners.

Preparation for this particular social studies lesson on the role of the United Nations was done on the spot the day previous. Mr. Woo and Mr. Viana agreed to the lesson's objectives and structure and then, on their own, planned their materials and the details of how they would structure their specific activities. Right before class, they checked with one another to be sure that they both still agreed to the class structure and their roles and to ensure that if either one had any questions or concerns, they were addressed before the students arrived.

This class period is divided into two parts. During the first part of the class, Mr. Woo takes the majority of the class and focuses on preparing them for a homework assignment on the history, role, and impact of the League of Nations and the United Nations. Mr. Viana works with the remaining smaller group of students, with whom he reviews the questions answered incorrectly on the previous day's test. Students will have a chance to retake the test and improve their score later in the week.

During the second half of the class, Mr. Woo assigns independent work in which students analyze international treaties and charters such as the Geneva Accord. Mr. Viana is available to answer questions from any of the students and monitors them as they work. Mr. Woo sits at a table at the side of the room and works with a small group of students who have voluntarily signed up in advance for more guided assistance in getting started on the assignment. Included are two students whom Mr. Woo and Mr. Viana asked to join the group, knowing they would need extra clarification and support to initiate this assignment.

ANALYZING THE COOPERATIVE PROCESS IN THE ■
PARALLEL CO-TEACHING VIGNETTES

The cooperative process as applied to parallel co-teaching can be quite varied, as illustrated by these elementary, middle level, and high school vignettes. Parallel co-teaching differs from supportive co-teaching, yet both can occur within the same lesson. Co-teacher roles and responsibilities shift based on the nature of the instructional activity, learners' needs, and other variables. In the case of the middle level co-teaching team, the desire to implement interdisciplinary thematic units helped the co-teachers decide how to divide the teaching responsibilities to capitalize on their strengths and interests. In parallel co-teaching, students do not necessarily have the opportunity to see their teachers collaborate in communication and instruction. It is clear, however, that students do experience the more intensive attention and monitoring that each co-teacher provides.

The five elements of the cooperative teaching process (face-to-face interaction, positive interdependence, interpersonal skills, monitoring, accountability) are illustrated in some way by all three of the co-teaching teams in the parallel co-teaching vignettes. All three teams experienced face-to-face interaction by including a preplanning component to their relationship. All teams met regularly in some configuration. Of the three teams, the middle level team was most deliberate in its planning, having arranged for a common preparation period to plan and process lesson implementation. The elementary educators met weekly, with on-the-spot briefing of the paraprofessional when she was unable to attend planning meetings. Even though the high school team used on-the-spot division of labor for its respective student subgroups and planned for the groups separately, the co-teachers met before instruction to check in with one another regarding their agreed-on teaching roles and the overall lesson plan.

All three co-teaching teams experienced positive interdependence, which is necessary for success in parallel co-teaching. In the elementary station-teaching example, all three teachers needed one another to facilitate each of the stations. The teachers' lively, physical demonstration of how to bring together two words to create a compound word is an excellent example of positive interdependence. Because parallel co-teachers teach separately from one another, they experience resource interdependence through their division of labor. The middle level team illustrated this when Ms. Kurtz gave Mr. Silva her resources so that he could take on her usual role of introducing the literature to be read in the unit and managing some social studies activities.

All three teams exercised interpersonal skills such as negotiation, consensual agreement, and creativity through their planning. Perhaps the most important quality required of and demonstrated by members of the three co-teaching teams is that of trust. The three elementary co-teachers had to trust that the other two would facilitate their respective stations as planned. In the middle level team, the language arts and social studies co-teacher had to trust that the math and science and special education co-teachers would introduce and use the literature as planned and deliver the lesson on the scientific roles of social agencies as planned. The high school co-teachers had to trust that each person would independently do the agreed-on individual planning and be prepared for the next day's parallel co-teaching.

Monitoring effectiveness and individual accountability is probably the most difficult to do in parallel versus other forms of co-teaching. Parallel co-teachers are not readily available to monitor and hold one another accountable for their instruction; they are engaged in teaching their own group and may not even be in the same physical space to observe and interact with each other. Monitoring effectiveness is implied in all three vignettes; the co-teachers all had planning times during which they could debrief about self-monitored successes or challenges of the lessons. Accountability also is implied because the co-teachers apparently trusted one another to deliver instruction without direct monitoring. Trust is built on past accountability. It may not be clearly stated, but can you see how the co-teachers were accountable for their roles and responsibilities?

FREQUENTLY ASKED QUESTIONS

The following are among the questions people ask when they are considering the use of parallel co-teaching.

1. If we group by disability labels, learning styles, perceived ability in a subject, or other traits such as gender, won't that produce stigmatization?

We warn against the possibility of creating a special class within a class by routinely grouping the same students in the same groups. We want to decrease the stigmatization that labels can create. In addition, homogeneously grouping students of low ability may result in lower achievement scores (Marzano, Pickering, and Pollock 2001, 84). We recommend that co-teachers deliberately assign students to groups to make them heterogeneous, whenever possible. Heterogeneous grouping allows students to learn with others who have different ways of approaching learning and thinking. Heterogeneous grouping stretches students to learn new ways of approaching problems, new questions to ask, and new styles of learning and yields positive achievement and social skills gains. Co-teachers are encouraged to group and regroup students frequently, as there are many different purposes for assigning students to work in a group. Frequent reassignment of group members reduces any stigmatization that would result if students with similar kinds of learning needs are permanently grouped for long periods of time.

2. Should students stay primarily with the same co-teacher?

In parallel co-teaching, as in other forms of co-teaching, it is beneficial for students to rotate among the different team members. This avoids stigmatization of students or teachers that might arise if someone other than the classroom teacher, such as the special educator or paraprofessional, always teaches one set of students. By interacting with multiple instructors, students stretch their thinking and learning approaches as they experience the differing content expertise and instructional approaches of each co-teacher. Rotating students among co-teachers ensures that the professional educators as well as paraprofessionals instruct all students, each of whom may have different strengths. In addition, struggling learners can benefit from the informed problem solving in which co-teachers can engage, given their firsthand knowledge of the students' learning characteristics.

3. How can we ensure quality control of the instruction provided by the other co-teacher(s) when we are busy with another group of students and may not even be in the same room?

This is a valid teacher concern, particularly when a co-teacher is a paraprofessional, a community volunteer, a student teacher, or an older cross-aged tutor, any of whom may have little experience taking full responsibility for a learning situation without direct teacher monitoring. Parallel co-teaching works best when co-teachers plan and debrief on a regular basis. Doing so provides the opportunity to include time to evaluate the successes and challenges that occurred while parallel co-teaching. Another way to enhance the likelihood that others will conduct their co-teaching responsibilities with integrity (i.e., as designed and intended) is for co-teachers to model briefly, before a lesson, each of the lesson's activities. Furthermore, during the co-teaching lesson, students may be assigned an independent task that does not require a co-teacher's guidance, thus releasing that co-teacher to observe, be available for questions, and provide guidance or feedback to other co-teachers. The idea here is to create structures before and during the operation of parallel co-teaching that allow for the co-teachers to be well prepared, confident in one another and in themselves, and available to each other.

6

The Complementary Co-Teaching Approach

Jacqueline S. Thousand

Complementary co-teaching is when a co-teacher does something to enhance the instruction provided by the other co-teacher(s). Within this approach, one co-teacher often takes primary responsibility for designing the lesson or presenting new academic content. Both co-teachers share in the delivery of the information, sometimes with a varied delivery method. One co-teacher may lecture or read aloud while the other writes notes on chart paper and shows students how to follow along in the study guide. For example, one co-teacher might paraphrase the other co-teacher's statements on a transparency. Sometimes, one of the complementary co-teaching partners preteaches the content of roles for successful cooperative group learning and then monitors as students practice the roles during the other co-teacher's lesson. The general educator might teach a lesson while the special educator demonstrates (on the overhead projector or the chalkboard) how to take notes on key points. Or the special educator might lecture while the general educator uses a graphic organizer on the overhead projector to assist students in organizing facts as differentiated from opinions.

Co-teachers who employ the complementary approach are cautioned not to forget to monitor the learners. Sometimes co-teachers get so excited "performing on the stage" with their colleague that they forget to monitor the learners as closely as they did when they employed the supportive or parallel co-teaching approaches. They also must guard against too much teacher talk, repeating one another's statements, or forgetting to solicit student input. Finally, complementary co-teachers can get in a rut, with one co-teacher always taking the role of content expert and the other, the complementary role. This can lead students to typecast the content teacher as the "real" teacher. To ward off this pitfall, be sure to plan for *role release*, the exchange of content and complementary roles, so that all co-teachers are perceived as "real" teachers. An added benefit of role release is that it gives the person who starts off as the complementary co-teacher the chance to really learn the content. As any teacher will testify, you really learn to understand a concept, skill, or procedure when you have to teach it to another person.

■ VIGNETTES: COMPLEMENTARY CO-TEACHING

Let's peek into the classrooms of the co-teaching teams to see how they teach standards-based lessons through complementary co-teaching. As shown in Table 6.1, they are demonstrating a variety of teaching and learning strategies, as well as different planning methods.

Table 6.1   The Many Faces of Co-Teaching: Co-Teaching Teams' Use of Complementary Co-Teaching

Meet the Co-Teachers	Co-Teacher Roles	Curriculum Area(s)	Teaching Learning Strategies	Planning Method
Elementary				
Ms. Gilpatrick, classroom teacher	Leads the lesson and explains the task, distributes materials, and monitors student progress	Science	Constructivist learning	Preplanning
Ms. Hernandez, paraprofessional	Incorporates art and music, distributes materials, and monitors student progress			
Ms. Nugent, speech and language therapist	Incorporates notes on blackboard, previews next activities, distributes materials, and monitors student progress			
Middle Level				
Ms. Kurtz, language arts and social studies teacher	Leads the lesson, explains the task, and monitors and gives feedback to students	Language arts	Multicultural education strategies	Preplanning and on-the-spot planning
Ms. Olvina, paraprofessional	Models how to play the game, and monitors and gives feedback to students		Game format for application practice	
High School				
Mr. Woo, social studies teacher	Leads the lesson	Social studies	Cooperative group learning (jigsaw with structured social and task roles)	Preplanning and on-the-spot planning
Mr. Viana, special educator	Records notes to model note taking and suggests future accommodations			

An Elementary Co-Teaching Team

In this lesson, Ms. Gilpatrick (the classroom teacher), Ms. Nugent (the speech and language therapist), and Ms. Hernandez (the paraprofessional) have complementary roles in a science lesson in which students compare and contrast the seeds of various fruits. In planning the lesson, all three met with the gifted and talented program coordinator for about 20 minutes to tap her expertise regarding multisensory activities. On the day of the lesson, the gifted and talented coordinator cannot be in the classroom, but her expertise is represented in the lesson's design.

Ms. Hernandez, who is musically talented, begins the class by playing a simple song about fruits that the students have been practicing. Students and co-teachers sing along. Ms. Gilpatrick then asks the students what they think they will be studying today, and they all chorally respond, "Fruit!" She says, "Yes" and begins holding up various fruits (e.g., grapes, banana, apple, peach, orange) as the students identify them in choral response. While she does this, Ms. Nugent, a talented artist, draws and colors in the fruits on the board with colored markers, also labeling each fruit as it is named.

Ms. Gilpatrick explains to the students that they are to work in pairs with their table-mates to create a chart about the seeds of each of five fruits. In the chart, they are to describe the color, shape, size, and amount of seeds in each fruit. As Ms. Gilpatrick explains the task, Ms. Hernandez passes out to each student a grape that has been cut in half so that the seeds inside can be seen. It should be noted here that Elisa, the student with autism, is seated with a classmate to whom she is especially responsive when she needs to stay on task.

As Ms. Gilpatrick asks students questions about each of the dimensions of the grape seed, Ms. Nugent records the students' responses on a large chart on the board. The dimensions— size, color, shape, and amount—also are written on the board so that students may refer to them when they are working with the other fruits:

Size	Tiny, small, big
Color	Brown, white, black, red
Shape	Oval, round
Amount	One, a few, lots

After showing this chart, Ms. Nugent distributes copies of it to each pair of students. At the same time, Ms. Gilpatrick checks for understanding by asking students to raise their hands if they know how to explain what to do; she calls on one of the seven students who raise their hands to explain and praises the student for sharing. All three co-teachers then distribute one fruit at a time for each pair to examine; each fruit has been cut in half so that students can see the seed(s) inside. The pairs study the fruit and complete the chart.

As students work in pairs, the three adults circulate around the room to monitor students' engagement and to probe them about their findings. Ms. Hernandez is assigned to keep a particular eye on Elisa and her partner to be sure that they are engaged and to provide redirection or support, if needed.

When students have completed their task, they are encouraged to draw and color the seeds for each of their fruits and to taste the fruits they have been examining. This "sponges up" what might otherwise be "dead time" for groups that finish early and provides students motivation for task completion.

Ms. Gilpatrick asks students to stand up around the room holding their charts. She calls on pairs randomly to share their findings, while Ms. Nugent records their results on a large chart on the board.

The lesson concludes with Ms. Hernandez leading the fruit song that the students already know. She introduces a new verse that celebrates the seeds of the fruits the students examined. She had composed the verse spontaneously as the groups were working and, with Ms. Gilpatrick's permission, wrote the words in large print on chart paper so that students can follow along. The students sing the new verse twice. Ms. Gilpatrick tells them that Ms. Hernandez created it especially for them and that they will have a chance to practice it all week. Finally, Ms. Nugent previews the follow-up activity to create a fruit-and-seed collage. Ms. Gilpatrick reminds them that they will continue to observe the plants that they have planted and will record the observations in their learning logs.

A Middle Level Co-Teaching Team

Ms. Kurtz (the language arts and social studies teacher) and Ms. Olvina (the paraprofessional) have been discussing the confusion that students often have in trying to differentiate among synonyms, antonyms, and homonyms. This conversation leads to an on-the-spot plan to use the game of Charades as an introduction to cooperative group-learning activities (round-robin, Go Fish–type of practice for determining synonyms, antonyms, and homonyms). Ms. Olvina volunteers to think of a few examples to use in Charades. As the class begins, Ms. Kurtz asks, "Who here knows how to play Charades or Go Fish?" She calls on a couple of students to explain the games briefly and then informs the class that today's lesson on synonyms, antonyms, and homonyms will involve both games.

Ms. Kurtz first provides a definition and gives several examples of antonyms, synonyms, and homonyms. She then says, "OK, let's play Charades for antonyms!" Ms. Olvina goes to the front of the class to model a charade for a pair of antonyms. The students guess until the correct answer is given. Ms. Olvina challenges them to an even tougher one, and students guess again. Ms. Kurtz then asks if any students have an antonym in mind to stump the class. Before they model them, she has the students who volunteer whisper the antonyms in her ear to be sure that they are, in fact, antonyms.

Ms. Olvina says that she is sure to be able to stump the class on her synonym charade. She performs it, and students guess. Again, two or three students volunteer model additional synonyms. Ms. Olvina repeats her challenge, this time for a homonym pair. New students act out homonym charades.

Ms. Kurtz sets up a transition to the next activity by telling students that, in pairs, they will have eight minutes to come up with at least two synonyms, two antonyms, and two homonyms that are really hard to figure out. She tells them that they have access to the computer, dictionaries, and thesauruses and that when they are finished, they are to come to her or Ms. Olvina to check their answers. Ms. Olvina projects an overhead transparency listing the student pairs that Ms. Kurtz had previously determined.

Ms. Kurtz and Ms. Olvina move around the room to monitor students' progress on the task, suggesting resources such as a thesaurus to pairs that appear to be struggling. Ms. Kurtz

(Continued)

(Continued)

has identified a few students whom she believes will need "starter" words. She has prepared a stack of cards, half of which she passes to Ms. Olvina. The two co-teachers share the responsibility for observing the pairs in which these students are working and are prepared to pass them a starter word, if needed.

After 10 minutes, Ms. Kurtz congratulates the pairs on their work and has them sign and pass their worksheets to Ms. Olvina. She then has two sets of partners sit at round tables to create six groups of four. A remaining pair is split across two quads to create two groups of five students. Each table has a can of popsicle sticks with words written on them. Ms. Kurtz explains that the students will have eight minutes to play a variation of Go Fish by taking turns drawing sticks from the can in a clockwise, round-robin manner and stating out loud a homonym, synonym, or antonym for the word they have drawn.

Teammates have two rounds to guess what the word on the stick might be, guessing homonyms, synonyms, or antonyms. When someone guesses correctly, the stick holder must show the stick. If no one guesses after two rounds, the students holding the popsicle sticks tell their tablemates what word is written on their sticks.

Ms. Kurtz sets a timer for eight minutes and tells the groups that the person in each group who is seated closest to her is the first person to select a stick. Then, both Ms. Kurtz and Ms. Olvina roam among the groups listening for examples of homonyms, antonyms, and synonyms to share with the class during the closure to the lesson.

Ms. Kurtz and Ms. Olvina wrap up the lesson by applauding the students for a great fishing expedition, and Ms. Kurtz asks for fish stories about a really difficult or funny synonym, antonym, or homonym pair. Ms. Kurtz and Ms. Olvina each share a couple of examples they heard as they monitored groups. Ms. Kurtz then announces a flash round. She offers a word, asking first for a homonym, next for an antonym, then for a synonym, and finally for the same word in another language. She asks Ms. Olvina to lead a second round, passing her a couple of words. They end the lesson by giving each other a high five with big smiles and laughs.

A High School Co-Teaching Team

The students in Mr. Woo's government class are preparing for two major assignments. The first is a field experience visiting a governmental meeting. The second is an interview of a public governmental official. Both of these field experiences are ones that the students have anticipated with excitement, and ones for which Mr. Woo has emphasized the importance of being prepared and behaving professionally. Today's lesson focuses on preparing students for their visitation to governmental meetings.

Mr. Woo begins the class by asking students, "What do you think we should be looking for? What do you think we should have as requirements for our report of the experience? How should the report be formatted? How long should the report be?" Within 15 minutes, the class comes to agreement on a structure for observing and then reporting about the meeting. By the time they are finished, Mr. Viana (the special educator) has typed this format into the computer, printed a form for every student, and quickly copied an overhead transparency of the form. As Mr. Woo briefly introduces a video of a meeting from the previous year, Mr. Viana distributes the form to all of the students. Mr. Woo directs them to use the form to take notes while they are watching the video. While the video is playing, Mr. Viana uses his transparency of the form to take notes about the meeting to create a model of what the students' reports should look like. Following the video, Mr. Woo leads the students through an examination of Mr. Viana's notes, so that they can compare their attempts with the standard the teachers expect of their actual meeting report.

In the second half of the class, Mr. Woo leads a similar discussion with the students about the content and format of their upcoming interview with a government official. Again, they develop an agreed-on format, which Mr. Viana types, prints, and distributes. As he does this, Mr. Woo offers the students a list of the possible local and regional officials whom they might interview and asks the students if they know of any others.

Mr. Woo then has students brainstorm possible questions that they might ask a governmental official. Mr. Viana records these on the board. All questions are accepted as potentially good questions. Mr. Woo describes the job of the president of the district's school board and asks students, in pairs, to generate three questions appropriate to ask this person. Mr. Woo samples at least one question from each pair while Mr. Viana records the questions on the board. Mr. Woo then teaches the students a process for prioritizing questions in which they each get four colored dots to vote for their preferred questions. They may distribute their four dots among one, two, three, or four questions. Students line up at the board to vote. Mr. Viana tallies the votes as Mr. Woo announces that the president of the school board will come to class the next day so that Mr. Woo can model the interviewing process using the students' most-voted-for questions.

The following day, Mr. Woo interviews the school board president, while Mr. Viana records the president's responses on the overhead projector, using the questions and formats that the class developed. The purpose of this exercise is to offer the students a concrete model of professional behavior in interviewing and the detail with which the instructors expect students to take notes in an interview. The school board president opens the class to a question-and-answer period for the students. After she leaves, Mr. Woo reviews the overhead notes and again engages the students in a discussion to determine the format, length, and due date of the interview report. Mr. Viana records these requirements and the format on the computer, prints copies, and distributes them to students while Mr. Woo goes over the list of officials whom students can interview. Mr. Woo closes the lesson by previewing the next day's class, in which students will sign up to meet particular officials, develop interviews, and rehearse questions with classmates.

After class, Mr. Viana suggests to Mr. Woo that some students may need some accommodations in how they perform and record the interviews. For example, he suggests that some students might feel more comfortable interviewing in pairs. He also suggests that for students who may have difficulty listening and simultaneously recording answers, they could be allowed to record their interview and transcribe it later. Finally, Mr. Viana suggests that it might be a good idea to pair all students thoughtfully so that students with differing strengths (e.g., interpersonal vs. verbal/linguistic, listening vs. writing) could support one another to create a better report. Mr. Woo agrees that all of these are great options for differentiating the assignment and suggests that in the next class, before they engage students in creating their interviews, Mr. Viana should discuss with the students the various options for conducting and recording the interview. Mr. Viana agrees, and they leave to teach their respective next-period classes.

■ ANALYZING THE COOPERATIVE PROCESS IN THE COMPLEMENTARY CO-TEACHING VIGNETTES

The five elements of the cooperative process differ when complementary co-teaching is applied at the various levels—elementary, middle level, and high school. The cooperative process gains in depth as the co-teaching team members shift from supplementary to parallel to complementary co-teaching. Co-teaching roles and responsibilities also shift based on the nature of the instructional activity, the preferences and experience of the members of the team, and the needs of their learners. Most important, students in classrooms where complementary co-teaching is practiced have the opportunity to see how their teachers communicate, establish equity and parity, and share authority.

As we have noted previously, the five elements of the cooperative process are face-to-face interaction, positive interdependence, interpersonal skills, monitoring, and accountability. In the complementary co-teaching vignettes, all three teams added a preplanning component to enrich their face-to-face interactions. Their division of labor allowed them to experience positive interdependence, perhaps most vividly portrayed by the elementary team, who allowed the students to experience their individual talents (music and artistic expression). The three teams exercised their interpersonal skills by communicating with each other both before and during the lessons. All three teams monitored their effectiveness during their debriefing sessions in preparation for the next day's lesson. It may not be clearly stated, but can you see how the team members held each other accountable for the roles and responsibilities that had developed?

We advocate that complementary co-teachers include as many elements of the cooperative process as possible. This happens when co-teachers experience frequent face-to-face interactions, realize exactly how they are positively interdependent, make opportunities to practice their social interpersonal skills, monitor how well they work together, and hold each other accountable for the tasks they have agreed to perform.

FREQUENTLY ASKED QUESTIONS

People ask several questions when they consider the option of complementary co-teaching. You might have similar questions.

1. As a complementary co-teacher, for what specifically am I responsible? I'm still unclear about this.

This is a good example of a question about role clarification. We suggest that people on the co-teaching team literally step apart from one another and write the following: "What are the questions that confuse you?" Questions about role clarification tend to fall into categories such as planning, instructing, grading, communicating with parents, and managing the discipline in the classroom. Here are a few examples:

- How do team members arrange to share their expertise?
- Who plans for what content?
- Who will adapt curriculum and instruction?

Do these questions sound familiar? They were first introduced within the context of roles and responsibilities. These questions continuously arise as co-teachers move from supportive to parallel to complementary to team-teaching co-teaching approaches. The answers to these questions will change depending on the experience of the co-teachers and the needs of the students for whom they are responsible.

Please forgive the ambiguity of the answer to this question. The answers are within each co-teaching team and must be collaboratively developed. Some co-teaching team members will need to envision the big picture to contextualize their role. Others will need a step-by-step (sometimes even a minute-by-minute) agenda. We encourage each co-teaching team member to be respectful of the others' learning and working styles.

2. How can you expect a special educator or a teacher of students who are learning English to be an effective complementary co-teacher in a high school science class where content mastery is so important?

It is to be expected that there will be a learning curve for anyone who is entering the science classroom—or the mathematics, foreign language, or social studies classroom. Co-teaching team members may need to structure observation and processing time for those who need to become familiar with the content and procedures of particular classes. We have great admiration for the co-teachers who have stepped up to the cognitive demands of learning enough of the subject matter—sometimes, seemingly, just barely enough—to stay one page or one chapter ahead of the students. As adults who have successfully completed their elementary, secondary, and postsecondary education opportunities, the special educator and the teacher of students who are learning English have the skills to acquire new knowledge, assimilate it, and support young people as they learn it. Science textbooks provide ample resources such as chapter outlines, previews, summaries, glossaries, and test banks. Students also can share what they know in the language of the beginner and thus better communicate with the co-teacher who is also a beginning learner in the subject. We, too, have experienced reluctance to jump into a new area of knowledge; yet each time we have done so, we have come through our trepidations with newfound knowledge, increased content mastery, enhanced skills and strategies, and improved self-confidence.

(Continued)

(Continued)

Finally, remember that not all members of the co-teaching team need to have the same level of curriculum content mastery and that, over time, all members of a co-teaching team can acquire the content knowledge and the skills modeled by their co-teaching partners. A benefit of co-teaching is that as co-teachers pool their respective expertise, they also exchange and enhance one another's diverse knowledge, skills, and strengths.

The Team-Teaching Co-Teaching Approach

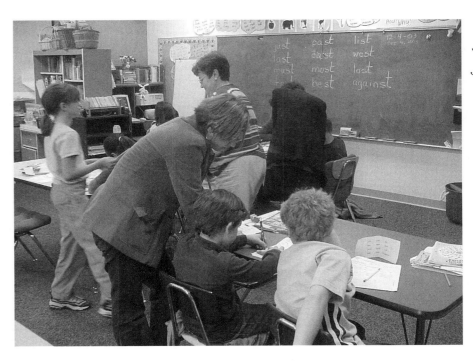

Erin Jarry

Topics Included in This Chapter:

- Vignettes: Team teaching co-teaching
- Analyzing the cooperative process in the team-teaching co-teaching vignettes
- Frequently asked questions
- Summary

Team teaching is when two or more people do what the traditional teacher used to do. Specifically, they share responsibility for planning, teaching, and assessing progress of students in the class(es) that they teach together. Team teaching is a sophisticated co-teaching process that has a beautiful flow to it. In keeping with the marriage analogy introduced earlier, when co-teachers use the team-teaching approach to co-teaching, they are like a married couple that dances beautifully together. Their dance is similar to a tango; it is complex, sophisticated, and intimate.

Both co-teachers plan and design the lesson or unit, and then they take turns delivering various components of the lesson. It may look as if they've divided the lesson in such a way that one person assumes greater responsibility for the introduction of the activities or the lesson and another person takes greater responsibility for the closure and facilitation of students' individual practice. Or it might look like tag-team teaching in which they consistently go back and forth and share responsibilities throughout the lesson. Some team-teaching teams rotate responsibility for the different aspects of each lesson or unit among the members each time they co-teach. It may take time for co-teachers to shift from supportive, parallel, and complementary co-teaching arrangements to achieve team teaching. Team teaching usually requires more face-to-face planning time than do the other approaches to co-teaching. Decisions about who teaches what are mutually determined and based on variables such as each person's curriculum content mastery, preferences, and training. The goal is for co-teachers to move in and out of each of the four co-teaching approaches, sometimes within a single lesson, based upon the needs of the diverse learners that they are teaching. As with complementary co-teaching, co-teachers employing the team-teaching approach must remember to not become too involved in the act of team teaching that they forget to closely monitor the learners in the class. They also must guard against too much teacher talk, repeating one another's statements or forgetting to solicit student input.

In team-teaching co-teaching arrangements, the equity and parity of the team members is obvious from their roles in the classroom. For example, you may find two teacher desks in the classroom and all teachers' names on the classroom door and on papers that are sent home. Moreover, all co-teachers participate equally at conferences as well as meetings with students' families.

■ VIGNETTES: TEAM TEACHING

Let's look into the classrooms for a final time as the team teach standards-based lessons. As summarized in Table 7.1, they are demonstrating a wide variety of best practices for instructional methods and a range of planning models as they team teach.

Table 7.1 The Many Faces of Co-Teaching: Co-Teaching Teams' Use of Team Teaching

Meet the Co-Teachers	Co-Teacher Roles	Curriculum Area(s)	Teaching Learning Strategies	Planning Method
Elementary				
Ms. Gilpatrick, classroom teacher	Distribute responsibility with joint delivery	Mathematics	Creative problem solving	Preplanning
Ms. Nugent, speech and language therapist				
Middle Level				
Mr. Silva, science and math teacher	Distribute responsibility with joint delivery	Science	Multiple intelligences theory Think-pair-share quick cooperative learning structure	Pre- and postplanning
Ms. Spaulding, special educator	Consult with from the paraprofessional and language arts teacher			
Ms. Kurtz, language arts and social studies teacher				
Ms. Olvina, paraprofessional				
High School				
Mr. Woo, social studies teacher	Distribute responsibility with joint delivery	Social studies		Preplanning
Mr. Viana, special educator				

An Elementary Co-Teaching Team

Ms. Gilpatrick (the classroom teacher) holds weekly class meetings with students and convenes additional meetings at other times as needed. She has been working with the students on problem solving since the beginning of the school year. At this weekly class meeting, she plans to problem solve repeated problems seen on the playground. Ms. Nugent (the speech and language therapist) arrives with a box that contains written note cards that describe some of the playground problems. The problem-solving process the two have agreed to use is SODAS (Hazel et al. 1995), one that Ms. Nugent has used successfully with students for years. SODAS is an acronym for Situation-Options-Disadvantages-Advantages-Solution. A template for the SODAS process is shown in Table 7.2.

Ms. Gilpatrick convenes and explains the purpose of this week's class meeting. The first problem randomly drawn from the box states, "A student calls another student's mother a name, and the students get into a fist fight on the playground." Ms. Gilpatrick puts a transparency of the SODAS template on the overhead projector as Ms. Nugent asks the students to identify the problem situation. Ms. Gilpatrick calls on a student who correctly identifies the problem situation. Ms. Nugent writes the identified situation on the overhead form. Ms. Nugent asks students to identify some options for solving this problem. Ms. Gilpatrick and Ms. Nugent alternate taking turns calling on students to share their ideas. Five options are generated, and Ms. Gilpatrick adds a sixth. Ms. Nugent records the information on the transparency.

The next step involves identifying disadvantages for each of the options. Ms. Nugent and Ms. Gilpatrick model how to talk about disadvantages of the first option, while Ms. Gilpatrick records disadvantages on the transparency. Then Ms. Nugent asks the students to turn to a neighbor and discuss possible disadvantages of the second option. After one minute, Ms. Gilpatrick calls on various students, and Ms. Nugent records the disadvantages that they share. The co-teachers repeat this process for the remaining options, alternating the roles of calling on the students and recording their answers.

Ms. Gilpatrick and Ms. Nugent model and record a discussion about the possible disadvantages of the first option and then ask the students to work in pairs to identify disadvantages for the remaining five options. Elisa, the student with autism, is partnered with a classmate who is especially good at giving Elisa the time she usually needs to generate ideas. When students are ready, Ms. Gilpatrick calls on them, and Ms. Nugent records their answers on the transparency. When this is done, Ms. Nugent rereads all of the disadvantages and asks the students to identify the worst disadvantages by raising their hands for no more than three choices when the item is read. Ms. Gilpatrick tallies their responses and puts a box around the three disadvantages that had the most votes.

Ms. Gilpatrick and Ms. Nugent repeat the process for the advantages. This time, Ms. Gilpatrick reads and Ms. Nugent tallies responses and puts a circle around the advantages with the most votes. Ms. Gilpatrick directs the students to turn to a different partner to identify the possible solution(s) that would achieve the best advantages and avoid the worst disadvantages. After a couple minutes, Ms. Nugent asks the students to report their answers, and Ms. Gilpatrick tallies the results. Ms. Gilpatrick explains that if the scenario were real, the two students who had fought would be expected to use SODAS to come up with an alternate response to fighting if a problem like this were to occur again.

Table 7.2   The SODAS Problem-Solving Process

SODAS

Situation (Define the problem)

_____

_____

_____

_____

Options

1._____ 2._____ 3._____

Disadvantages

a._____ a._____ a._____

b._____ b._____ b._____

c._____ c._____ c._____

d._____ d._____ d._____

Advantages

a._____ a._____ a._____

b._____ b._____ b._____

c._____ c._____ c._____

d._____ d._____ d._____

Solution

_____

_____

_____

If you agree to a solution, make a plan.
(Who will do what, when? How you know if the plan is working?)

_____

_____

_____

_____

_____

(Continued)

(Continued)

Ms. Nugent asks students how the SODAS problem-solving process might help them solve problems on the playground, in class, and at home. Ms. Gilpatrick and Ms. Nugent close the lesson by each sharing an example of how they have used SODAS in their personal lives and telling the students that they will practice using SODAS to solve problems throughout the year.

A Middle Level Co-Teaching Team

Mr. Silva (the science and math teacher) recently attended a workshop where he heard Thomas Armstrong talk about the use of multiple intelligences (MI) theory (Armstrong 2000). In the workshop, Armstrong gave an example of how MI theory could be used to teach Boyle's law. Boyle's law explains the inverse relationship between the volume and pressure of a gas if temperature remains constant. Coincidentally, Boyle's law is related to one of the seventh- and eighth-grade standards in physics that Mr. Silva must teach.

Mr. Silva explains MI theory and Boyle's law to both Ms. Spaulding (the special educator) and Ms. Olvina (the paraprofessional) during a planning session. Ms. Spaulding agrees that using MI theory would be a great way to teach Boyle's law. She is already familiar with MI theory and is really looking forward to team teaching this lesson and having the chance to apply MI theory in a content area.

While planning, Mr. Silva and Ms. Spaulding prepare a visual presentation. Ms. Olvina spontaneously creates a rap that reinforces the main concepts of the law. She records it on a tape so that it can be played in the class, even though she is not going to be there because she will be co-teaching with Ms. Kurtz (the language arts teacher) at that time.

Ms. Spaulding starts the lesson with an overview of MI theory and the eight intelligences—verbal/linguistic (word smart), logical/mathematical (logic smart), visual/spatial (picture smart), bodily/kinesthetic (body smart), musical (music smart), naturalist (nature smart), interpersonal (people smart), and intrapersonal (self smart). As Ms. Spaulding describes each intelligence, Mr. Silva points to its representation on the MI Pizza transparency, which is reproduced in Figure 7.1.

Mr. Silva then asks students to identify their own top two intelligences and one that is currently least developed for them. He explains that everyone has all intelligences in different proportions and that intelligence may change over time with opportunities to learn. Like a muscle, intelligence grows with exercise.

As Mr. Silva names each intelligence, students raise their hands if it is one of their top two. Ms. Spaulding tallies responses on the MI Pizza transparency and creates a class profile of strength intelligences. Ms. Spaulding uses this as an opportunity to talk about how no one intelligence is better than another. Ms. Spaulding reveals her strength intelligences (i.e., body smart, people smart, picture smart), and Mr. Silva reveals his (i.e., logic smart, word smart, nature smart). Ms. Olvina and Ms. Kurtz have given permission to reveal their strengths; they both are people smart. In addition, Ms. Olvina is music smart and Ms. Kurtz is word smart.

Mr. Silva states, "Today we are planning to teach you about a gas law named after a man, Robert Boyle. Now be honest, how many of you are excited to learn about this law?" Of the 26 students, 5 raise their hands. Mr. Silva asks, "How many of you might be interested in learning about this law if it was taught through the use of MI?" Now 22 of the 26 students raise their hands.

Mr. Silva says that some students who are word smart might understand by reading the definition of Boyle's law, which Ms. Spaulding projects on a screen. Ms. Spaulding reads the law and asks, "How many of you understand Boyle's law by reading the definition or hearing me read it to you?" Only a few students raise their hands. Mr. Silva says, "Some of you are logic smart, so you might understand if I give you the formula." Ms. Spaulding projects the formula and briefly explains it. She asks, "How many of you now think you understand Boyle's law?" A few more students raise their hands.

Figure 7.1   The Multiple Intelligence Pizza

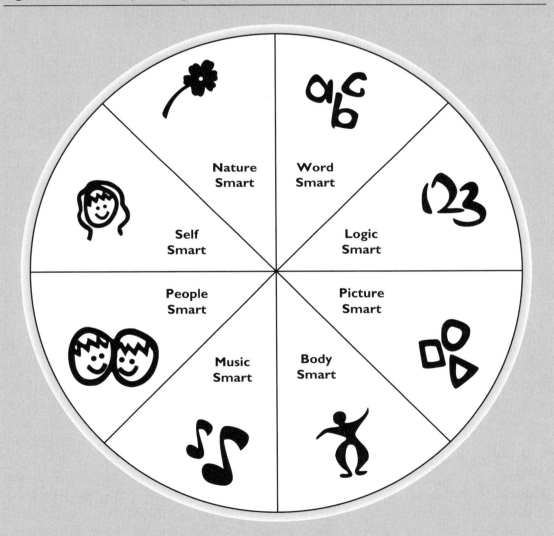

(Continued)

(Continued)

To use bodily/kinesthetic (body smart) intelligence to facilitate understanding, Mr. Silva asks the students to suck oxygen into their mouths and inflate both cheeks. Ms. Spaulding models this. Mr. Silva then has everyone push all of the air into one cheek, and asks, "What happened to the pressure in the one cheek when the volume was decreased?" The students answer that they felt that one side had more pressure when the volume was cut in half.

To use visual/spatial (picture smart) intelligence, Mr. Silva passes out balloons while Ms. Spaulding directs students to blow up and tie their balloons. Mr. Silva then has students squeeze the balloon to decrease the balloon's volume. As the students comply, several balloons pop. Ms. Spaulding asks the students to describe what just happened. As they do, Mr. Silva draws a V (volume) and a P (pressure) on the board, with an arrow pointing down next to the V and an arrow pointing up next to the P, graphically illustrating that as the volume of a gas goes down, the pressure goes up. Mr. Silva next holds up a balloon pinched midway by his hand. When he has the students' attention, he releases his hand, and the pressure releases.

Ms. Spaulding asks students to speculate about the relationship between volume and pressure that he has just illustrated. As they correctly respond, Ms. Spaulding draws an arrow pointing up next to the V and an arrow pointing down next to the P, indicating that as the volume increases, the pressure decreases.

To use the naturalist (nature smart) intelligence to help students learn about Boyle's law, Mr. Silva, a scuba diver, explains how when people dive, they have to control their rate of assent to the surface to avoid getting the bends. He explains this in terms of Boyle's law—the inverse relationship between the pressure and volume of a gas.

To use musical intelligences to activate learning, Mr. Silva plays the tape recording of Ms. Olvina's rap about Boyle's law while Ms. Spaulding projects the words of the song on a screen. Students listen once and then, as a class, all sing "The Boyle's Law Rap."

Mr. Silva and Ms. Spaulding use students' interpersonal (people smart) intelligence in a think-pair-share cooperative activity in which students explain Boyle's law in their own words to a partner and then identify the intelligence activities that most helped them understand the law and why.

To use the intrapersonal (self smart) intelligence to help students learn about Boyle's law, Mr. Silva asks them to think of a time when they felt under lots of pressure and to identify how much psychological or thinking space (or volume) they felt they had. Then Ms. Silva asks the students to think of a time when the pressure was low and to identify how much psychological space (volume) was available to them. The students are asked to record their observations in their learning logs and to be prepared to share their answers at the beginning of the next day's class.

To close, Mr. Silva asks, "Who now completely understands Boyle's law?" All but two students raise their hands. Ms. Spaulding asks, "Who found MI helpful in learning about Boyle's law?" Everybody raises his or her hands. They do the same when she asks if they want to use MI to learn other things in science. In the remaining minutes of the class, the MI rap is played again, and the students join in the rap.

In a debriefing session after the lesson, Mr. Silva and Ms. Spaulding excitedly talk about how enlightening the lesson had been. Mr. Silva said, "I think we can use multiple intelligences in other ways, too. We can use it to assess learning in different ways, like Ms. Olvina showing understanding of Boyle's law by using her musical intelligence to develop a rap." Ms. Spaulding agrees, and the two brainstorm ways to use MI theory to promote and assess students' learning in the next week's lessons.

A High School Co-Teaching Team

Mr. Woo (the social studies teacher) and Mr. Viana (the special educator) spent two planning sessions getting ready for a two-week unit in which students will learn about primaries, campaign finance, conventions, and election processes, including the Electoral College. In the first session, Mr. Viana admitted that he has always been a little confused about why, in a democracy, it is not simple majority rule. Mr. Woo said, "I am sure you are not alone, so let's arrange for our students to discuss whether the Electoral College process should be maintained or abolished."

To examine the Electoral College, they decided to use a classic jigsaw cooperative group methodology, with base teams and expert groups. The four-day lesson would start with students preparing in expert groups on the first day. On the second day, experts teach one another in base teams and come to decisions about whether the Electoral College should be abolished or maintained. On the third day, students share results of surveys of community members' understanding of and desire to keep or abolish the Electoral College and develop a class-wide summary chart of survey results. On the fourth day, base teams synthesize their work by composing a 200- to 300-word letter to the editor of the local newspaper explaining their position on the Electoral College's value and how they came to that position (e.g., community opinion survey, outcomes of past presidents elected through this process). What follows are details of the first two days of the lesson.

Mr. Woo begins by asking students, "What do you know about the process of getting to become president of the United States?" Someone states that the majority of people voting elect the president. Several students disagree and speak about the Electoral College. One student says that you can be elected even if you do not have the majority of votes. Mr. Woo asks the students how the Electoral College works. The students admit that they don't really understand the process. Mr. Viana admits to the students that he is not clear on how it works either. Mr. Woo states that by the end of the day's class, everyone should understand the process.

Mr. Woo assigns students to small cooperative groups and explains the cooperative group jigsaw in which each person is responsible for learning and teaching critical content to the base team. He says that the ultimate goals of each team are to determine the pros and cons of maintaining or abolishing the Electoral College system and to reach consensus about whether to maintain or abolish the Electoral College and provide rationale to support the group's decision.

Within each base team, the members are given a vignette in which a president came into power not by majority vote, but by election within the Electoral College or a decision made within the House of Representatives. Included in the vignette is the actual election process along with the historical context of the time that this president was in office and the significant accomplishments or perceived failures (or both) within his or her presidential term. Members are given an overview of the Electoral College—how it came about, the rationale for it, and how it works.

Mr. Viana explains that students will first work individually to become experts on their materials, as they are responsible for teaching it to the other members of the team. After all members have read and studied their materials, they are paired with a person from another team who has the exact same materials in order to check jointly for understanding and prepare the key points for instructing the other team members about their content. While the students are working, both teachers monitor students' work by walking around the room.

After 10 minutes, Mr. Viana directs the pairs of students to get into a larger expert group with people from the remaining groups that have been studying the same content. In the expert

(Continued)

(Continued)

group, they are to review the content and prepare materials—visuals, flowcharts, bullet points, and so on—that will help them teach their classmates. Twenty minutes later, Mr. Woo disbands the expert groups and sends students back to their base teams. Mr. Viana and Mr. Woo provide the students with feedback on their use of cooperative, academic, and social skills; thank them for their great work; and briefly describe what students will do the next day in base teams.

On the second day, Mr. Woo asks students, "What is it that we did yesterday to prepare for today? What is the task we are going to complete by the end of the day?" He and Mr. Viana randomly call on students to answer the questions. Mr. Woo then tells the students that they will have 30 minutes for base team members to teach their information to one another.

Mr. Woo describes the rotating roles of speaker, clarifier, and timekeeper. The speaker has seven minutes to teach information and three minutes to answer questions. The clarifier is responsible for leading listeners to ask clarifying questions in the last three minutes. The timekeeper gives the speaker five-, seven-, and nine-minute warnings as time elapses. Mr. Viana checks students' understanding of the three roles.

Mr. Viana clarifies the social skills that the students will be expected to use (i.e., active listening, taking turns, and encouraging others to speak) by reviewing charts of what each social skill looks and sounds like, which the students prepared earlier in the year. Mr. Woo tells the students that both teachers will observe them to be sure they are using the social skills while working.

Mr. Woo and Mr. Viana rotate among the base teams, complimenting members on their teaching and use of social skills. At the end of the instructional period, Mr. Viana asks students to give examples of active listening demonstrated by their team. Both he and Mr. Woo provide additional examples from their observations. Mr. Woo asks the students to identify the pros and cons of maintaining the Electoral College, and Mr. Viana records the information on an overhead transparency. Mr. Viana asks for the results of the various groups' decisions either to maintain or to abolish the Electoral College. Mr. Woo records these data. Mr. Woo and Mr. Viana assign homework, which is for each person to interview at least four people, no more than two of whom are family members. They are to ask the following:

- *How does the Electoral College work?*
- *Should it be maintained or abolished?*
- *Why should it be maintained or abolished?*

Mr. Woo distributes forms for students to use to record information gathered during the interviews while Mr. Viana previews the unit activities and timelines.

■ ANALYZING THE COOPERATIVE PROCESS IN THE TEAM-TEACHING CO-TEACHING VIGNETTES

In these vignettes, you might have noticed that team teaching requires more trust, confidence, communication, and face-to-face planning time than the other co-teaching approaches. As stated previously, the five elements of the cooperative process are face-to-face interaction, positive interdependence, interpersonal skills, monitoring, and accountability. In the team-teaching vignettes, all three teams relied on preplanning face-to-face interaction. The elementary team spent the least amount of time engaged in formal preplanning, indicating that they had a high level of trust and had taught in a similar fashion previously. In its preplanning, the middle level team included other persons who had different areas of strength as a resource when designing the lesson. A division of labor allowed all three team-teaching teams to experience positive interdependence. All three teams rotated some of the responsibilities among the team members, and, in addition, the high school team divided some tasks among the members based on content mastery. For example, the classroom teacher had a greater role in explaining the academic content, and the special educator assumed greater responsibility for explaining social skills and facilitating students' use of the social skills when they worked in cooperative learning groups. The three teams exercised their interpersonal skills by communicating with each other both before and during the lessons. Monitoring effectiveness was strongest among the members of the middle level team during their debriefing of the lesson in preparation for future lessons. Accountability can be detected in the teams monitoring their effectiveness and was strongest among the members of the middle level team as they debriefed about lessons in preparation for future lessons. We advocate that team teaching co-teachers incorporate as many elements of the cooperative process as possible into their interactions before, during, and after co-teaching.

FREQUENTLY ASKED QUESTIONS

The following are among the questions people ask when they are considering the use of team teaching.

1. Should personnel who are team teaching remain together, or should one of them follow the students whom they have been supporting to the next grade level, working with new teachers at that level?

We know it takes time to develop the team-teaching relationship. We've heard from many classroom teachers that attempting to team teach can be really frustrating for them when personnel changes from year to year. They work together for an entire year, become familiar with each other's style, and then they have to start over again the following year with a brand new person. Classroom teachers often report that changing co-teaching partners often thwarts their development as co-teachers. Support personnel such as special educators, Title I personnel, instructors for students learning English, and those who provide gifted and talented education also express concern about changing co-teaching partners. Their concern, particularly at the middle and high school levels, has to do with mastering new content. For example, they might have been assigned to co-teach in a specific content area (e.g., biology), acquiring more familiarity with the content, and then they are transferred to another academic

(Continued)

(Continued)

area (e.g., algebra) in which they will learn a whole new set of academic principles, concepts, facts, and skills.

On the other hand, there are benefits to the students and to the new teachers of students who are at risk for school failure if teaching personnel who know the students accompany them to the next grade and work with other teacher(s) at that level. If the students go to a new class with someone who has supported them before, such as a special educator, students are less likely to fall through the cracks. The new teacher immediately has access to a knowledgeable, built-in resource person.

In co-teaching, as in life, there are no perfect solutions. There are advantages and disadvantages associated with staying with the teacher or accompanying the students. It is up to the team members to explore the advantages and disadvantages of each option and to choose the solution that is best for the students they teach. Our observations of co-teaching teams reveal that in elementary schools, about half of the teams decide to stay together and half decide to follow the students. In the upper grades, we tend to see more co-teaching teams who stay together, with team members citing mastering the complex curriculum as one of the main reasons for doing so.

2. How long will it take for co-teaching teams to evolve to the team-teaching stage?

First, we want to emphasize that each co-teaching approach is a valid option. Second, we encourage you to avoid referring to "evolving" or "stages" because these terms imply a hierarchy. Although it is true that many co-teachers begin with the supportive and parallel co-teaching approaches, others often start with team teaching. Third, there is no one answer to this question—only multiple options.

Some teachers decide to use the team-teaching approach within a few weeks of working together. Other teachers may require a year or more to see that the team-teaching approach might be useful given the needs of their students and the curricula they are teaching. The amount of time required varies because of many factors, including the teaching competencies and subject matter expertise of the co-teachers, the time co-teachers devote to the cooperative process itself, the time available for collaborative planning and teaching, the willingness to develop a working relationship among the members of the co-teaching team, and the needs of the students.

In fact, one of the best ways to learn to co-teach is to co-teach, to learn by doing. We have each learned a new skill this way, in particular when we practice with someone who is just a little bit more skilled than we are. We propose a framework to help guide the decisions about who should co-teach; this framework is based on two of the many factors involved:

willingness to co-teach and skills or ability to co-teach. The Willingness to Co-Teach scale can vary from *low willingness* to *high willingness*. The Capability to Co-Teach scale also varies from *low capability* to *high capability*. As shown in Figure 7.2, this results in a four-quadrant taxonomy.

Figure 7.2   The Zone of Proximal Development for Co-Teachers

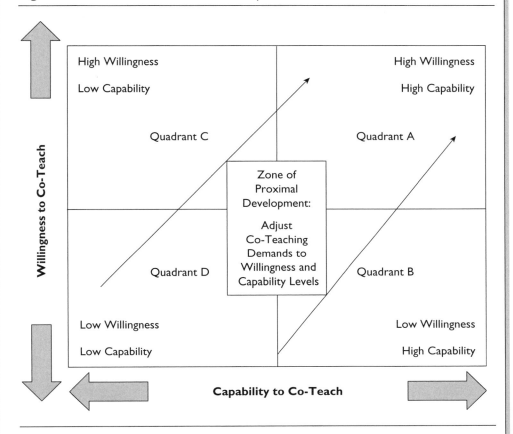

In Quadrant A, when co-teachers are both capable and willing, their use of all four approaches to co-teaching can be developed quickly. For co-teachers in Quadrant B, who are capable but not so willing, it may take a little more time. For co-teachers in Quadrant C, who are willing but not so capable, more time may be needed for them to develop the teaching competencies that are needed for successful co-teaching to occur.

For those in Quadrant D, who are neither willing nor capable, it may be necessary to provide systematic professional development opportunities such as those described in Chapter 11 and logistical administrative supports such as those described in Chapter 10. The Zone of Proximal Development (Vygotsky 1987) offers a theoretical framework to describe how teachers learn from each other while they actually conduct co-teaching activities. A *Zone of Proximal Development* (ZPD) is defined as a particular

(Continued)

(Continued)

range of ability with and without assistance from a teacher or a more capable peer (Vygotsky 1987). Vygotsky emphasizes that what children can do with the assistance of others is even more indicative of their mental development than what they can do alone. We believe that this is also true for teachers: what teachers can do with the assistance of others is even more indicative of their capabilities than what they can do alone.

To scaffold teachers effectively within their ZPDs, there should be an awareness of the reciprocal roles that can be assumed throughout the co-teaching process: A teacher-peer models the co-teaching behavior, that co-teaching behavior is then imitated, the model fades out instruction, and the teacher practices reciprocal teaching (scaffolding others) until the co-teaching skill is mastered. Supports and demands for co-teaching may be adjusted depending on the co-teacher's placement in the taxonomy.

To illustrate, when co-teachers are neither willing nor capable (Quadrant D), a lower demand for co-teaching would be expected, along with more support to learn the skills and develop the willingness. Teachers in Quadrant D might start with one period a day as a supportive co-teacher and then move to a parallel teaching arrangement as they experience the natural reinforcement of seeing children succeed.

When co-teachers are willing and capable (Quadrant A), they can continue to accept a high level of responsibility for co-teaching assignments and, at the same time, expand their skills to mentoring and coaching others. Co-teachers who are capable but not so willing (Quadrant B) might take the opportunity to interview other co-teaching teams in action to discover how perceived barriers were addressed. In this way, the unwilling co-teachers might become more willing to co-teach. When co-teachers are willing but not so capable (Quadrant C), specific supports for developing teaching skills such as cooperative learning would help the co-teachers learn the communication and leadership skills necessary for children to be successful in group work and, at the same time, co-teachers would be learning the skills to practice within their own co-teaching team work.

In summary, it is important to honor where people are in their co-teaching journeys and treat them with respect, regardless of the quadrant in which you or they may currently fall. Also remember that you and your co-teachers can and are obliged to lobby for professional development and administrative support so that you and your students can experience the benefits of co-teaching.

PART II SUMMARY ■

As you read about each of the co-teaching approaches in the previous chapters, you may have used the advance organizer presented in Figure II.1 in the introduction to Part II to compare and contrast what you learned about the four approaches. Did you detect key features (i.e., differences) of each approach? What were some cautions for using each of the four approaches? What did you conclude were some common features or similarities across the four co-teaching approaches? Whether or not you used the advance organizer to summarize your discoveries regarding the four co-teaching approaches, you may find the comparisons among the approaches presented in Figure II.2 on the following page useful as a summary of Chapters 4 through 7. Note that the content of this table is not intended to present all that there is to know about the four approaches, but is a selection of some of the common and differing dimensions as well as cautions associated with the supportive, parallel, complementary, and team-teaching approaches.

Figure II.2 Similarities and Differences of Supportive, Parallel, Complementary and Team Teaching Co-Teaching Approaches

Similarities Among the Four Co-Teaching Approaches

- Two or more co-teachers are in the classroom.
- They capitalize on specific strengths and expertise of co-teachers.
- They provide greater teacher-to-student ratios and additional one-on-one support for students in the classroom.
- All approaches have benefits and cautions associated with their use.
- Students are heterogeneously grouped by mixed abilities and interests.
- There are shared responsibilities.
- Each approach requires trust, communication, planning time, and coordination of effort. (Note: The need for all of these elements increases as you move from supportive to parallel, parallel to complementary, and complementary to team teaching co-teaching.)

Supportive Differences	Parallel Differences	Complementary Differences	Team-Teaching Differences
One co-teacher is in the lead role; the other provides support. Who is in lead and who provides support may change during the lesson.	Co-teachers work with different groups of students in the same room. (There are at least seven different options for arranging the groups.)	One co-teacher teaches content; the other clarifies, paraphrases, simplifies, or records content. One co-teacher may preteach specific study or social skills and monitors students' use of them; the other teaches the academic content.	Both co-teachers are equally responsible for planning, instruction of content, assessment, and grade assignment. This approach requires the greatest amount of planning time, trust, communication, and coordination of effort.
Supportive Cautions	Parallel Cautions	Complementary Cautions	Team-Teaching Cautions
Beware of the "Velcro effect," whereby a supportive co-teacher hovers over one or selected students, stigmatizing both students and the co-teacher. Beware making the supportive co-teacher the "discipline police," materials copier, or in-class paper grader rather than an instructor. Beware of ineffective use of the supportive co-teacher's (e.g., special educator) expertise Beware of resentment if the supportive co-teacher's (e.g., special educator) skills are not being used or the lead co-teacher (e.g., content teacher) feels an unequal burden of responsibility. Beware of staying in the supportive role due to lack of planning time.	Beware of creating a special class within the class and lowering student achievement by homogeneously grouping lower-performing students together (Marzano, Pickering, and Pollack 2001, 84). Beware that the noise level can become uncomfortably high when numerous activities are occurring in the same room. Beware failing to adequately prepare other co-teachers to ensure that they deliver instruction as intended, since you cannot monitor each other while you all are simultaneously co-teaching.	Beware of not monitoring the students who need it. Beware of too much teacher talk, repetition, and lack of student-student interaction. Beware of "typecasting" the co-teacher delivering content as the "expert" or "real" teacher. Beware of failing to plan for "role release" so that all co-teachers can teach the content.	Beware of not monitoring the students who need it. Beware of too much teacher talk, repetition, and lack of student-student interaction.

PART III

Changing Roles and Responsibilities

The two chapters in Part III examine how the role of paraprofessionals and students change when they are engaged as co-teachers in the classroom. Chapter 8 traces the history of paraprofessionals in schools; introduces a paraprofessional and her team; and follows her team as she engages in supportive, parallel, and complementary co-teaching roles in a single lesson. This vignette is followed by an examination of the benefits of having paraprofessionals co-teach, the unique challenges faced by paraprofessional co-teachers, and cautions for paraprofessional co-teachers to avoid when engaged in each of the four co-teaching approaches.

Chapter 9 looks at the role of students as co-teachers and introduces five vignettes in which elementary through high school students engage as instructors in very different ways. The remainder of the chapter examines the emerging research base on students as co-teachers and offers suggestions on how to prepare students for and assess them in the co-teaching role.

The Role of Paraprofessionals in Co-Teaching

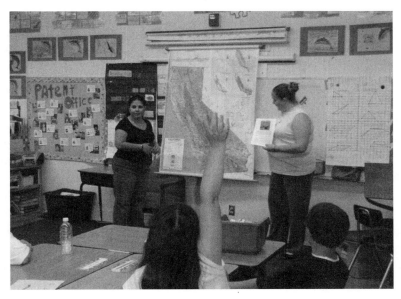

Lauren Etting

Topics Included in This Chapter:

- History of paraprofessionals in education
- Meet a paraprofessional and her elementary co-teachers
- A paraprofessional in the role of supportive, parallel, and complementary co-teacher
- Benefits of paraprofessionals as co-teachers
- Challenges for paraprofessionals as co-teachers
- Cautions to paraprofessionals as co-teachers
- Assessing paraprofessionals as co-teachers

Have you ever wondered about the role of paraprofessionals in co-teaching? In our work with co-teachers, we have faced numerous questions about the various roles of paraprofessionals in inclusive classrooms. In this chapter, we examine these roles. Through a vignette, we offer examples of how a paraprofessional can contribute effectively as a co-teacher in the classroom. We summarize potential benefits of having a paraprofessional in the classroom as a co-teacher. We also examine the critical issues of paraprofessional training and supervision as well as cautions about employing paraprofessionals as co-teachers.

■ HISTORY OF PARAPROFESSIONALS IN EDUCATION

The history of paraprofessionals began in the 1950s, when paraprofessionals were introduced into schools to provide teachers with more time for planning for instruction. For the most part, early paraprofessionals performed clerical services such as duplication of materials or management of students in noninstructional settings (e.g., lunch room, playground). Then in the 1970s, federal legislation was passed that guaranteed students with disabilities access to free public education. With steady movement toward general education being the preferred primary placement for students with disabilities, the paraprofessional's role has transformed to being primarily instructional in nature, especially when supporting students in the general education setting (Giangreco, Smith, and Pinckney 2006; Pickett and Gerlach 1997, 2003).

The increased reliance on paraprofessionals to assist in differentiating instruction in the classroom is evidenced by the numbers. For example, a comprehensive study of K–12 staffing patterns in all 50 U.S. states revealed that from 1993 to 2000, the number of paraprofessionals in classrooms increased 65%, from approximately 319,000 to over 525,000 (National Center for Education Statistics 2000). Of these, 55% were employed in inclusive and other educational settings supporting students with disabilities, 25% were assigned to support students in compensatory programs (e.g., as Title I aides or multilingual aides), and the remaining 20% worked in learning environments such as libraries, media centers, and computer laboratories. These data reveal the predominant instructional nature of today's paraprofessionals, as do the various titles given to individuals in this position—teaching assistant, paraeducator, instructional aide, and educational technician, to name a few.

Given that hundreds of thousands of paraprofessionals are assigned to instruct in elementary, middle level, and high school classrooms, the following three questions naturally arise:

1. Can paraprofessionals be co-teachers?

2. What are the appropriate co-teaching roles for paraprofessionals?

3. What supports do paraprofessionals need to become and perform as effective co-teachers?

Let's examine the first question by revisiting the teaching teams introduced in Chapter 3. Recall that in the elementary team, Ms. Hernandez, the part-time paraprofessional who attends the university in hopes of becoming a teacher, joins the first-grade classroom teacher, Ms. Gilpatrick, for three hours a day during literacy instruction. Also, Ms. Nugent, the school's new speech and language therapist, joins the team as a collaborating teacher. Recall also the transdisciplinary middle level teaching team. This team comprises two content area teachers—Mr. Silva, the bilingual math and science teacher, and Ms. Kurtz, the language arts and social studies teacher—Ms. Spaulding, the team's special educator, and Ms. Olvina, the paraprofessional who is assigned to one of Mr. Silva's science classes and one of his math classes. With the addition of a paraprofessional as integral to each team, students were more likely to receive individualized instruction to meet their needs.

To approach the second question—whether a paraprofessional can play any of the supportive, parallel, complementary, and team-teaching roles—take a moment to revisit Chapters 4 through 7, which describe the co-teaching approaches. As we track the elementary team members through their experiences with the four co-teaching approaches, we learn how Ms. Hernandez successfully works with her collaborating teachers using the supportive, parallel, and complementary co-teaching approaches. As we trace the middle level team's journey from supportive to team-teaching instructional arrangements, we learn how Ms. Olvina naturally uses all four of the co-teaching approaches. For all four approaches, then, it is possible for paraprofessionals to provide meaningful instruction, although our experience has been that to use the complementary and team-teaching approaches, the paraprofessional's roles and responsibilities require, at the very least, time for planning, careful training, and supervision. Issues of paraprofessional training and supervision for co-teaching are critical ones that are frequently discussed in the literature (Ashbaker and Morgan 2005; French 2002; Gerlach 2006; Picket and Gerlach 2003). Therefore, at the end of this chapter, we examine these issues and offer some advice to co-teachers.

Meet a Paraprofessional and her Elementary Co-Teachers

The role of the paraprofessional as a co-teacher is best illustrated by examples. To supplement the examples of the elementary and middle level co-teaching teams described in Chapters 4 through 7, we introduce you to the following elementary team, on which Ms. Katz is the assigned paraprofessional.

Who Are Our Co-Teachers?

Table 8.1 introduces you to the team members by name, job role, and the curriculum area(s) for which each person is responsible.

(Continued)

(Continued)

Table 8.1   Meet the Co-Teaching Team Members

Co-Teaching Team Members	Co-Teaching Role	Curriculum Area(s)
Mr. Jeffries	Fourth-grade classroom teacher	All core areas
Ms. Katz	Paraprofessional	Language arts, science/health
Mr. Riehl	Speech and language therapist	Social studies
Ms. Hoosokowa	Special educator	Math

Mr. Jeffries, a fourth-grade teacher, has been teaching for three years. Currently, he teaches 26 students—three are eligible for special education as well as speech and language services, one is eligible for gifted and talented services, five are eligible for Title I support, and three are students who are learning English. Two students are eligible for special education. Andreas, a boy with Autism, and Wendy, a girl with Down Syndrome, require additional peer, adult, or technological support at times throughout the day.

As a first-year co-teacher, Mr. Jeffries is eager to appear competent to all who enter his classroom but fears that his teacher preparation program and previous experiences have not adequately prepared him to co-teach or design lessons for such a diverse array of students. He acknowledges that the composition of his class is more diverse than previous years. He has been assigned to co-teach and collaboratively plan with a variety of people. He is to co-teach with Ms. Katz, a paraprofessional, daily during language arts and three times a week in science/health; with Mr. Riehl, a speech and language therapist, three times a week during social studies; and with Ms. Hoosokowa, a special educator, four times a week during math. In addition to meeting and planning with these folks, Mr. Jeffries is expected to collaboratively plan monthly with the teacher who works with students eligible for free and reduced lunch, the consultant who works with students who are gifted and talented, and the teacher for students learning English. Although Mr. Jeffries welcomes all of the support, he feels a bit overwhelmed with the number of people with whom he must interact and with the number of meetings that he must attend.

Ms. Katz has worked as a paraprofessional in the same school district for four years. This is her first year at this particular elementary school. In previous years, she provided instruction and support to students who were seated at the back of classrooms, or she supported certain students by sitting next to them during other class activities. Also, she has performed many clerical duties (e.g., copying worksheets, recording grades, making modified materials). Her supervisor, Ms. Hoosokowa, tells Ms. Katz that she will now function primarily as a supportive or parallel co-teacher with Mr. Jeffries during language arts and science/health classes. She learns about the various learning profiles of the students in Mr. Jeffries's class and is told that her responsibility is to promote independence and interaction with peers rather than codependence with the paraprofessional. Ms. Katz comments that this is a departure from her traditional responsibilities and is uncertain about how to function in the classroom. She wonders how acceptable these new responsibilities and roles will be to Mr. Jeffries. Ms. Hoosokowa promises to meet with Ms. Katz and Mr. Jeffries weekly and to occasionally observe, coach, or co-teach to model practices and approaches for Mr. Jeffries and Ms. Katz to use during their team-taught language arts and science/ health classes.

Getting Ready to Co-Teach

Ms. Katz is required to attend two days of training prior to the beginning of the school year. The training, designed and delivered by Ms. Hoosokowa and Mr. Riehl, emphasizes skills development for paraprofessionals. However, when Mr. Jeffries reviews the list of strategies Ms. Katz would learn (i.e., developing positive supports for responding to challenging behavior, differentiating instruction based on learning profiles, using educational technology to support diverse learners, facilitating peer support, co-teaching, and learning the roles and responsibilities in inclusive classrooms), he asked if he could attend. Ms. Hoosokowa and Ms. Katz were thrilled that he wanted to attend. Ms. Hoosokowa talked with Mr. Riehl, and they decided to open the training session to any professional staff member who might want to participate. Ms. Katz learns that she will participate in twice-monthly, hour-and-a-half training meetings for all district paraprofessionals. Mr. Jeffries is surprised and impressed that Ms. Katz will have ongoing professional development while co-teaching in his class.

Ongoing Planning for Co-Teaching

During the first week of school, Ms. Katz, Ms. Hoosokowa, and Mr. Jeffries identify the need for and initiate a weekly 45-minute collaborative meeting time. Once a month when they review the progress of target students and discuss further accommodations or modifications for any learner who appears to be struggling, they are joined by Mr. Riehl as well as the teacher who works with students eligible for free and reduced lunch, the consultant who works with students who are gifted and talented, and the teacher for students learning English. On a daily basis, Ms. Katz meets with Mr. Jeffries for 10 minutes before the language arts class in order to review and finalize the procedures that each will follow during the lesson. Ms. Katz is comfortable meeting with Ms. Hoosokowa on an as-needed basis.

A PARAPROFESSIONAL IN THE ■ ROLE OF SUPPORTIVE, PARALLEL, AND COMPLEMENTARY CO-TEACHER

The Big Picture

It is one month into the school year, and Ms. Katz is feeling comfortable in her role as a member of the teaching team. Ms. Hoosokowa has observed and given feedback three times. In meetings with Mr. Jeffries, Ms. Katz feels her ideas are respected and welcomed. Mr. Jeffries has said on more than one occasion that her contributions in the classroom are valued. Ms. Katz is especially pleased that Ms. Hoosokowa has noticed academic, social, and communication progress shown by both Andreas, a boy with autism, and Wendy, a girl with Down Syndrome.

Mr. Jeffries is amazed at how efficient and productive the weekly planning meetings have become. He, too, has noticed and is excited about the progress all of his students are making. He is pleased with the lessons that the team has implemented. He has shared the lessons with other fourth-grade teachers, noting how grateful he's become of his teammates' knowledge and perspectives. He would like to continue to learn effective teaching strategies and has decided to earn a master's degree in special education or instructional leadership.

A Sample Lesson: Supportive, Parallel, and Complementary Co-Teaching in Action

Mr. Jeffries and Ms. Katz outline a three-day language arts lesson on character development and plot for the next week (see Resource G for the lesson plan). As usual, they agree to create a positive tone by greeting students as they enter the classroom. Mr. Jeffries opens the lesson with an anticipatory set, a brief reading, and a minilecture on and review of character development and plot. Meanwhile, Ms. Katz is in the supportive co-teaching role, positions herself near Andreas because he sometimes gets confused about expectations for the lesson. Most of the time, Andreas wants to join the activity, and sometimes he needs a short break prior to settling into the activity. At these times, Ms. Katz suggests that he move to a table at the side of the room for a few moments or go for a walk prior to beginning the activity. Being in the supportive co-teaching role, Ms. Katz is free to provide the adult support or supervision that Andreas needs.

Strategically seated close to the front of the room near Mr. Jeffries, Wendy works with a group of her peers who can be strong academic, social, and communication models for her. At the beginning of a language arts activity, Wendy sometimes needs to be reminded to put away her other materials and get organized for the current activity. Again, because Ms. Katz is in the supportive co-teaching role at the opening of the lesson, she is free to assist Wendy, if needed. Also, Ms. Katz works in the supportive role at the beginning of the lesson by circulating among all of the students to check their completion of the language arts homework.

After the anticipatory set, minilecture, and a brief reading, Mr. Jeffries asks students questions about the characters in the story and the plot. Ms. Katz shifts to the complementary co-teaching role. She complements Mr. Jeffries's teaching by writing clarifying comments or examples of his questions on the board. Next, Ms. Katz switches roles with Mr. Jeffries; she takes the lead, assigning students to one of three learning stations. In this parallel co-teaching arrangement, one group, of which Andreas is a member, works at Station 1 with Mr. Jeffries to examine character development in a trade book they all read together. A second group works with Ms. Katz at Station 2, where students compose and illustrate their own stories. Ms. Katz is ready to explain how students might develop their characters fully and how they can make the plot more interesting. She coaches the students at her station to provide peer-editing suggestions to improve each other's characters and plots.

Wendy is a member of the third group of students, who are working independently at Station 3. These students choose their own stories, read, and then focus on the character and plot development. Here, students have the choice of accessing content either by reading alone, reading the same book with a peer, or reading with text-to-speech software, an accommodation for Wendy's Individual Education Program. Wendy and all of her classmates know that if she needs help with her computer, headset, or the text-to-speech software, she is expected to ask a peer for assistance before asking for help from Mr. Katz or Mr. Jeffries. Wendy is often joined by two other classmates who like to use the text-to-speech software because it helps them learn correct pronunciation of English vocabulary.

Students rotate through each of the three stations over the course of three days. On the third day, Mr. Jeffries and Ms. Katz exchange stations. Mr. Jeffries facilitates student writing at Station 2, and Ms. Katz is at Station 1, where students all read the same book together. They agreed to do this strategic swap in parallel co-teaching roles so that Mr. Jeffries can observe Wendy, whose turn it is at Station 2, and thus authentically assess her present level of performance in writing and illustrating an original story (one of the fourth-grade standards on the high-stakes statewide assessment test). As accommodations for Wendy, the co-teaching team has set up this station so that (a) she can first dictate parts of her story to a peer or to Mr. Jeffries, who writes her ideas, and (b) the dictated notes are then transferred to text with the *Alpha*, a keyboarding and writing tool. Peers are available to assist with illustrating, if Wendy so desires. Andreas is working at the independent reading station, with Ms. Katz as the group facilitator. A different book, at a more difficult reading level, will be assigned for the group to read at this station on the third day.

Both Andreas and Wendy have individualized behavior contracts and checklists that Ms. Hoosokowa developed and provided to Mr. Jeffries. At the end of each language arts period, Ms. Katz, in the parallel co-teacher role, meets with Wendy and then Andreas to discuss and record measures of their academic, social, communication, and independent behaviors; concurrently, Mr. Jeffries assigns homework and directs the other students to clean up the classroom. Wendy and Andreas then take their checklists to Mr. Jeffries, who reviews them and awards their earned points. He exchanges exuberant high fives with many of the students who are happy with the products they have created.

At their subsequent planning meeting, Mr. Jeffries and Ms. Katz reflect on the three-day lesson (see Resource G for the lesson plan). They agree that they liked the flow in and out of supportive, complementary, and parallel co-teaching approaches so much that they want to continue designing lessons this way. They brainstorm how to include others (e.g., parent volunteers, fifth or sixth graders, the librarian) who could facilitate a fourth learning station, so as to increase the amount of individualized attention and coaching that each student could then enjoy. They decide to ask Ms. Hoosokowa to facilitate a learning station. This would allow her to directly observe how the students with disabilities are not only surviving but thriving in the co-taught classroom.

Analyzing the Cooperative Process for a Paraprofessional as a Co-Teacher

Because you were introduced to the five basic elements that comprise the cooperative process for working within co-teaching teams in Chapters 4 through 7, we invite you to analyze this co-teaching team. In what ways have Ms. Katz, Mr. Jeffries, and Ms. Hoosokowa structured their work together? Do you see how they have set up frequent face-to-face interaction (daily as well as monthly), setting mutual goals so that they reciprocate and exchange roles (positive interdependence)? What specific interpersonal skills do you think were important in ensuring the success of this co-teaching team? In what ways were supervision and training provided to all team members? How did Mr. Jeffries and Ms. Katz share the monitoring of student progress and accountability? Do you agree that this team has mastered the cooperative process for creating a viable co-teaching team? What other considerations for determining effectiveness did they consider?

■ BENEFITS OF PARAPROFESSIONALS AS CO-TEACHERS

Researchers and practitioners alike agree that multiple benefits occur when paraprofessionals join co-teacher teams. The benefits are organized by their role in inclusion and differentiation of instruction, their role as cultural ambassadors, and their role in recruiting paraprofessionals into the teaching force.

Inclusion and Differentiation of Instruction

Researchers and practitioners mention the importance of and need for instructional assistants in order to instruct students with identified disabilities alongside their general education peers (Downing, Ryndak, and Clark 2000; Marks, Schrader, and Levine 1999; Mueller and Murphy 2001; Piletic, Davis, and Aschemeier 2005; Riggs and Mueller 2001). Co-teachers in inclusive settings have not been silent about their reliance on and appreciation of paraprofessionals (e.g., Salazar and Nevin 2005). For instance, Nevin et al. (2007) describe co-teachers' perceptions of the added value that paraprofessionals bring. In particular, the teacher-to-student ratio is increased, thus allowing for increased personalization of instructional programs.

Cultural Ambassadors

In their comprehensive study of paraprofessionals in two large school districts in Southern California, Rueda and Monzo (2002) state that the knowledge of the multicultural and multilingual communities from which paraprofessionals hail is essential in helping teachers tap into their students' prior knowledge and interests. This is especially true if a teacher is monolingual and his or her students are culturally and linguistically diverse. As a caution Rueda and Monzo note that if school cultures don't support collaboration among teachers and paraprofessionals, teachers can remain unaware of the knowledge that paraprofessionals possess about students' cultures. Thus, teachers can fail to tap their paraprofessionals' expertise as cultural ambassadors.

Teacher Recruitment

As preservice teacher educators, we have met paraprofessionals who decide to become certified teachers; they are among the best first-year teachers who show high levels of confidence meeting the needs of diverse learners. Therefore, one benefit of having paraprofessionals serve as co-teachers, particularly in inclusive general education classrooms, is that they provide a solid foundation upon which to apply the theory and practices to which they are introduced in their teacher preparation studies. There are currently teacher preparation programs in special education from which paraprofessionals are actively recruited for teaching certification (Littleton 1998; Rueda and Monzo 2002).

CHALLENGES FOR PARAPROFESSIONALS ■ AS CO-TEACHERS

Poorly Defined Roles

In the vignette above that describes Mr. Jeffries, Ms. Katz, and their support team, did you detect the variety of roles that Ms. Katz performed in the classroom? Research studies conducted over the last decade reveal a broad range of roles that paraprofessionals can and do play. For example, bilingual paraprofessionals have served as both instructors and translators for children who speak languages other than English (Ashbaker and Morgan 2005; Wenger et al. 2004). Paraprofessionals are instructors of small groups (Ashbaker and Morgan 2005), behavior managers (Perez and Murdock 1999; Young 1997), assistants in speech and language therapy (Radaszewski-Byrne 1997), and even job coaches (Rogan and Held 1999).

The range and flexibility of paraprofessionals' roles can be viewed as both a gift and a burden. On the one hand, role flexibility gives teachers and paraprofessionals the discretion to adjust a paraprofessional's job description based on the current needs of the students in a classroom. On the other hand, if job expectations are not clear, it can be confusing, not only to the paraprofessional but also to the teacher and students. Villa and Thousand (2005) emphasize the importance of at least some fundamental job clarity regarding collaborative partnerships:

Job titles and formal definitions determine the way that people behave. Thus, to further signal a change in culture (from a previously isolationist perspective of only one teacher in a classroom), we should formulate new policies and job descriptions that expect, inspect, and respect a collaborative ethic. (p. 69)

Doyle (2002), who has developed comprehensive paraprofessional training materials and guidelines, suggests that paraprofessionals and their co-teachers articulate roles for at least the following five key areas: lesson planning, delivery of instruction, responses to students' behaviors (both proactive and reactive), strategies to promote ongoing communication, and methods of student evaluation. Pickett and Gerlach (2003) offer two inventories. One assesses potential responsibilities of a paraprofessional in a classroom or school (i.e., delivery of instruction, activity preparation, supervision of groups of students, behavior management, ethics, team participation and membership, clerical work, home school communication, and other special education duties). The other examines the skills and confidence of the paraprofessional in these same areas. A comparison of the lists of responsibilities can inform which tasks become immediate job responsibilities and which require further preparation. Especially important for co-teaching is a clear description of what are and are not a paraprofessional's job functions, which can include instruction, behavior management, materials preparation, collecting assessment information, and legal and ethical conduct.

Ambiguity in Supervision Responsibilities

Etscheidt (2005), in a comprehensive legal analysis of paraprofessional services for students with disabilities, reminds us that "paraprofessionals may not serve as the sole designer, delivery, or evaluator of a student's program" (p. 68). In other words, it is the teacher who has the responsibility for the education of all learners even when instructional and other tasks are delegated or mutually decided upon by a teaching team. Paraprofessionals are school employees who teach under the supervision of other professional staff responsible for the design, modification, implementation, and assessment of instruction and learner progress. Thus, as national leaders in the training and supervision of paraprofessionals emphasize (Pickett and Gerlach 2003), supervision of paraprofessionals must occur. Yet ambiguity about who is responsible for the supervision of paraprofessionals and how supervision should be accomplished remains a premier problem. Clearly, co-teaching among educators and paraprofessionals creates a unique opportunity for the regular, authentic, and ongoing observation, analysis, and coaching of paraprofessional effectiveness that is recommended by Morgan and Ashbaker (2001).

Inconsistent Initial and Ongoing Professional Development

Mueller (2002) refers to the *paraprofessional paradox* when she writes that "we have developed a service delivery system that depends heavily on relatively untrained, underpaid, and devalued staff members to provide complex instructional and behavioral programs to our most challenging students. Hello, what's wrong with this picture?" (p. 64). Clearly, administrators, teachers, and paraprofessionals themselves want to avoid this paradox, and there are no arguments against the notion that the best way to address such a paradox is to provide adequate preparation and supervision of paraprofessionals. The literature is rich in comprehensive paraprofessional development options (e.g., Bueno Center for Multicultural Education 1997; French 2002; Morgan, Forbush, & Avis 2001). A valuable resource to add to your support system is the annotated bibliography of paraprofessional training resources, which is updated regularly and published on the Web by the National Resource Center for Paraprofessionals (http://www.nrcpara.org/bibliography).

CAUTIONS TO PARAPROFESSIONALS ■
AS CO-TEACHERS

At the end of the chapters on each of the four approaches to co-teaching, there are frequently asked questions that serve as cautions for co-teachers engaged in each of the approaches. The cautions apply equally to paraprofessionals. Several are worthy of repeating here, as they especially apply to paraprofessionals. For paraprofessionals in the supportive co-teaching role, be mindful not to become "Velcro-ed" to individual students or function as hovercraft vehicles blocking students' interactions with other students. This can result in isolation of both the student and the paraprofessional, leading other students to perceive that the support teacher and the student being supported are not genuine members of the classroom.

For paraprofessionals in the parallel co-teaching role, remember that it is possible to create a special class within a class by routinely working with the same group of students who are clustered homogeneously based on some dimension such as perceived ability, eligibility for special education, or status as an English learner. This can stigmatize the students and the paraprofessional as well as remove the opportunity for students to learn from other students who learn in different ways, which occurs when students are grouped heterogeneously.

For paraprofessionals in the complementary co-teaching role, remember that, like a new co-teacher assigned to an unfamiliar content area, it is impossible for a paraprofessional to have complete knowledge of the content area from the very start. There are many ways to become more proficient in a content area (see the second frequently asked question in Chapter 6). Be sure to take the initiative and learn about what you don't know in whatever way is best for you to access and absorb new information. Also, remember that it is possible to step on the toes of a co-teaching partner when restating points. To ensure that this type of clarification for students is not perceived as a correction or evaluation, be sure to have the conversation about when and how it is OK to complement instruction. It may be that you have to work out a signaling system so that you know when one co-teacher wishes to jump in and add value to another's teaching.

For paraprofessionals who are fortunate enough to reach the point in their partnership with a co-teacher to team teach, remember that any paraprofessional may be reassigned at any point in time, no matter how great the co-teaching relationship is. It may be to students' benefit that you follow them to the next grade. It may be that there is a greater need for in-class support from a paraprofessional in another classroom, with another teacher, or in another subject area.

■ ASSESSING PARAPROFESSIONALS AS CO-TEACHERS

As is true of professional certificated or credentialed teachers who engage in co-teaching, paraprofessionals who work as co-teachers benefit and grow from receiving constructive feedback from colleagues or by evaluating their own performance against some standard. That standard might be the job description crafted for the paraprofessional position. Or it might be the results of assessing oneself using the survey instrument Are We Really Co-Teachers? We created this 34-item checklist to support co-teachers in their professional development. For ideas on how to use the checklist, see Table 11.3 in Chapter 11.

The Role of Students as Co-Teachers

Jacqueline S. Thousand

Topics Included in This Chapter:

- Vignettes: Students in co-teaching roles
- Analyzing the cooperative process in the student co-teaching vignettes
- Preparing students to be co-teachers
- The research base for students as co-teachers
- Assessing students as co-teachers
- Frequently asked questions

Recently, we observed a classroom of fourth and fifth graders who were actually co-teaching! In this chapter, we begin by defining *teaching* so that it is feasible to consider students as co-teachers. We briefly explain methods that allow students to become co-teachers, and through a variety of vignettes, we show the student co-teachers in action. We summarize the emerging research base on students as co-teachers (including the barriers and disadvantages to students as co-teachers), provide a method for student co-teachers to be assessed, and pose and answer frequently asked questions to address the major barriers to implementing students as co-teachers.

What is teaching? We believe that to tap the vast resources the student body offers, we should use the broadest possible answers to this question. If you consult any dictionary, you will find multiple meanings that the English language attributes to the word *teaching*. For example, to teach is to impart knowledge or skills. To teach is to give instruction. To teach is to cause to learn by experience or example. To teach is to advocate or preach. On the other hand, to instruct or to tutor or to train to educate implies methodological knowledge in addition to content knowledge. Students can and should become co-teachers. They effectively collaborate in school activities such as serving on school committees, advocating for classmates and themselves, planning and evaluating instruction from their teachers, and providing assistance in making friends (Villa and Thousand 2004). In fact, children and youth who learn and practice being student co-teachers are more likely to grow into adults who are more effective advocates for themselves. They are likely to become more effective members of work teams, their families, and their communities. In other words, when students are co-teachers, they can embody all the verbs that are associated with the word *teaching*. They can tutor, instruct, impart knowledge, assess progress, demonstrate examples, act out the procedures as a model, and so on. In Chapter 2, we emphasized the reasons co-teaching is important in twenty-first-century schools. We want to emphasize here our most important reason for co-teaching: it allows students to experience and imitate the cooperative and collaborative skills that teachers show when they co-teach. All students benefit when their teachers share ideas, work cooperatively, and contribute to one another's learning. This often results in students becoming co-teachers themselves, as the following vignettes illustrate.

■ VIGNETTES: STUDENTS IN CO-TEACHING ROLES

Just as there are many faces of adult co-teachers, there are many ways for students to be co-teachers. Table 9.1 provides an overview of the roles and methods used by the student co-teacher teams described in this chapter.

Table 9.1 The Many Faces of Students as Co-Teachers

Meet the Student Partners	Co-Teacher Partner(s)	Curriculum Areas	Co-Teaching Approach
Bill, a high school senior, attending college-level classes in math during junior and senior years	Sharon, a high school math teacher	Sharon supports Bill in acquiring a deeper understanding of math, assisting fellow students, and exploring teaching as a career	Supportive for the first three weeks, complementary for the next few weeks, team teaching for the remaining time
Christine, a high school student with special needs Cat, a high school student who wants to develop her teaching skills		Cat tutors Christine in the content of the eleventh-grade health class so that Christine learns to teach a unit on personal safety to a third-grade class	Supportive and complementary
Dave and Juan, reciprocal co-teachers	Elaine, a third-grade classroom teacher, and Laurie, a special educator	Elaine and Laurie teach reciprocal teaching to all students and structure a learning contract for Dave and Juan to be more successful in mathematics (acquisition of facts)	Complementary (each serves as teacher and as learner)
Denny, a fifth-grade student who is gifted and talented and has challenging interpersonal skills	Cathy, a fifth-grade mathematics teacher, and Shamonique, the gifted and talented teacher	Cathy and Shamonique teach Friendly Disagreeing skills and math problem solving with an emphasis on explaining the reasoning processes	Parallel (for acquiring the friendly disagreeing skills) and supportive (for applying the friendly disagreeing skills)
Co-teaching students	Ms. Marquez, teacher of 25 ethnically and linguistically diverse first, second, and third graders	Ms. Marquez teaches students to teach each other computer and other educational technology skills that they know	Complementary

Meet Bill and Sharon

During his senior year in high school, Bill experienced a unique partnership with his mathematics teacher that evolved from supportive, to parallel, to complementary co-teaching and culminated in team teaching.

"It is pretty neat when you can help out students who are having trouble learning, challenge someone like me at the same time, and it doesn't cost the school district a dime." Bill made this statement after he had exhausted his school's mathematics curriculum by his sophomore year and attended university mathematics courses in his junior and senior years. In his senior year, he arranged an independent study in mathematics that included team teaching with Sharon, who taught the high school's most advanced math class. Bill wanted to refine his instructional skills even though he also tutored many students in mathematics after school.

During the first week of the team-teaching arrangement, Bill observed Sharon. At the end of the second week, he began teaching the last 10 minutes of the class; he was responsible for introducing the math concept or operation that would be taught in the next day's lesson. Sharon and Bill met daily to review and approve Bill's instructional plan for the minilessons. After a month, Bill taught his first full-length class and continued for the rest of the semester. When he was not instructing the group as a whole, he worked individually with students who had missed class or who had difficulty with a concept. He continued to observe Sharon's methods and conferred with her on a daily basis to receive feedback on his own teaching. Bill also asked for feedback from the students. He was available to help after school, and some students even called him at home for help. One student in the class commented, "Bill is easier to understand compared with the other teacher, and he uses better examples."

Bill's inclusion in the mathematics teaching team had other positive effects. He reported that he was advancing his math education and learning about people at the same time. He also noted that his self-confidence had improved. Having been a student in the same class only two years earlier, he empathized with the students' struggles with the material. He believed that the students recognized and appreciated this empathy. Sharon was impressed with the professional and serious manner with which Bill conducted himself, the students' positive responses to his presence as her co-teacher, and his progress in using effective instructional strategies.

Meet Christine and Cat

When Christine made a presentation before 200 parents, teachers, and administrators at her high school graduation, she stumbled slightly. The stumble came as she read something she had written three years earlier for a school newspaper article. She decided on the spot to make a modification. "I have . . . nothing . . . and I'm not handicapped," the 19-year-old proclaimed, and she immediately received a well-earned round of applause.

The applause came because the audience could see the newspaper article projected on the screen at the front of the room. In the article that she wrote as part of a journalism class she and her tutor had been taking, Christine explained, "I have Down Syndrome, but I'm not handicapped." The modification represented Christine's anger at the labels placed on her and her refusal to accept the limitations that some labels imply.

Throughout her high school career, Christine enjoyed several types of peer support that made her full inclusion into a public high school possible. The peer support helped Christine enjoy meaningful relationships with those who became her tutors, tutees, friends, advocates, and recipients of her advocacy. During her freshman year, the peer support came in the form of the cheerleading squad of which Christine was the student manager. During her sophomore year, Christine participated in a journalism class responsible for the production of a weekly school newspaper. Because it took her nearly five times longer to complete class assignments, her teachers sought a full-time partner for her. Cat, a fellow student journalist who had a study hall during the same period as Christine, volunteered. The two worked together twice a week during class and every day in the computer lab during study hall to produce "Christine's Corner," a column featuring the unique accomplishments of various students in the school.

During her junior year, Christine and Cat enrolled as second-year journalism students, resuming their partnership. Cat arranged to receive credit as a peer tutor for Christine. She planned, implemented, and evaluated daily lessons designed to assist Christine in completing health, journalism, and history assignments. She met weekly with her supervisor (a special educator who coordinated Christine's educational services), kept a journal, and learned Madeline Hunter's model of effective teaching (M. Hunter 1988, 1994; R. Hunter and Hunter 2006). With Christine as her tutee, Cat embarked on what developed into her future career as a teacher. Cat reported in her journal, "Not many kids my age get to sample the job that they hope to have five or six years down the road. Thanks to Christine, I get to do that. My transcript and portfolio will show that I've chosen this as an individualized course of study, and that should help me to get into the college I want."

Christine appreciated Cat's support. She explained, "It's boring having my teachers all day. I like having Cat as my tutor because we're friends and she is fun." Cat also participated with Christine in meetings with teachers, advocates, and administrators to plan for a smooth transition from high school to adult life. Christine noted, "I get scared. I don't know all those people, and sometimes I cry. That's why Cat helps me. She tells me it's okay, and she will stick up for me. After those meetings, we go to McDonald's and talk it over."

As much as Christine enjoyed the tutor-tutee relationship with Cat, she also wanted to reverse that arrangement so that she, too, was in the helping role. Christine did not have the content knowledge to assist Cat in all of her academic courses, so other opportunities were explored. What resulted was a weekly health lesson that Christine team taught with a third-grade teacher. Christine applied the knowledge she was acquiring in her 11th-grade health course to the personal safety unit offered to the third graders. Christine then evaluated her own performance by summarizing the lessons and the outcomes to Cat, who planned to be an elementary teacher. "I learned from Christine what worked and didn't work for little kids," Cat relayed. "By sharing her experiences with me, she helped me see that younger students have shorter attention spans. I'll remember that someday when I have a class of my own."

The coordinator for Christine's high school services wrote, "I feel extremely fortunate. . . . Christine, in my opinion, is a remarkable woman who has freely shared her thoughts and feelings with others. In return, she has been the recipient of support, respect, and

(Continued)

(Continued)

unabashed admiration from some of the most unsuspecting and extraordinary adolescents I have known. She and her friends have taught me that camaraderie and common sense are far more useful than a master's degree and that some of the best educational resources come free of charge" (as reported by Harris 1994, 300).

Christine and Cat not only experienced the unique feeling that comes from helping; Christine developed a new co-teaching relationship with the third-grade teacher, which served as a key performance demonstration of her Individual Education Plan (IEP) speech and behavioral goals. Christine made extra effort to improve her articulation and to model appropriate behavior for the third graders she taught each week. Her skills in the academic classes she was taking improved steadily as she learned to translate into her own words what she was learning. Cat, similarly, experienced the benefits of practicing her own career goals in meaningful and realistic ways.

Meet Dave and Juan

All the students in Elaine and Laurie's third-grade classroom learned how to be reciprocal co-teachers for acquisition of math facts. Each student co-teacher practiced sequential co-teaching steps using auditory, verbal, and written directions to match different learning styles. Elaine, the classroom teacher, and Laurie, a special educator, scheduled at least one opportunity per day for the student co-teachers to practice—approximately 10 minutes to allow for each partner to play the role of teacher and then switch to the role of learner. The students focused on six math facts per session (four known and two unknown or as yet not mastered), practicing with activities that matched various learning styles (e.g., auditory, visual, kinesthetic) until mastery occurred.

They noticed that Dave and Juan were two student co-teachers who frequently used derogatory put-down statements and failed to use praise, feedback, or other appropriate social skills they had learned during training. They also fought over the materials. Their progress in acquiring math facts as well as their written feedback, however, indicated that they perceived the sessions to be going well. When Elaine interviewed them about these concerns, Dave and Juan each accused the other. As reported by LaPlant and Zane (2002), Laurie provided additional social skills training, and both Laurie and Elaine demonstrated the social skills and supervised the tutoring sessions frequently. Dave and Juan developed more skills in making positive statements and sustaining positive interactions with one another. Elaine and Laurie then added two items to Dave and Juan's data-collection procedures: saying nice things and saying "thank you." Both Dave and Juan also kept a graph to give them a visual representation of their performance. Finally, Elaine and Laurie set up a contract whereby Dave and Juan collected jointly accrued points based on the number of times they both made positive statements. The points could be traded later for activities they both enjoyed (e.g., learning games, lunch with the supervisor). Not only were they learning more math facts, they treated each other with more respect, became friends, and eagerly volunteered to serve as co-teachers with other classmates.

Meet Denny, Cathy, and Shamonique

Denny (a pseudonym), a fifth-grade student who was gifted and talented and had challenging interpersonal behaviors, was in Cathy and Shamonique's classroom with 24 peers (Conn-Powers

2002). He often insisted that his ideas were the only correct ones and ridiculed his classmates. During a social studies lesson that required debate skills, Shamonique, the gifted and talented education co-teacher, taught the students a new skill—encouraging others by asking them, in a friendly way, to share their ideas for solutions—to use when they worked in groups. In this cooperative lesson, students were expected to use the skill at least twice during a 40-minute problem-solving session taught by Cathy, the fifth-grade mathematics co-teacher. In their groups, students were expected to solve an equation, explain their reasoning, apply computational skills, and use friendly disagreeing skills they had learned during social studies. Each group kept track of its friendly disagreeing skills by tallying members' use of the five ways to disagree. They referred to the posters that they had created in a previous lesson, which prominently displayed the five ways to disagree (see Table 9.2).

Table 9.2   Examples of Friendly Disagreeing Skills

Friendly Disagreeing Skills	What Words Might You Say?	What Might You See and Hear?
Ask for different opinions	Why do you think that is best? What is your answer?	Lean in, friendly face, mild tone of voice
Ask others to explain why	Will you show me how that works? Will you help me see how to solve the problem?	Lean in, friendly face, quizzical tone of voice
Add on or modify	Could we expand on your answer? How about if we added . . . ? Is it ok to change . . . ?	Lean in, friendly face, questioning tone of voice
Offer alternatives	Wouldn't this work too? What do you think about . . . ?	Lean in, friendly face, mild tone of voice
State disagreement	I have a different idea. Can I show you how my answer is different?	Lean in, friendly face, excited tone of voice

In addition, each group recorded its problem-solving strategies on the poster paper. The lesson overall was quite successful. All six groups met the criteria. Denny participated for the entire lesson, and his team members praised him for encouraging them to disagree with him. The impact of this positive peer pressure was powerful. While Denny played tetherball with another group from his class at recess, Shamonique overheard him use one of the friendly disagreeing skills, the alternative-idea method: "What do you think about this way to hit the ball?"

(Continued)

(Continued)

Meet Student Co-Teachers for Computer Use

Ms. Marquez, a classroom teacher in an ethnically and culturally diverse elementary magnet school for computing and technology, was considered an outstanding teacher. Her class consisted of 25 first, second, and third graders: 15 Anglo children, 8 Mexican Americans, 1 Chinese American, and 1 African American. The classroom seating and the placement of computers were flexible and adaptable to students' needs and the specific learning activity.

Ms. Marquez noticed that the children used the computers individually, in pairs, in larger groups, or with the teacher depending on the task and the students' computer skills or preferences. She assigned each student to be a study buddy with another student and reminded them that sharing and helping were expected. Study buddies were taught specific social skills for cooperation (e.g., sharing ideas, explaining answers) and were expected to produce an academic product from either a teacher assignment or a student-selected assignment.

Learning styles and cultural differences were easily accommodated because Ms. Marquez selected software with animated graphics, sound output, sound input, or visual text to meet the auditory or visual learning styles of many children. In addition, the keyboard and mouse required kinesthetic learning (for more on effective instructional practices for students who are learning English, see Gersten and Baker 2000).

When it came to grouping students, Ms. Marquez reflected on Chisholm's (1995) research, which highlights the fact that gender is the only factor that appears when children are able to select their working groups: "Cross-gender groups at the computer were essentially non-existent" (p. 170). Consequently, Ms. Marquez ensured cross-gender groupings by assigning male and female students to work together on certain assignments. Later, one child explained that she worked with everybody (meaning both boys and girls), thus showcasing the egalitarian nature of the classroom.

■ ANALYZING THE COOPERATIVE PROCESS IN THE STUDENT CO-TEACHING VIGNETTES

These examples of student co-teachers illustrate the five elements of the cooperative process—face-to-face interaction, positive interdependence, interpersonal skills, monitoring, and accountability. We emphasize again that when these elements are present in a co-teaching partnership, in this case a student co-teaching partnership, the quality of the relationship often is more creative and yields better outcomes. The face-to-face interactions included student co-teachers in one-to-one tutorials (e.g., Dave and Juan, Christine and Cat during journalism class), small-group instruction (Ms. Marquez's students co-teaching each other computer skills, Denny and his classmates co-teaching their reasoning for math problem solving and keeping track of friendly disagreeing skills), and large-group instruction (Bill and Sharon co-teaching the math class). Positive interdependence varied according to the age and grade level of the student co-teachers (e.g., goal interdependence for Bill and Christine, reward interdependence for Dave and Juan). Social skills also varied according to the ages and needs of the student co-teachers (e.g., Christine improved her articulation so that the third graders could understand her, Denny learned to disagree in a friendly way that even helped him with a playground event). Methods to monitor and be accountable for progress included Dave and Juan's self-recorded graphs and the frequent feedback sessions between Bill and Sharon.

PREPARING STUDENTS TO BE CO-TEACHERS ■

In this section, we describe the vital role that adults play in creating successful student co-teachers. We describe several instructional methods that support students to serve in co-teaching roles: cooperative learning, peer tutoring, dialogue teaching, and instructional conversation.

The vignettes show that adult co-teachers play a vital role in creating successful student co-teachers. For example, Bill needed the agreement of Sharon, the math teacher, to become her co-teacher. Christine and Cat exchanged teacher and learner roles during the debriefing session for Christine's teaching of the safety unit for third grade. In this way, Cat could hear how differently third graders learn compared with Christine's learning needs. Elaine and Laurie explicitly taught reciprocal peer tutoring skills to their third graders and provided additional supports for Dave and Juan. Denny's co-teachers, Cathy and Shamonique, arranged for all the fifth graders to learn how to disagree in a friendly way.

Students are more likely to become effective co-teachers when their co-teachers explicitly teach how to tutor or work as study buddies. Co-teachers with successful student co-teachers also make sure that student co-teachers enjoy the reciprocity involved in being both teacher and learner. Co-teachers create more opportunities for students to practice co-teaching skills when they set up *cooperative group learning* so that all members of the group can practice the communication skills involved in teaching others what they know. Denny's co-teachers used cooperative group learning with an emphasis on teaching the social skill of friendly disagreeing. Dave and Juan's co-teachers used structured peer tutoring to help students with emotional challenges become kinder and more effective partner learners. Ms. Marquez was a co-teacher with her students to ensure improved computer skills for all the children. Bill and Christine benefited from having their co-teachers (Sharon and Cat) work with them as coaches in developing teaching skills.

Co-teachers who rely on cooperative group learning make sure that students are responsible not only for their own learning but also for the learning of the other members of their group. They are responsible for showing certain social behaviors with their peers. The co-teacher's role shifts from that of a presenter of information to a facilitator of learning. There are five major tasks in a cooperative lesson: (1) clearly specifying the objectives, (2) making decisions about placing students in learning groups to ensure heterogeneity, (3) clearly explaining what learning activities are expected of the students and how they will demonstrate positive interdependence, (4) monitoring the cooperative interactions and intervening to provide task assistance (e.g., answer questions, teach task-related skills) or to increase students' interpersonal and group skills, and (5) evaluating student achievement and group effectiveness (Johnson, Johnson, and Holubec 1998).

There are several other instructional methods that encourage and prepare students to be co-teachers. *Dialogue teaching* may be the perfect method for those who have been silenced (e.g., students of color, those at risk, second language learners, students with disabilities). Dialogue teaching means that students help to generate the curriculum, design their own instructional methods, and report their progress within a framework of consciousness-raising group dynamics (Kluth et al. 2002). Dialogue teaching also involves changing the pace of classroom speaking to allow more time to think before responding, valuing different types of contributions (e.g., laughter, gestures, typed words on a communication board), and making sure topics are important to the students (e.g., issues related to race, gender, class, ability). Co-teachers who practice dialogue teaching develop skills in listening to and differentially responding to their students' linguistic habits and verbal styles, especially for the students who are learning English as a second language or the students who are non-verbal. Student co-teachers who practice dialogue teaching can acquire a new awareness of their strengths and contributions.

Achievement increases when learners receive appropriate scaffolding of content instruction to help them learn English (Echevarria and Graves 1998; Graves, Gersten, and Haager 2004). Achievement also improves when teachers provide interactive and direct approaches to instruction for oral language, literacy, and academic content (Genesee et al. 2002). Other effective techniques include guided practice, active learning, opportunities for frequent conversation in English, instructional presentations with multiple media, and curriculum modifications.

Instructional conversation (Garcia 2002, 2005), also referred to as the *discourse of sheltered instruction* (Echevarria and Graves 1998), is a particularly compelling teaching-learning process to use when the student co-teachers are also students who are learning English and are fluent in other languages. Student co-teachers who use instructional conversation learn how to encourage talking. They, as well as their partners in the co-teaching relationship, practice the give-and-take that is a hallmark of authentic conversation. This is different from the typical one-way teacher-to-student talk that often dominates classrooms, in which the teacher asks questions and the student answers. Instead, the co-teacher who uses instructional conversation accepts responses in either language (e.g., Spanish or English) and, in a response, models the English phraseology through restatements and furthering comments to discover more about what the speaker knows. The co-teacher who uses instructional conversation also ignores inappropriate responses or inaccurate usage, such as incomplete utterances to convey meaning, rather than providing immediate correction as is the usual method in traditional instruction. Instead, the co-teacher models appropriate constructive social interaction by continuing the conversation while modeling the correct usage. Co-teachers who practice instructional conversation often add a visual component by writing the words and sentence structures on a chalkboard or chart paper (an especially helpful technique for the specialized vocabulary that often appears in science and math subjects).

A common characteristic of these teaching and learning activities is that they encourage students in the co-teacher role. The outcome is that students receive the benefits of a more active role in communicating their understanding of the academic content. This, in turn, leads to increased retention and achievement.

THE RESEARCH BASE FOR ■ STUDENTS AS CO-TEACHERS

In this section, we summarize recent research in several areas: peer tutoring, partner learning, students in coaching roles in cooperative groups, and student-led conferences. Several theoretical frameworks undergird the research and practice base for students as co-teachers. For example, cognitive psychologists have verified that *reciprocal teaching* (see Palinscar and Brown 1984) is effective in significantly raising and maintaining the reading comprehension scores of poor readers. In a reciprocal teaching exchange, students alternate being the teacher who coaches the comprehension skills being practiced, similar to the way that Dave and Juan interacted to learn their math facts. Another theoretical framework that explains the success of students as co-teachers is *social learning theory* (Johnson and Johnson 1989). When students work as co-teachers, they form an interdependent relationship that allows them to learn from each other as they teach.

First, there is a strong body of research about the benefits of peer tutoring. Fuchs, Fuchs, Mathes et al. (2002) and Fuchs, Fuchs, Thompson et al. (2000), for example, show that peer tutoring helps teachers individualize learning materials to address a broader range of instructional needs. Students at risk for school failure in urban multicultural and disadvantaged neighborhoods also have increased their reading skills when the whole class engaged in peer tutoring (Kourea, Cartledge, and Musti-Rao 2007). When students co-teach in a peer-tutoring system, there are more opportunities to respond to and practice academic content than in more conventional teacher-directed lessons. There is also evidence that peer tutoring facilitates positive changes in students' social behaviors and school adjustment (Fuchs, Fuchs, Mathes et al. 2002). Moreover, Faltis (1993) and Walter (1998) cite peer tutoring and cooperative group learning as methods that are especially beneficial for students who are learning English.

Similarly, a rich research base documents the benefits of students as co-teachers within cooperative group-learning formats, especially for building relationships among diverse populations. Johnson and Johnson (1989, 2000, 2002) summarize the impact of cooperative learning on the processes of acceptance and rejection. When students experience cooperative group learning (i.e., positive interdependence, positive interpersonal social interactions, systematic feedback on their academic and social skills progress), they show more frequent and open communication, deeper understanding of other perspectives, more clearly differentiated views of each other, improved self-esteem, more successful achievement and productivity, and increased willingness to interact with others who are different from them. When students work in co-teaching roles, they experience elements similar to cooperative group learning. For example, positive interdependence occurs through shared goals and division of labor, student co-teachers must show good interpersonal and communication skills in the teacher role, and they both assess how their teaching is affecting their learners and receive feedback about their performance from the educator working with them in the co-teacher role.

In addition, there is a nascent body of literature that should encourage educators to continue exploring how best to achieve the student co-teacher role. For example, when students took on the role of reporting their own progress at family-teacher conferences, Countryman and Schroeder (1996) found that the positive evaluation data from students, parents, and teachers resulted in the decision to continue the practice for future conferences. Teachers at a middle school included their students as co-presenters when holding family-teacher conferences. The students led the meetings by introducing their family members to the teacher, showing their parents or family members selected examples of their work, explaining the progress they had made, and outlining the goals for the next marking period. Evaluation comments focused on the students' honesty in reporting their progress, increased student empowerment to be responsible for their own educational programs, and improved school-community relationships because of the more personal format.

■ ASSESSING STUDENTS AS CO-TEACHERS

One way to assess students as they develop their co-teaching skills is to encourage them to self-evaluate by using the checklist shown in Table 9.3. Individually, each student co-teacher can use the checklist and then compare with his or her student co-teachers the Yes versus Not Yet assessments. This allows team members to have a starting point to discuss the strengths of the student co-teacher partnership thus far and target areas for improvement.

Student co-teachers can also complete the checklist jointly. Rather than coming to consensus on an item, we suggest that the team use a different approach to self-rating. We suggest that, for a team to give an item a *yes* rating, every member must definitively agree that a *yes* is appropriate. If any one team member is not sure about a *yes* rating, the response must remain *not yet*. This reduces the temptation to pressure the person with a differing perception to give in for the sake of consensus and, instead, encourages a real dialogue about the differing perspectives, perceptions, and experiences of members of a co-teaching team.

Others who are not on the team but who are requested to respond or who have a responsibility to observe the student co-teachers can use the checklist to provide constructive feedback (in much the same way that Laurie and Elaine did for Dave and Juan). We encourage student co-teachers to revisit the list frequently, talk about the items, and select some items to focus on for improvement. This is how independent, self-regulated learning develops!

Table 9.3   Checklist: Are You Really a Student Co-Teacher?

Directions: If you wonder whether or not your students are co-teachers, ask your students to check *Yes* or *Not Yet* in response to each of the following statements. Then add the number of responses in each column to discover their current Student Co-Teacher Score.

We know we are student co-teachers when we . . .	*Yes*	*Not Yet*
1. Explain instructional goals or objectives of a lesson.	_____	_____
2. Apply a scoring guide (rubric) to grade work produced.	_____	_____
3. Detect mistakes or misunderstandings.	_____	_____
4. Provide instructional feedback to correct mistakes without giving away the answers.	_____	_____
5. Celebrate the successes of our students.	_____	_____
6. Communicate with other co-teachers to plan, teach, and evaluate lessons.	_____	_____
7. Discuss concerns or disagreements freely with co-teaching partners.	_____	_____
8. Use a problem-solving method when faced with conflicts.	_____	_____
9. Ask for help when necessary.	_____	_____
10. Add item of interest to your own situation _____.	_____	_____
Total	_____	_____

FREQUENTLY ASKED QUESTIONS

1. Isn't it true that students are not developmentally mature enough to be capable of co-teaching? After all, it takes four years of college for teachers to learn the profession.

Yes, it is true that certification of teachers requires at least a four-year college degree, methods classes, and understanding of learning and assessment techniques. However, we suggest that the goal is not to have students perform at the same level of proficiency as certified teachers. The most important strategy for overcoming the belief that students are not developmentally mature enough to serve as co-teachers is for the teacher to explicitly model and implement those strategies that facilitate students in partner-learning roles. School personnel must ensure that student co-teachers are trained, monitored, and provided with ongoing coaching and support. Moreover, school personnel can select instructional methods that set the context for students to practice co-teaching roles, such as cooperative group learning, peer tutoring, and dialogue teaching (as described earlier).

2. How can teachers justify taking time away from teaching the curriculum and helping students meet the standards for graduation to teach instructional methods to student co-teachers?

We agree that a major disadvantage of the use of student co-teachers is that it seems there isn't enough time in the school day to provide for all the required subjects. Conscientious teachers often worry that the time required to prepare students adequately to serve as co-teachers is time that could be better spent on teaching the curriculum. The structure of the typical school day requires that teachers guarantee that a specified number of minutes are used to teach mandated subjects. It could be argued that the time required to prepare students as co-teachers is time well spent; when students are trained as co-teachers, there is more one-on-one time available to meet the unique learning needs of more students.

In addition, we know there are standards that call for students to engage in service-learning activities as part of graduation requirements. Co-teaching roles can fulfill the spirit of service learning.

In fact, celebrating students as co-teachers can be perceived as the ultimate goal for teachers who practice co-teaching. Whether they use supportive, parallel, complementary, or team-teaching approaches, co-teachers model collaboration and communication for their students. Co-teaching teams can set the expectation among their students, other educators, and specialists that students will be members not only of student governance but also of peer support teams; learning teams; teams to plan Individual Education Programs; and teams to plan transitions from elementary to middle school, middle school to high school, or high school to life after school. Student co-teachers themselves become the most effective voice for showing and telling about the results. Creating a variety of methods for students to share their successes, trials, tribulations, and unexpected positive outcomes of being co-teachers is a powerful way to overcome barriers and disadvantages.

PART IV

Administrative Support and Professional Development

Part IV features three chapters that examine the logistical aspects of co-teaching and an Epilogue that illustrates the logistics in action with a co-teaching partnership. Chapter 10 is specifically written to provide administrators with ideas for facilitating change toward co-teaching by attending to five variables—vision, skills, incentives, resources, and action planning. Chapter 11 describes how co-teachers can mesh planning with co-teaching by suggesting ways for creating and efficiently using planning time, providing an easy-to-use co-teaching lesson plan template, and offering an Are We Really Co-Teachers? self-assessment for promoting co-teachers' professional development. Chapter 12 builds upon the content of Chapter 11 and provides some advanced tips for avoiding potential pitfalls, tips that include communication, interpersonal relationship building, and conflict management. The Epilogue pulls the content of the book together through the story of Nancy Keller and Lia Cravedi-Cheng's two-year journey of developing a shared voice through co-teaching. Throughout the story, tips introduced in Chapter 11 are highlighted to illustrate how these two co-teachers worked to make their partnership flourish.

10

Training and Logistical Administrative Support for Co-Teaching

> **Topics Included in This Chapter:**
>
> - Building a vision
> - Building the skills and capacity for co-teaching
> - Incentives to engage people in co-teaching
> - Resources for co-teaching
> - Getting started: Planning and taking action
> - Summary
> - Frequently asked questions

Do you wonder how administrators spark an interest in co-teaching among their staff? Do you want to know the kinds of organizational support that administrators provide to facilitate the effective implementation of co-teaching approaches? Are you interested in learning how schools allocate resources to support co-teaching? These and other administrative, training, and logistical issues are discussed in this chapter as we examine five variables—vision, skills, incentives, resources, and action planning—that factor into a formula for facilitating change toward co-teaching (Villa and Thousand 2004).

More specifically, this chapter describes ways to (1) build a vision of collaboration in planning and teaching within a school; (2) develop educators' skills and confidence as co-teachers; (3) create meaningful incentives for people to take the risk to embark on a co-teaching journey; (4) reorganize, schedule, and expand human and other resources for co-teaching; and (5) plan for and take actions designed to get school personnel excited about implementing co-teaching approaches.

■ BUILDING A VISION

School leaders involved in co-teaching stress the importance of clarifying for themselves, school personnel, and the community a vision based on assumptions that (1) all children are capable of learning, (2) all children have a right to an education with their peers in their community's schools, (3) everyone who provides instruction shares responsibility for the learning of every child in the school, and (4) co-teaching is an organizational and instructional strategy that benefits students and educators alike. Simply stating a vision, however, is not enough. School leaders need to foster widespread understanding and consensus regarding the vision.

Consensus Building Through an Examination of Rationales for Co-Teaching

One strategy for building a vision and consensus for co-teaching is to educate people about the rationales for and benefits of co-teaching, as discussed in

Chapter 2 and illustrated in the vignettes and discussions throughout this book. Our experience tells us that in the process of building consensus, different people will find different rationales compelling. If we are to have any hope of shifting a person's belief in favor of co-teaching, we must first listen to and identify the person's concerns (questions, fears, nightmares, confusions) regarding co-teaching and supply him or her with the appropriate rationale that addresses those concerns.

Stated otherwise, as change agents, we first must solicit and listen to the concerns of everyone affected by a shift to co-teaching (which may be just about everyone—teachers, parents, students, community members). Next, we must use this information to determine which of the rationales speak to each individual's priority concerns. Fiscal and legal matters may speak to administrators and school board members; disappointing efficacy data about pullout programs versus inclusion and co-teaching may speak to parents and students; the fragmented and poorly coordinated nature of categorical support programs such as Title I, special education, gifted and talented education, and instruction of students learning English may speak to educators tired of isolation and endless hours of paperwork

Information about the rationales that are important to various individuals may be communicated in any number of ways—through the structure of inservice training events, distribution of readings with follow-up discussions, videotapes of co-teachers, or visits to schools that have adopted co-teaching. Finally, once we are knowledgeable of concerns, we are in the position to address them seriously in any planning or implementation process by regularly and vigilantly asking, "How can we ensure that people's worst nightmares (concerns) about co-teaching do not come true?"

Consensus Building Through Respecting What We Expect

A vision and consensus for co-teaching can be fostered by actively respecting what we expect—that is, encouraging, recognizing, and publicly acknowledging those educators who plunge in as early innovators and pioneers to model and actively promote the philosophy and practice of co-teaching. To determine what teachers find to be meaningful recognition, administrators need to ask them directly what they consider rewarding. For some teachers, public recognition for engaging in an innovation is rewarding. For others, public recognition would be embarrassing, but an opportunity to attend a conference on co-teaching would be a treat.

Building consensus for a vision is really about replacing an old culture with a new one and managing the personal loss that inevitably accompanies cultural change. New heroes and heroines, rituals and symbols, and histories must be constructed. New histories replace old ones when traditional solutions (e.g., adding yet another new pullout program or professional when children with new differences arrive at school) are publicly pointed out to be ineffective, inefficient, and counter to the desired vision and when collaboration among staff in planning and co-teaching is regularly and routinely celebrated.

Consensus Building by Clarifying How and When to Use Co-Teaching as a Strategy to Support Diverse Learners

Some school personnel appear to be confused about the purpose of co-teaching and when to engage in the practice. In some schools, co-teaching is incorrectly viewed as the only way to support students with disabilities in inclusive settings. Not every student eligible for special education needs to be placed in a co-taught classroom. Table 10.1 provides an overview of the various levels of support, including co-teaching, that can be made available for individual students. Members of the Individual Educational Program (IEP) team who are responsible for making placement decisions for students with disabilities are encouraged to review the table and identify the level of support that is needed.

Some students with and without disabilities may require additional support (e.g., study skills training, homework support, remediation) that school personnel may not be able to address adequately within the time available in a co-taught classroom. In response to this situation, many schools establish learning centers where all students can receive extra support and targeted instruction. Students may be assigned to a learning center during study hall or as an alternative to an elective for one period a day, or they may attend only as long as is necessary for them to master a specific skill. Staff members at one high school with which we are familiar use their library media center as the learning center. Every period of every day, one general education teacher and one special educator are assigned, as an official duty, to work with students in the learning center, which is housed in the library media center. In addition to the library media director and the general and special education personnel, trained peer tutors are available to provide tutorial and other assistance to their fellow students. Such an arrangement avoids stigmatization of students receiving support and allows all students, whether or not they are eligible for a particular support program, to receive assistance from teachers and peers on an as-needed basis.

■ BUILDING THE SKILLS AND CAPACITY FOR CO-TEACHING

Unless educators believe they have the skills to co-teach, they will doubt their capacity to be good co-teachers. The more diverse the student body, the more skilled educators must be as a collective instructional force. We highlight the word *collective* to emphasize that educators of a co-teaching team need not have the same content and instructional skills; they do, however, need easy access to one another so that they can share their skills across students and classrooms. We further believe there is a core set of skills and strategies that all co-teachers need to acquire (over time) to meet diverse student needs and realize the research promise of co-teaching.

No matter how exciting or promising an innovation like co-teaching is, educators need training, guided practice, feedback, and opportunities to problem solve with colleagues and clarify the nuances of co-teaching. Furthermore, for the innovation to become the new culture, people must come to understand its significance for their personal and professional growth and for the growth of

Table 10.1   Levels of Student Support

- Classroom Companion—Students assume responsibility for supporting other students' participation in academic or elective classes. This may include helping with mobility to and from class, carrying or remembering materials, taking notes, assisting in task completion, facilitating communication, and being role models for social/friendship interaction.

- Consultation—Support staff meet regularly with the general education teacher to keep track of student progress, assess the need for supplemental materials, problem solve, and maintain positive and open communication. Students know that they can stop in or request assistance from support staff on a specific assignment or for general support.

- Stop-In Support—Support staff observe students on a regular or irregular basis to determine possible needs or to set up peer support systems. They maintain open communication with the classroom teacher and the students.

- Part-Time Daily Support—Support staff provide support to students at a predetermined time, on a rotating basis, or for specific assignments activities. Staff should maintain awareness of curriculum and assignments to encourage student productivity and tutorial or organizational support. Staff may also supply supplemental materials for classroom use.

- Team/Co-Teaching—Support staff assume half of the responsibility for teaching the curriculum, as prearranged by all involved staff members, who assume responsibility for the development of multilevel curriculum, appropriate strategies, grading the learning environment, and student arrangements.

- Daily In-Class Staff Support—Support staff assist all students by moving around the room, providing support as needed. Staff collaborate with general education teacher to develop and plan for specific support strategies and student needs. Staff may supervise or teach small groups within the class or based on a pullout model, as needed.

- Total Staff Support—Support staff remain seated in close proximity to the students. Support staff also assume responsibility for developing or acquiring the strategies and materials that will support each student's success.

their students. Within the context of co-teaching, this places training front and center as a strategy for reducing anxiety and transforming the culture of the school. Because so many teachers report that neither their professional preparation nor their relatively isolated teaching experiences have adequately prepared them for co-teaching, it becomes a local school district's responsibility to develop and provide an ongoing comprehensive inservice training agenda. We emphasize the importance of giving people choice as to how they receive training (e.g., courses, mentoring, team teaching, summer institutes, workshop series, videotapes, book studies).

Who Receives Training?

As emphasized throughout this book, any member of the school and the greater community is a candidate for training because anyone can become a co-teacher. Although training may initially be organized for and delivered to innovators and early adopters in the school, eventually everyone involved—teachers, administrators, paraprofessionals, related service personnel, and students—needs to acquire a common core of knowledge about co-teaching. To excuse those who are reluctant, resistant, or apathetic from acquiring the disposition and skills to implement co-teaching divides people, promotes the development of factions, fosters resentment toward those who don't participate, reinforces a "this too will pass" mentality, and generally works against the development of a unified new culture.

Common Core of Training

At a minimum, staff members need training in collaborative planning (Thousand and Villa 2000; Villa 2002a) and approaches to co-teaching such as those discussed throughout this text (Bauwens and Mueller 2000; Friend 1996; Villa 2002b). Other content includes differentiation and universal design approaches to instruction (Thousand, Villa, and Nevin 2007a, 2007b; Tomlinson 1999; Udvari-Solner, Villa, and Thousand 2002), cooperative group learning (Johnson and Johnson 1999), and other areas (e.g., discipline) that they self-identify as priority areas for mutual skill development.

■ INCENTIVES TO ENGAGE PEOPLE IN CO-TEACHING

Without incentives that are meaningful to each person affected by the change toward co-teaching, the outcome may be passive or active resistance rather than excited engagement. Promoting co-teaching requires structuring incentives, notably a menu of incentives. In developing this, first be sure to focus on teams as well as individuals in order to highlight the importance of and pride in collaborative teaching efforts. Second, spend time "in the trenches" with teachers, support staff, and students who are involved in co-teaching. Discover what they are doing well that can be privately and publicly acknowledged. Third, ask staff members and students what they value as incentives. What is rewarding to one person may be of little significance to another. Some commonly identified teacher incentives include the following:

- Short notes of praise (e.g., "The students in your co-taught class seem excited about learning. Thanks for taking the risk and embarking on a co-teaching journey. I know you will have fun along the way.")
- Special training opportunities
- Mentoring of others new to co-teaching practices
- Travel to conferences or other schools engaged in co-teaching
- Regular forums for airing concerns and generating viable solutions
- Opportunities to make presentations at conferences, school board meetings, parent-teacher organizations, and community gatherings
- Visits to co-taught classrooms to become familiar with other co-teachers and the practices they employ
- Off-campus retreats for collaborative planning efforts

Time: The Universal Incentive

Although many incentives are unique to individuals, one incentive is common to and highly valued by everyone engaged in co-teaching and other educational reforms: time—time for face-to-face interaction and time to plan, share, and reflect with colleagues. Many classroom teachers have told us that it is difficult to develop a co-teaching relationship when you cannot spend adequate time with your co-teaching partner(s). These teachers report that it is almost impossible to develop a trusting relationship with a co-teaching partner when there is little planning time, when a partner fails to show up, when one partner is frequently pulled from the co-teaching classroom to handle emergencies, or when co-teachers are assigned to co-teach only one or two days a week.

The reality is that many special education and other support personnel have other mandated responsibilities and emergency situations that sometimes pull them out of co-taught classrooms. Administrators need to understand the necessity for continuity among co-teachers and work with classroom and support personnel to decrease the amount of time that support personnel are pulled from general education classrooms to handle behavioral emergencies, attend meetings, conduct assessments, and do paperwork.

Recognizing that forming a trusting co-teaching relationship is contingent on several variables (including frequency of contact, capability, willingness, and dependability), many school administrators promise general education teachers co-teaching support for a minimum of four out of five days a week. The fifth day, the day that the support personnel are not necessarily in the class, is the same day each week, and the fact that the classroom teacher will be teaching alone that day is considered in the co-planning of instructional activities for that day. Support personnel use the fifth day for paperwork, assessment, and meetings.

In addition, some schools schedule a meeting among support personnel for part of the fifth day so that they can collaboratively brainstorm strategies and supports that can be brought back to the co-taught classroom to support struggling learners. Consider the following example: A speech and language therapist is co-teaching several classes but is unable to provide direct service to all learners eligible for speech and language services in every classroom. Special educators, however, are co-teaching in all classrooms that include students eligible for speech and language services. During the weekly meeting occurring on the fifth day, the speech and language therapist can provide indirect service to the eligible learners by mentoring the special educators and enabling them to target oral and written language goals for eligible students in their co-taught classes. We encourage you to look at Table 11.1 in Chapter 11 to see how schools provide the valuable incentive of time for collaborative meeting and planning.

Scheduling as an Incentive

Co-teaching is closely linked to scheduling. Scheduling practices can provide a powerful incentive or disincentive for co-teaching. For example, the scheduling practice of tracking students into ability groups and classes, such as concentrating special education–eligible and other at-risk students into the lower-track classes, is a huge barrier or disincentive for co-teaching. A research-supported, best educational practice is to group students heterogeneously by perceived ability or achievement. This means that classrooms should have a composition that reflects the natural proportion of students with and without identified special needs. On average in schools across the United States, 10% to 12% of students are eligible for special education. In any given classroom, therefore, the ideal would be to have not many more than that proportion of the students eligible for IEPs.

Some congregation of students with disabilities occurs when scheduling co-teaching personnel into the classes, but by keeping the number at no more than 4% to 5% above the mean for that school, the natural proportion of students with disabilities to peers without disabilities is maintained. A natural proportion allows for academic, social, and communication models; avoids stigmatization of students and personnel who support them; and follows the research-supported alternative of heterogeneous grouping (Johnson and Johnson 1999).

Professional Development as an Incentive

Many educators are motivated by professional development of their skills and knowledge (Cook 2004; Cramer et al. 2006; Hall and Hord 2001). Co-teaching experiences empower teachers to meet nationally recognized sets of standards specified for novice teachers (either the Interstate Teacher Assessment and Support Consortium [INTASC] Standards or the Council for Exceptional Children [CEC] standards for beginning special educators) and for veteran teachers (National Board for Professional Teaching Standards [NBPTS]). The standards include competencies related to collaboration in order to differentiate instruction so as to increase student achievement. Once initial knowledge about a new instructional practice such as co-teaching has been acquired, follow-up application activities should reflect the best practices (Roy 2005). We like to say, "Learning to co-teach is a journey, not a destination!" We have worked diligently with co-teachers and their administrators to prepare two professional development multimedia programs for co-teaching and differentiated instruction (Thousand, Villa, and Nevin 2007a, 2007b; Villa, Thousand, and Nevin 2008).

Intrinsic Incentives

Although all of these extrinsic incentives are important, we have learned that genuine and sustainable changes in culture and dedication to co-teaching depend on people who are also reinforced by intrinsic motivators—their emotions, values, beliefs, and social bonds with colleagues. Intrinsic motivation includes recognizing one's increased effectiveness as evidenced by student success and happiness, feeling the pride in one's own professional risk taking and growth that accompanies recognition from respected colleagues and from students, and experiencing personal satisfaction with one's professional accomplishments.

RESOURCES FOR CO-TEACHING ■

Resources for co-teaching may be technical and material (e.g., technology, curriculum materials) or organizational (e.g., how the school day, week, and year as well as the people within the organization are organized). Time is an example of an organizational resource (and incentive) that is in short supply in many schools. The previous discussion on incentives examined ways to gain more time for educators to plan, reflect, and collaborate with others. Clearly, educators' perception of the adequacy of the technical, material, and organizational resources available to them influences their work satisfaction. Nevertheless, the human resource—teachers' relationships with other adults and with the students, as well as the unique gifts, talents, and traits that each person offers— is most important to school health and improvement and to the success of co-teaching.

Redefining Roles

We propose that for educators to access most readily the resources of other educational personnel, everyone in the school system must stop thinking and acting in standard, isolated ways. Everyone must relinquish traditional roles, drop distinct professional labels, and redistribute job functions across any number of other people. Flexibility and fluidity are the main aims of role redefinition. Exactly who does what from one year to the next should evolve, determined by the needs of students and the complementary skills (and needs) of the educators distributing job functions among themselves.

Job titles and formal definitions sometimes determine how people behave. Thus, to further signal and symbolize a change in culture, new policies and job descriptions should be formulated to expect, inspect, and respect the collaborative ethic and practice of co-teaching. We are familiar with a number of school districts that have done this by creating a single job description for all professional educators (e.g., classroom teachers, special educators, school nurse, guidance personnel) that identifies collaboration in planning and teaching as expected job functions.

Allocating Resources for Co-Teaching

Allocating human resources to classrooms for the purpose of co-teaching should ideally be a collaborative responsibility involving general education classroom teachers, support personnel, and administrators of both general and special education programs (Thousand, Villa, and Nevin 2006). The overall responsibility for allocating or scheduling human resources resides with the administrator who can design a master schedule to allow the special educators and other support personnel—such as Title 1, gifted and talented, and English-language instructors, as well as speech and language personnel—to be free to co-teach with their general education co-teaching partners. There is no one way to schedule co-teaching, but scheduling should always be based on an in-depth understanding of both student needs and existing human resources. What follows are elementary, middle level, and high school examples of resource allocation through scheduling.

Resource Allocation at the Elementary Level

In some elementary schools committed to co-teaching, classroom teachers are told that they will receive co-teaching support in at least two academic content areas. Elementary classroom teachers typically identify language arts and math as the content areas in which they want co-teaching support. This can be problematic because most elementary classroom teachers prefer to teach language arts first thing in the morning. The solution to this dilemma is twofold. First, the number of personnel available to co-teach must be increased by utilizing all available personnel (e.g., Title I, special education, gifted and talented, and English-language instructors; school counselors; paraprofessionals; students) to co-teach during language arts and math classes. Second, if the number of personnel is still insufficient to allow co-teaching to occur at the same time in various classrooms, administrators develop a schedule that rotates language arts or math instructional time throughout the day, thereby allowing the necessary support to occur during the instructional time identified as most important by the classroom teachers. Some schools change the order of rotation each marking period, allowing all personnel to teach language arts during their preferred time of day during at least one marking period of the school year.

Resource Allocation at the Middle and High School Levels

There is no one way to do most anything in education, including constructing co-teaching configurations. All of the scheduling examples described in this section are meant to illustrate that there is no correct way to allocate resources for co-teaching. Every solution has advantages and disadvantages. It is up to the teachers and administrators to think creatively, be inventive, take a risk, try new and different things, form unconventional partnerships, and trust their intuition in order to conceive of solutions that will be advantageous to their students.

Traditional Structure Scheduling

In middle and high schools that structure the day into forty- to fifty-minute blocks, special educators may co-teach daily in four of six instructional periods and provide direct tutorial services or do paperwork and attend meetings for the remaining two periods of the school day.

Interdisciplinary Content Scheduling

Many middle level and high school administrators have encouraged the formation of interdisciplinary teams (i.e., math, science, social studies, language arts) and designed master schedules, which provide two planning periods per day. One planning period is set aside for common planning time among all team members, including the support personnel assigned to that team (e.g., Title I reading teacher, speech and language therapist, instructor of English learners), and the other planning period is used for individual or co-teaching team planning.

Natural Proportion Scheduling

Some middle and high schools have chosen to distribute all students heterogeneously across all subjects and grade levels and rely on regularly scheduled consultation and some co-teaching to support the students and general education classroom teachers. A major concern with this approach is that individual student needs may not be met and the co-teaching relationships may not evolve.

Differing Levels of Support Scheduling

There are at least two approaches for scheduling differing levels of co-teaching support at the middle and high school levels. For illustrative purposes, each of the two scheduling scenarios assumes that there are six sections of a particular core curriculum area (e.g., biology) available at any grade level. These scheduling scenarios would work in schools structured into traditional forty- to fifty-minute blocks as well as schools employing extended block scheduling or a combination of both approaches.

In the first scenario, students who are eligible for special education and require co-teaching support are placed in two of the six classes where co-teaching will occur. Students with IEPs requiring consultation and part-time co-teaching support from a professional or paraprofessional are placed in one of two other classes where consultation time between general education and special education teachers will occur weekly and basic skills or paraprofessional personnel will provide part-time co-teaching support. The remaining students with disabilities who require minimal accommodations and modifications are placed in the remaining two classes, where the classroom teacher assumes responsibility for implementing and monitoring the effectiveness of the accommodations and maintaining communication with the special educator.

In the second scenario of differentiated support, two classroom teachers of the same grade level or content area team up with a special educator and a special education paraprofessional. The students eligible for special education are divided evenly across the two classrooms, and the team determines when the special educator will co-teach with the classroom teacher. While the special educator is in one of the two classes, the paraprofessional works in the other class, providing support to the other classroom teacher and the students eligible for special education. Students who require basic skills or English language support are evenly divided among two of the other four content classes, and other support personnel (e.g., Title I personnel, teachers of English learners, reading specialists, curriculum consultants) provide co-teaching support to those classes. In this scheduling scenario, the remaining two sections do not have students eligible for special education or other categorical support programs. School personnel implementing this approach monitor the percentage of students eligible for special education who are placed in the co-taught classes to avoid violating the principle of natural proportion discussed earlier.

Scheduling Everyone for Co-Teaching Over Time

Many schools have made a conscious decision to rotate, over time, co-teaching responsibilities across all personnel. For example, given the six sections of a particular core content area used in the scheduling scenarios just described, the two content area classroom teachers assigned to co-teaching would rotate every two years, resulting in all classroom teachers having two years of co-teaching responsibilities and experience over a six-year period.

Department, Grade Level, or Content Emphasis Scheduling

Some schools have chosen to assign special educators to departments; some have chosen to assign them to grade levels. Some schools assign special educators to co-teach in the two primary areas of special education eligibility (language arts and math) because these are the two most high-stakes assessment areas. In these schools, if co-teaching is needed in science or social studies, a paraprofessional is assigned (and supervised) as the co-teacher.

Scheduling General Educators to Co-Teach

Across the nation, many other creative and novel co-teaching structures have been successfully implemented. In one Pennsylvania middle school, the special educators co-teach in science and social studies and provide consultation in math and language arts. It was decided that the best way to support the students in this school who were eligible for special education in math and language arts was to have two general educators co-teach. Math and language arts teachers teach alone for three of their four 1.5-hour extended block periods. Teachers have staggered preparation periods, during which the first half is used for planning and the second half is dedicated to co-teaching with another same-content teacher, helping students apply information taught in the first half of the period. This co-teaching support is reciprocated during one of each teacher's three instructional periods. The teachers enjoy this unique collaborative arrangement, and the students are succeeding.

Forming Outside Partnerships to Access Resources to Support Co-Teaching

Developing partnerships with personnel in state departments of education, faculty of institutions of higher education, and staff in other school districts with a similar interest in co-teaching is another way to gain much-needed human, political, and fiscal resources. State department of education personnel may provide fiscal incentives or regulatory relief for innovations. They may provide valuable public relations support, articulating in circulars, publications, and public presentations the need for co-teaching. Higher education–school district collaboration offers mutual benefits to both organizations. Together, the two organizations can design and solicit state or federal support for model demonstrations; arrange for valuable internship experiences for students in teacher preparation programs; conduct research to document the challenges, solutions, and impacts of co-teaching practices; or deliver coursework to help develop the new roles or skills necessary for co-teaching. Finally, schools with a common vision of co-teaching should join forces to share or exchange resources, including personnel (e.g., reciprocal inservice presenters, joint hiring of a specialist in augmentative communication); resolve barriers to change; form coalitions to advocate for change in outdated teacher preparation programs and state-level funding policies; and celebrate successes together.

GETTING STARTED: PLANNING ■
AND TAKING ACTION

If co-teaching is to become an integral part of the school culture, the administrative leaders must have an action plan for building consensus for the vision, helping staff members acquire competence, providing meaningful incentives, and allocating the necessary resources. Action planning means attending to all of these variables and being thoughtful and communicative about the process of change—how, with whom, and in what sequence the steps or stages of change are formulated, communicated, and set into motion. Action plans for co-teaching require the right mix of planning versus action and the continual involvement of the many people affected by the change. Resource K is an Action Plan Template that administrators can use to ensure that all planned activities are delineated and articulated to those who are involved in creating and executing the plan. A sample one-year plan for establishing co-teaching in a school district is presented in Figure 10.1 to show how each activity is delineated, timelines are set, success is measured, and actual outcomes of the activity are noted. We highly recommend that leaders who initiate any change, including co-teaching, use this or a similar planning format to inform and hold accountable those engaged in the change process.

Benefits of Involvement and Communication in Planning

Engaging people in action planning for co-teaching is important for at least two reasons. First, participatory planning promotes individuals' personal ownership of the coming changes. Second, it helps prepare people for change by getting them to believe that change really will occur. Planning is the alarm signaling to everyone that things will no longer be the same. For planning to accomplish this, administrators need to be up-front and effective communicators who can articulate the desired future and get people to see clearly how it can be achieved and what part each person will play.

An integral part of action planning is regular and continuous evaluation. What is worthy of evaluation? Clearly, in the case of co-teaching, we want to know whether students and staff benefit from this organizational and instructional arrangement. We also want to know about affective and process variables such as educators' feelings at various points during the change process. Both outcome and affective process evaluations provide change agents the information needed to adjust the action plan or undertake new actions to deal with concerns, failures, and successes.

Working With the Unwilling

Obviously, the best-case scenario is when school personnel choose to co-teach rather than do it simply because they're required to. Likewise, co-teaching may initially work best if the partners not only choose to co-teach but are also able to choose the colleague(s) with whom they will co-teach. However, this is not always possible. Sometimes administrators have to assign staff to co-teach. Collaboration in planning and teaching cannot be viewed as a voluntary activity. For educators to think that they have a choice as to whether or not to collaborate is similar to a team of health care professionals perceiving that they have a choice as to whether or not to collaborate in performing an operation, following the patient's progress, and providing follow-up care. Students and families have a right to expect educators to collaborate in planning and teaching, and educators have a professional, legal, and ethical responsibility to do so.

Administrators need to understand that a teacher's initial reluctance to co-teach is not necessarily a permanent barrier to implementing co-teaching or any other innovation. McLaughlin (1991) found that teachers' commitment to an innovation only comes after they have acquired initial competence in the new skills necessary to implement the innovation. The key is for administrators to support school personnel in implementing co-teaching so that they acquire the skills and feel successful. Administrators can take actions to expand the number of personnel willing and able to co-teach. Table 10.1, shown earlier in this chapter, describes the levels of support to students—from classroom peer support and specialist consultation to full-time staff support—that an administrator can facilitate. Table 10.2 suggests other administrative actions, such as creating a master schedule that includes time for co-teachers to meet.

Another strategy to assist personnel in overcoming their initial reluctance is to highlight how co-teaching can help teachers meet their own basic psychological needs (see Chapter 12). Administrators also report being able to overcome resistance from some staff members by clarifying teaching personnel's legal responsibilities for educating students with disabilities in the least restrictive environment by providing any necessary supplemental supports, aids, and services (e.g., co-teaching) identified by the IEP team within general education classrooms.

Schools initiating co-teaching often start small, with teachers who volunteer to try co-teaching as a pilot project. As explained in Figure 7.2 in Chapter 7, co-teachers may need various levels of support to co-teach successfully,

Table 10.2 Administrator Actions to Promote Co-Teaching

✓ Publicly articulate the rationale for co-teaching.

✓ Redefine staff roles (i.e., in the job description of classroom teachers and support personnel) so that all are expected to participate in collaborative planning and teaching.

✓ Assess the staff's need for collaboration (e.g., With whom do I need to collaborate to adapt instruction successfully? From which colleagues can I acquire skills through modeling and coaching?).

✓ Create a master schedule that allows for collaboration (e.g., common planning and lunch periods).

✓ Change length of the workday or school year (e.g., provide teachers with 220-day instead of 185-day contracts; early dismissal of students).

✓ Establish professional support groups to help staff learn about and begin to practice co-teaching.

✓ Provide time for co-teachers to meet by relieving them from noninstructional duties that other staff members who are not co-teaching are required to perform (e.g., bus duty, lunchroom supervision).

✓ Provide training in collaborative planning (e.g., courses and workshops, mentoring and peer coaching systems, job shadowing, clinical supervision, and the pairing of new co-teaching teams with veteran co-teaching teams).

✓ Educate school and community members about the accomplishments of collaborative planning and teaching teams.

✓ Periodically provide additional time for co-teaching teams to meet (e.g., hire substitutes, use inservice time, provide release time).

✓ Provide incentives for co-teaching (e.g., recognize *co-teaching teams accomplishments*, offer additional training, provide release time for co-teaching teams to observe one another teaching, attend conferences, and make presentations about their accomplishments).

depending on their competence and willingness to co-teach. Administrators need to assess the support needs of beginning co-teachers and provide that support, whether it be training, incentives (e.g., common meeting time), coaching and mentoring, or opportunities for reflective analysis for improvement. Pilot projects can then be extended to other teachers and classrooms as the word gets out about the successes and benefits for students and teachers.

Put It in Writing

People do best if their decisions are put into some systematic written format (action plan) that specifies in some detail who will do what, by when, and to meet what criterion. Therefore, we encourage administrators to work with general education teachers, categorical support personnel, paraprofessionals, and others to develop a written plan that addresses actions that will be taken to (1) build support for the vision of co-teaching; (2) develop educators' skills and confidence to be co-teachers; (3) create meaningful incentives for co-teachers; and (4) reorganize, schedule, and expand human and other resources for co-teaching. Figure 10.1 offers an action-planning template that school personnel can use to plan and then fully embark on a co-teaching journey.

■ SUMMARY

Reengineering educational practices can be a complex and seemingly overwhelming proposition. Yet an increasing number of communities are making the choice to implement co-teaching approaches with integrity and quality. The good news is that we now know some things about how to facilitate change so that co-teaching becomes part of the daily schooling routine. We know, for example, that schools have cultures and that to actualize a new vision of schooling and schooling practices, a new culture must come to replace the old one. We know that change inevitably creates cognitive and interpersonal conflict that can be managed through perspective taking, effective communication, collaboration, conflict resolution, and creative problem solving. We know that for fundamental change to occur, the roles, rules, relationships, and responsibilities for everyone (students included) will be redefined; hierarchical power relationships have to be altered so that everyone affected by the impending change has a voice and a role in decision making. We know that change is not necessarily progress; only close attention to valued outcomes will tell us if change equals progress. We know that action planning is important and that resources, incentives, and skill building make a difference. We know that commitment to a change often does not occur until people have developed skills and gained experience with the change. Finally, we know that effective school organizations can be crafted, and they are crafted by individuals—individuals who choose to ensure the success of all students by being courageous and engaged in a school community during the change process.

Figure 10.1 Sample One-Year Action Plan

	Activities	Success Measure	Responsible Person(s)	Date	Outcomes
	• Major activities • Chronological order • Preparation steps • Implementation steps	"We will know we are successful if . . ." • What is measured? • Who will measure? • When to measure?			
Building Consensus for a Vision of Co-Teaching	At the beginning of the new school year, tell teachers that the district will implement a co-teaching approach at each site in one year's time; explain that this year the approach will be piloted with volunteers at each site during the second semester	Message communicated at August inservice	Dr. Nash (superintendent)	August 23	Message communicated verbally and in writing at August 23 meeting
Skill Development	Provide districtwide inservice on rationales for and approaches to co-teaching for all administrative, general special education, related services, and other support program personnel and paraprofessionals	Presenter hired	Ms. Dome (director of instructional services and staff development)	Hire speaker by July 1	Speaker hired July 15
		Training occurs	Ms. Dome	October 5	3-hour inservice provided
	Purchase co-teaching books for pilot team	Books purchased	Ms. Dome	July 1	Books purchased June 15 and arrived on June 30
	Set up book study groups in each building	Book study groups established at each site	Building principals	September 15	Groups established in five of seven sites by target date and in other two by September 30

(Continued)

Figure 10.1 (Continued)

	Activities	Success Measure	Responsible Person(s)	Date	Outcomes
Incentives	Arrange for visit to neighboring schools to see examples of co-teaching	Visits occur	Building principals and Ms. Dome	September, October, November	Each site sent teams to observe veteran co-teaching teams in other schools; 15 visits to area schools occurred over three months
	Arrange for substitute coverage once a month to allow piloting co-teachers to plan during the school day	Substitutes hired, and teachers meet	Building principals and co-teaching teams at each campus	Monthly, October–June	Substitute coverage provided monthly for all teams except in December; when subs were not available for three teams; these teams were given substitute coverage for an additional planning meeting in January or February
	Co-teachers re-create co-taught lessons for faculty colleagues to participate in as if they were students in these classes	Co-teachers teach lessons to colleagues	Ms. Dome, building principals, and pilot co-teacher teams	March 15	Occurred at all school sites on March 15
Resources	Identify who will pilot co-teaching in first year of implementation	A minimum of five co-teaching teams recruited at each building	Building principals	September 15	Five teams recruited at all but one site, where four were recruited
	Develop a master schedule that provides common planning and teaching time for the pilot co-teaching partnerships	Master schedule completed	Building principals and guidance counselors	December 10	Target met
	Identify co-teachers for second year of implementation	A minimum of five additional co-teaching teams recruited at each site	Building principals	March 20	Target achieved at all campus sites

FREQUENTLY ASKED QUESTIONS

The following questions are ones that administrators and teachers often ask when co-teaching is being considered as an initiative or when they have not experienced administrative support.

1. My teachers complain about all the initiatives we "throw" at them. We are asking them to employ research-based strategies, differentiate instruction, and include students with disabilities in general education classes and curriculum. I am concerned that my teachers will be overwhelmed if I also ask them to co-teach. Isn't there a limit to the number of new things to which I can ask my teachers to commit?

Without a doubt, there are numerous initiatives that are being introduced in schools today. We acknowledge that many of our teacher and administrator colleagues feel overwhelmed. We know teachers do not burn out from too much work; they burn out from a lack of support. Providing the training and other logistical support described in this chapter can help teachers feel less overwhelmed and more supported as they broaden their repertoires to include new skills and strategies.

Our work with successful educational leaders has taught us that teachers can be motivated to take on a new initiative such as co-teaching if they are given the information to show how the initiative connects to the overall mission of the school and how the initiative is connected to what they already are doing. It is interesting to note that co-teaching has been shown to be an important vehicle for teachers to deliver the very initiatives you mentioned (i.e., research-based strategies, differentiated instruction, inclusive education). Once teachers have this information, they will be able to see how co-teaching links with, supports, and makes more efficient the implementation of other best practices initiatives. This can motivate teachers to take on co-teaching as part of their collaborative teaching repertoire.

2. I don't have administrative support where I work. We have received no training on how to co-teach and we don't have common planning time. Very few of the classroom teachers are interested in co-teaching. I am a special educator and believe co-teaching is a valuable practice that will allow my students to succeed in general education classrooms. But I am only one person working in a bureaucracy. What can one person do?

While we firmly believe that it is an administrative responsibility to provide time for co-teachers to meet and plan and to arrange for professional development to support co-teaching teams in acquiring new skills and becoming proficient in their use, we recognize that not all teachers are fortunate enough to work in a school system that provides these types of administrative support.

(Continued)

(Continued)

We know teachers like you who have designed and employed a variety of strategies to promote co-teaching in their school. Perhaps some of the actions they have taken could work for you:

- Share this chapter with an administrator. Ask him or her to read it so that you can sit down together to discuss how the strategies outlined in the chapter might be adjusted to fit your school situation.
- Locate training on co-teaching in your area. Find someone—a teaching colleague and/or an administrator—to go with you.
- With an administrator and/or a general education colleague, visit co-taught classes in another school.
- Start a book study of this co-teaching book with colleagues who agree to read about and try using the four co-teaching approaches described in it.
- Talk with someone from your central office (e.g., special education director, curriculum coordinator), and advocate that your school purchase the media kit (Villa, Thousand, and Nevin 2008) to accompany this book and use the suggestions in the kit's facilitator's guide to design training in co-teaching for yourself and others.
- Begin small, wherever and whenever you can. Find a general education colleague who is willing to experiment in co-teaching with you. Remember that whatever small steps you take, you are making a positive difference for yourself, a colleague, and students you teach. Over time, others will notice the success of your co-teaching and perhaps be motivated to try it as well.

Meshing Planning With Co-Teaching

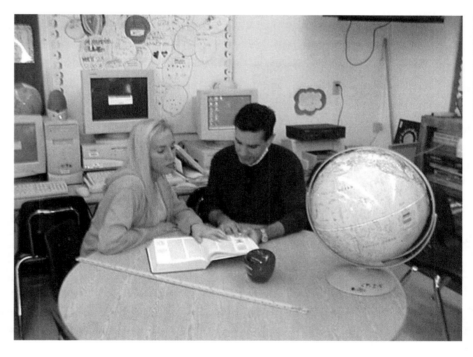

Susan Cushman

Topics Included in This Chapter:

- Planning for starting out as co-teachers
- Finding and creating time for ongoing planning and reflection
- Effective and efficient use of planning time
- Lesson planning as co-teachers
- Planning for professional growth and future partnerships
- Frequently asked question

Failing to plan is a plan to fail.

People usually do not plan to fail; they simply sometimes fail to plan adequately, which results in a failed or less-than-effective effort. This holds as true with co-teaching partners as with co-workers in any other organization where there is a desired outcome or product. In a co-teaching partnership, the desired outcome is the effective execution of a co-taught lesson that yields effective student learning.

What, then, must be considered and addressed for co-teachers to plan to teach effectively, to mesh teaching and planning effectively? First, there is a set of planning considerations involved in getting a co-teaching relationship up and running. Second, there is the challenge of finding and creating time to meet and plan. Third, there are tools to ensure that the time spent planning is, in fact, effective and efficient. Fourth, co-teachers need a lesson plan format that they can understand, implement, and use to communicate their teaching actions to one another. A final area of planning concerns how co-teachers plan for their own professional growth and for continuation, expansion, or other future changes in their partnerships.

■ PLANNING FOR STARTING OUT AS CO-TEACHERS

Even if you have been in a co-teaching relationship before, as a co-teacher in a new co-teaching relationship, you begin all over again in getting started. If you have the opportunity to choose your co-teaching partners, you need to invite them into the co-teaching relationship. You need to be clear about your rationale and objectives for co-teaching so that you can communicate this information to your partner(s), your administrator(s), your students' parents, and the students themselves. It is also necessary so that you can motivate and assess yourself against the objectives you have set for your co-teaching efforts.

In terms of up-front planning, you need to determine with your co-teachers a specific time to sit down and address the role and responsibility issues identified in Chapter 3 (Tables 3.2 and 3.3). Namely, you need to discuss and agree on how, where, when, and how often you will meet to plan. You will need to decide on global issues regarding how you will get to know the learning characteristics of the students, what content you will teach, the instructional procedures you will and will not use, and the ways in which you will assess student learning. You will have to agree on which of the four types of co-teaching partnerships you will start using. You will need to decide how discipline will be handled in the classroom and how communication with families, administrators, and others will occur. There are many logistical questions as well, from how student and teacher spaces will be arranged to how you will refer to each other in front of students to how decisions will be made when there is disagreement among co-teachers.

FINDING AND CREATING TIME FOR ONGOING ■ PLANNING AND REFLECTION

As stated earlier in this book, although many incentives are unique to individuals, one incentive is common to and highly valued by everyone engaged in education: time—time for planning and shared reflection. "The time necessary to examine, reflect on, amend, and redesign programs is not auxiliary to teaching responsibilities—nor is it 'released time' from them. It is absolutely central to such responsibilities, and essential to making school succeed" (Raywid 1993, 34).

Time is a finite resource. Its use must be planned and allocated efficaciously because it is the basic dimension through which co-teachers' work can be constructed and evaluated. Time often defines the possibilities and limitations of co-teachers' ability to successfully perform and deliver in the classroom. Table 11.1 highlights ways in which some schools can and have attempted to meet the time challenges that all co-teachers will face throughout their partnerships.

EFFECTIVE AND EFFICIENT USE ■ OF PLANNING TIME

In addition to the challenge of finding time to plan, co-teachers often are confronted with the challenge of using effectively what little time they actually create, expand, rearrange, or find. Often it is not how much time is finally set aside for planning, but how that resource is used. The real issue is not just adding or manipulating time, but changing the fundamental way that teachers do business when they do sit down face-to-face to plan.

Co-teaching planning meetings are more likely to be both effective and efficient when co-teachers consistently use a structured agenda to guide their conversations. Co-teachers have found the Co-Teaching Planning Meeting Agenda Format that is presented in Resource L to be useful in helping them get to all of their discussion topics in a timely and efficient way. This meeting format ensures that the five elements of the cooperative process that are present when co-teachers engage in co-teaching are also present when co-teachers meet to plan (Thousand and Villa 2000). Table 11.2 shows how the elementary co-teaching team featured in this book used the Co-Teaching Planning Meeting Agenda Format to plan the language arts lesson that used differentiated learning stations. You will find this lesson described in Chapter 5; the plan for this lesson is shown in Resource D.

An element of the cooperative process is face-to-face interaction. This element is prompted and recognized with the "public" recording of who is present, late, and absent from the meeting. Positive interdependence also is structured when leadership is distributed through rotating roles. Roles may be task related (e.g., timekeeper, recorder) or relationship oriented (e.g., encourager, observer). As Table 11.2 indicates, roles are assigned in advance of the next meeting. This ensures that each person has the materials needed to carry out his or her role (e.g., the timekeeper has a watch or timer, the recorder has chart

Table 11.1 Strategies for Expanding Time for Planning

Borrowed Time

1. Rearrange the school day so there is a 50- to 60-minute block of time before or after school for co-teachers to plan.

2. Lengthen the school day for students by 15 to 30 minutes on four days, allowing for early student dismissal on the fifth, thus gaining a long (i.e., 1- to 2-hour) time block for co-teachers to meet.

Common Time

3. Ask co-teachers to identify when during the day and week they prefer to plan and redesign the master schedule to accommodate this with a block for common preparation time.

Tiered Time

4. Layer preparation time with existing functions such as lunch and recess.

Rescheduled Time

5. Use staff development days for co-teachers to do more long-range planning.

6. Use faculty meeting time to problem solve common co-teaching issues of either immediate or long-range importance.

7. Build into the school schedule at least one co-teacher planning day per marking period or month.

8. Build in time for more intensive co-teacher planning sessions by lengthening the school year for teachers but not for students, or shortening the school year for students but not teachers.

Released Time

9. Go to year-round schooling with three-week breaks every quarter; devote four or five of the 3-week intersession days to co-teacher planning as professional development days.

Freed-Up Time

10. Institute a community service component to the curriculum; when students are in the community (e.g., Thursday afternoon), co-teachers meet to plan.

11. Schedule "specials" (e.g., art, music, physical education), clubs, and tutorials during the same time blocks (e.g., first and second period) so that co-teachers have at least that extra time block to plan.

12. Engage parents and community members in conducting half-day or full-day exploratory, craft, hobby (e.g., gourmet cooking, puppetry, photography), theater, or other experiential programs to free up time for co-teachers to plan.

13. Partner with colleges and universities; have their faculty teach in the school, provide demonstrations, or conduction university-campus experiences to free up time for co-teachers to plan.

Purchased Time

14. Hire permanent substitutes to free up co-teachers to plan during the day rather than before or after school.

15. Compensate co-teachers for spending vacation or holiday time planning with pay or compensatory time during noninstructional school-year days.

Found Time

16. Strategically use serendipitous times that occasionally occur (e.g., snow day, student assembly) to plan.

New Time

17. In what ways might the school administration provide co-teachers with incentives that would motivate the use of their own time to plan?

paper and markers or a computer to record minutes). Assigning roles in advance also prompts co-teachers to rotate roles and thus create a sense of distributed responsibility and positive interdependence.

The Co-Teaching Planning Meeting Agenda also increases co-teachers' accountability for task completion and use of interpersonal skills through the monitoring and group processing of task and relationship behaviors. This occurs both midway through and at the end of the meeting. By prompting the assignment of action items to individual team members and the setting of due dates in the Minutes of Outcomes section of the worksheet, the agenda further develops co-teachers' accountability for completing the actions to which they commit. Finally, the building of the next meeting's agenda ensures that co-teachers will come together again face-to-face to do more planning.

■ LESSON PLANNING AS CO-TEACHERS

Figure 11.1 presents a suggested Co-Teaching Daily Lesson Plan Format that we have found to be effective in constructing co-taught lessons (Thousand, Liston, and Nevin 2006). This template also is included as a reproducible template in Resource B. The plan prompts co-teachers to think about the essential elements of any good lesson plan, such as the content objectives, the curriculum standard(s) addressed in the lesson, the materials needed by each partner, how student learning will be assessed, and any accommodations or modifications that might be needed for particular students. Note that co-teachers are prompted to go to Resource A: A Checklist of Sample Supplemental Supports, Aids, and Services. This helps spark ideas for individual supports that will be the least intrusive, only as special as necessary, and the most natural to the context of the classroom.

Because this is a lesson plan for two or more co-teachers, it prompts co-teachers to deliberately consider the following:

1. Which of the four types of co-teaching arrangements will the team be using?

2. How will the room be arranged so that each co-teacher has the needed space to deliver instruction? Will instruction be delivered by one or more co-teacher in another space outside of the classroom, such as a learning center or the school library, for all or part of the lesson?

3. Exactly what will each co-teacher be doing before, during, and after the lesson?

Collaboratively deciding how to answer these three questions ensures that all partners in the co-teaching venture are clear about their own and each other's instructional roles and responsibilities.

The final question in the lesson plan is the following: Where, when, and how do co-teachers debrief and evaluate the outcomes of the lesson? This question is designed to prompt co-teachers to plan—to engage fully and systematically in a recurring planning-analysis-reflection cycle that promotes not only co-teachers' communication with one another, but also the overall quality of their instruction.

Table 11.2   Elementary Team's Use of Co-Teaching Planning Meeting Agenda Format

People Present	Absentees	Others Who Need to Know
Ms. Gilpatrick, classroom teacher	None	No one
Ms. Nugent, speech and language therapist		
Ms. Hernandez, paraprofessional		
Roles	This meeting	Next meeting
Timekeeper	Ms. Nugent	Ms. Hernandez
Recorder	Ms. Gilpatrick	Ms. Nugent
Other		

Agenda	
Agenda Items	Time Limit
1. Review agenda and positive comments	5 minutes
2. Identify objectives and standards	3 minutes
3. Identify student learning preferences and needed supports	5 minutes
4. Brainstorm number and types of stations	7 minutes
5. Identify necessary materials	5 minutes
6. Discuss assessment of student progress	5 minutes
6. Complete Co-Teaching Lesson Plan	20 minutes
7. Processing of task and relationships	5 minutes

Minutes of Outcomes		
Action Items	Persons Responsible	By When?
1. The way we will communicate outcomes to absent members and others	N/A	
2. Division of labor	Refer to lesson plan	

Agenda Building for Next Meeting		
Date: Following day	Time: 7:45 am	Location: Ms. Gilpatrick's room

Expected agenda items
1. Review previous day's lessons
2. Brainstorm and make any necessary adjustments

To show how easy it is to use the Co-Teaching Daily Lesson Plan Format with the supportive, parallel, complementary, and team-teaching co-teaching approaches, we have translated one team scenario from each of Chapters 4 through 7 into a lesson plan and included them as Resources C through F. Resource C shows the high school supportive co-teaching example from Chapter 4. Resources D and F translate the elementary team scenarios from Chapters 5 and 7 to illustrate parallel and team-teaching co-teaching approaches. The middle level team scenario from Chapter 6 is used in Resource E to show a complementary co-teaching lesson plan. Resource G features the lesson plan for the paraprofessional as a co-teacher featured in Chapter 8. Resource H illustrates students as co-teachers by translating the lesson for the third-grade mathematics reciprocal peer-tutoring scenario from Chapter 9.

Prior to examining each lesson plan, we recommend that you review the scenario on which it is based to familiarize yourself with the team members and the overall flow of the lesson. We found the lesson plan format easy to use to describe each co-teacher's responsibilities, clarify the expected student outcomes, note any needed adjustments for particular students, and ensure co-teacher communication.

■ PLANNING FOR PROFESSIONAL GROWTH AND FUTURE PARTNERSHIPS

Anyone who has been involved in teaching for any length of time has heard people talk about the importance of educators being reflective practitioners. Reflective practitioners strive to improve their teaching by gathering data on the effectiveness of their instruction through examining student performance and soliciting feedback on their instructional performance from other instructors and from students themselves. Reflective practitioners think about these data and feedback to make better instructional decisions in future lessons or to arrange for additional training, coaching, or mentoring. People who co-teach are in an ideal situation to spur their own professional growth through dialogue with their co-teachers. They can ask teammates to observe and provide direct feedback, and they can set joint professional goals and receive support and encouragement from their partners.

Co-teachers can also reach outside of their co-teaching team and ask others who have expertise in an area in which improvement is desired to observe, mentor, or more formally provide instruction in that area of expertise. Co-teachers can take workshops, seminars, or courses together to learn and practice jointly innovations that the team considers important to use with their students, including improving the quality with which they use each of the four co-teaching approaches described in this book.

It is important for co-teachers to know what the desired co-teaching behaviors are so that they are able to self-assess and reflect on the degree or quality with which they engaged in these behaviors. For this purpose, we have created the 34-item Are We Really Co-Teachers? self-assessment checklist presented in Resource M. This checklist can be reproduced and used in a number of ways to

Figure 11.1 Co-Teaching Daily Lesson Plan Format

Co-Teaching Daily Lesson Plan

Date: _____

Co-Teachers: _____
(Names)

Content Area(s): _____

Lesson Objectives

Content Standards Addressed

Circle the Co-Teaching Model(s) Used:

Supportive   Parallel   Complementary   Team Teaching

What is the room arrangement? Will other spaces outside of the classroom be used?
(Draw a picture of the room arrangement.)

What materials do the co-teachers need?

How is student learning assessed by co-teachers?

What specific supports, aids, or services do select students need? (See Appendix A for suggestions.)

(Continued)

Figure 11.1 (Continued)

What does each co-teacher do before, during, and after the lesson?

Co-Teacher Name:		
What are the specific tasks that I do *before* the lesson?		
What are the specific tasks that I do *during* the lesson?		
What are the specific tasks that I do *after* the lesson?		

Where, when, and how do co-teachers debrief and evaluate the outcomes of the lesson?

promote team members' professional development. Each co-teacher can rate the co-teaching partnership individually on the 34 items and then compare *Yes* versus *No* assessments. Doing so provides team members with a starting point for discussion about the strengths of the partnership thus far and enables them to target areas for improvement. The team can also complete the assessment jointly. Rather than coming to consensus on an item, we suggest that the team use a different approach to self-rating. We suggest the rule that every member must definitively agree to the *Yes* rating. If any team member is unsure that a *Yes* rating is merited, then the score must remain *No*. This reduces the temptation to pressure a person with a differing perception to give in for the sake of consensus and, instead, encourages a real dialogue about differing perspectives, perceptions, and experiences as members of a co-teaching team. Others who are not on the team but who are requested to respond or who have a responsibility to observe the co-teachers can use the checklist to provide constructive feedback, which can lead to professional reflection and team-member growth. The completed Are We Really Co-Teachers? self-assessment shown in Table 11.3 is an example of the results of a principal's observations of a mature co-teaching team, which has many strengths and just a few areas for targeted growth.

Table 11.3 Self-Assessment: Are We Really Co-Teachers?

Directions: Check Yes or No to each of the following statements to determine your co-teaching score at this point in time.

Yes	No	In our co-teaching partnership:
X	___	1. We decide which co-teaching approach we are going to use in a lesson based on the benefits to the students and the co-teachers.
X	___	2. We share ideas, information, and materials.
X	___	3. We identify the resources and talents of the co-teachers.
X	___	4. We teach different groups of students at the same time.
___	X	5. We are aware of what one another is doing even when we are not directly in one another's presence.
X	___	6. We share responsibility for deciding what to teach.
X	___	7. We agree on the curriculum standards that will be addressed in a lesson.
X	___	8. We share responsibility for deciding how to teach.
X	___	9. We share responsibility for deciding who teaches what part of a lesson.
X	___	10. We are flexible and make changes as needed during a lesson.
X	___	11. We identify student strengths and needs.
X	___	12. We share responsibility for differentiating instruction.
___	X	13. We include other people when their expertise or experience is needed.
X	___	14. We share responsibility for how student learning is assessed.
X	___	15. We can show that students are learning when we co-teach.
X	___	16. We agree on discipline procedures and jointly carry them out.
X	___	17. We give feedback to one another on what goes on in the classroom.
X	___	18. We make improvements in our lessons based on what happens.

Yes	No	*In our co-teaching partnership:*
X	___	19. We communicate freely our concerns.
X	___	20. We have a process for resolving our disagreements and use it when faced with problems and conflicts.
X	___	21. We celebrate the process of co-teaching and the outcomes and successes.
X	___	22. We have fun with the students and each other when we co-teach.
X	___	23. We have regularly scheduled times to meet and discuss our work.
X	___	24. We use our meeting time productively.
X	___	25. We can effectively co-teach even when we don't have time to plan.
___	X	26. We explain the benefits of co-teaching to the students and their families.
X	___	27. We model collaboration and teamwork for our students.
X	___	28. We are each viewed by our students as their teacher.
___	X	29. We include students in the co-teaching role.
X	___	30. We depend on one another to follow through on tasks and responsibilities.
X	___	31. We seek and enjoy additional training to make our co-teaching better.
___	___	32. We are mentors to others who want to co-teach.
X	___	33. We can use a variety of co-teaching approaches (i.e., supportive, parallel, complementary, team teaching)
X	___	34. We communicate our need for logistical support and resources to our administrators.

TOTAL   YES: 29   NO: 5

FREQUENTLY ASKED QUESTION

1. My co-teacher and I co-teach two class periods together. We have a common planning time but we also have many other responsibilities and demands placed on our time. How important is common planning time to the success of our co-teaching team?

Educators today face many tasks and demands that compete for their time. In essence, they are asked to run and reinvent schools at the same time. Our experience has taught us that purposeful planning is essential to the development of a highly effective co-teaching team. While there are exceptions, co-teachers who regularly co-plan seem to be the ones who are able to broaden their repertoire to include all four of the co-teaching approaches. Those who do not set aside time to plan end up planning on the spot and, as a result, tend to primarily employ the supportive co-teaching approach. While a supportive co-teaching approach has benefits, it is not always the most effective use of professional expertise to support diverse students.

We suggest that you and your co-teaching partner discuss the various demands, including co-teaching, with which you are charged and prioritize them in order of importance. Also determine which of these responsibilities the two of you must absolutely address jointly and which you could do on your own. We also suggest that, at least initially, you and your co-teacher commit to meeting at least twice a week for at least 30 minutes to discuss students, design lessons, and divide up tasks to be completed before, during, and after the two classes in which you co-teach. We encourage you to reflect on your co-teaching team's effectiveness when you do spend time planning as compared to when you do not. Were you more flexible and responsive to student needs and differences? Did you feel more comfortable and competent? Did you have more fun? Did you go beyond supportive co-teaching and use parallel, complementary, and/or team-teaching co-teaching approaches in your lessons?

12

From Surviving to Thriving

Tips for Getting Along With Your Co-Teachers

Topics Included in This Chapter:

- Advice from co-teachers
- Keeping communication alive
- Understanding the developmental nature of co-teaching relationships
- Managing conflict
- Tips for dealing with challenging and unproductive behavior
- Tips for avoiding potential problems

In this chapter, we discuss how you can thrive as a co-teacher. We begin by sharing some advice from co-teachers. Then we explain the communication skills and psychological supports that may help you move beyond survival mode, especially when experiencing the conflicts that co-teachers typically face. We emphasize that understanding the developmental nature of co-teaching relationships can help resolve conflicts. Finally, we offer practical tips to avoid potential problems.

■ ADVICE FROM CO-TEACHERS

R. Whitehouse, a member of a first-grade teaching team, explained the following:

Co-teaching can be viewed as the vehicle for teaching professionals the social skills of openness and honesty in communication, flexibility, compromise, and acceptance of difference. Because we stress the importance of feeling that we do not always need to be perfect, that we can make mistakes in front of one another, it's OK to fail now. I'm more likely to try new things. It's easier to try new things if you have someone to take the risk with—someone to laugh with.

A student co-teacher wrote,

I learned to lose my shyness and let the story I was reading aloud to my partner come to life through me. I enjoyed making voices and facial expressions, but most of all, I enjoyed the acceptance [of my partners]. . . . I became a more patient person. . . . [My partners] taught me to be outgoing and always try new things. Once I actually danced in the middle of the group as we were playing a game. I would never have guessed I would be brave enough to do that in front of people. Yet it was all because I was a co-teacher.

A co-teacher member of a multicultural teaching team wrote,

I have really changed. I teach in a completely different way. I am no longer so threatened by difference. When I admit I do not understand a particular perspective, my [co-teachers] actually try to help me understand.

A high school co-teacher of students learning English explained,

I have always considered myself a good teacher, but with the changes that I have made in an effort to be more responsive, I am now becoming my best.

Finally, a junior high school science co-teacher and her special education co-teacher wrote,

We also became comfortable talking about our interpersonal interactions and our progress as co-teachers. Although at times these discussions were difficult, they yielded tremendous results for us. We both are better teachers as a result of these open and honest discussions.

KEEPING COMMUNICATION ALIVE ■

A common characteristic that shows up in these comments from co-teachers is that they have discovered that the underlying key to success are the three C's of co-teaching: communicate, communicate a different way, and communicate again! This is similar to the idea contained in the adage, "If at first you don't succeed, try, try again." The more flexible and versatile your communication skills, the more likely you are to communicate successfully with your co-teachers. There are three strategies in particular that co-teachers can use to communicate more effectively: helping to meet each other's psychological needs, adjusting to each other's learning styles, and coaxing each other out of distress patterns.

First, use your communication skills creatively to help meet the basic psychological needs of you and your fellow co-teachers. Recall that, previously, you learned of Glasser's (1999) belief that people choose to do what they do because it satisfies one or more of the five basic human needs: survival, power over or control of one's life, freedom and choice, a sense of belonging, and fun. By communicating your respect and appreciation for your co-teachers' personal commitment or work accomplishments, you help them meet their needs for survival and power. By working in a co-teacher relationship and enjoying the give and take, you and your co-teachers may experience a sense of belonging and freedom from isolation by having others with whom to share the responsibility for accomplishing the challenging tasks of teaching in classrooms of diverse students. It can be fun to problem solve creatively and to engage in stimulating adult dialogue and social interactions, especially when your co-teachers acknowledge the humor and enthusiasm that each brings to the partnership.

Second, successful co-teachers know they are more effective communicators when they use words their partners understand, pay attention to their partners' preferred learning styles (e.g., visual, auditory, kinesthetic), and change the tone of voice and gestures they use when speaking. Co-teachers can strengthen their communications by using predicates (verbs, adverbs, and adjectives to describe a subject) that reflect their listeners' visual, auditory, or kinesthetic learning styles and preferences. As defined by the communication framework known as *neurolinguistic programming* (NLP), predicates are used to identify which representational system a person prefers to use in processing communication—visual, auditory, or kinesthetic. Co-teachers who use visual predicates such as "Do you see what I mean?" are more likely to connect with their partners who have a visual learning style. Co-teachers who use auditory predicates such as "Does that sound right to you?" are more likely to be heard by their partners who prefer an auditory learning style. Similarly, when co-teachers use kinesthetic predicates such as "Will you put me in touch with your ideas about what we're doing?" they are more likely to get action from their partners with a kinesthetic learning style.

A third strategy co-teachers can use to communicate more effectively is to practice the skill of the *process communication model* (PCM). PCM research suggests that communication mismatches abound in American schools (Bradley, Pauley, and Pauley 2006; Kahler 1982; Pauley, Bradley, and Pauley 2002). Mismatches between co-teacher personality types can result in the failure to connect and collaborate effectively with one another. PCM identifies six personality types (i.e., reactor/feeler, workaholic/thinker, persister/believer, dreamer/imaginer, rebel/funster, promoter/do-er) based on individual behavior patterns, needs, motivators, and perceptions. Each person possesses a personality structure comprising these six personality types, with relative strengths differing from one person to the next. No one type or personality is better or more successful than another. Although everyone has all six, each person is able to communicate easily with two or three but struggles with the other three or four. Co-teachers whose most well-developed personality types match tend to do well communicating with each other. Those who have personality structures that differ can be expected to have difficulty communicating unless they become familiar with the needs, motivations, and perceptions associated with their own strongest personality types and the needs, motivations, and perceptions associated with their partners' strongest personality types. Keefe, Moore, and Duff (2004) corroborate the premises of PCM in their study of creating and maintaining co-teacher relationships. They found that effective co-teachers must know not only their students and their content, but also themselves and their co-teacher partners.

PCM can create a more supportive and responsive classroom and working relationship with co-teachers who are the most difficult to reach. When co-teachers match their communication patterns to meet the communication preferences and personality types of their partners, they can experience increased achievement and satisfaction in what they are doing both individually and jointly. In other words, if we want our co-teachers to listen to what we are saying, we need to speak their language. In fact, PCM can create a more supportive and responsive relationship with co-teachers who are the most difficult to reach.

Co-teachers must address multiple issues related to assessment, accountability, lack of time for planning or even taking care of personal needs, dealing with challenging students and families, individualizing instruction for a wide range of diverse students, and lack of praise and recognition (Pauley et al. 2002). When co-teachers have their psychological needs met on a daily basis and help meet their partners' needs as well, they are more likely to thrive despite these multiple stressors. For example, co-teachers who have a preference for perceiving the world through feelings may overadapt by continuously trying to please others when they are distressed; then they may make mistakes and lack assertiveness. The result may be that they are rejected by their co-teachers. When these co-teachers are appreciated for who they are and provided with sensory stimulation (e.g., flowers, scented candles), however, their distress patterns may disappear. Similarly, co-teachers with a preference for perceiving the world through ideas may overthink for their co-teacher partners, overcontrol and criticize their co-teachers' thinking skills, and, finally, reject their co-teachers. When their psychological need for recognition of their work is met, they are less likely to criticize others.

Some co-teachers perceive the world through their opinions and convictions. Their distress patterns move from focusing on what their partners are doing wrong, to pushing their beliefs and preaching, and then to forsaking their partners as having no commitment. When their psychological needs are met through recognition of their work and opinions, they are much less likely to show these distress patterns. Some co-teachers have a need for solitude, and when that need is not met, their distress pattern moves from being inattentive to their partners, to passively waiting or avoiding their partners, to being left out of activities altogether.

Co-teachers who thrive on fun activities will try hard to do what is asked of them and then begin blaming things, situations, or their co-teachers for what goes wrong, and finally they will become vengeful. When their psychological need for fun and their strong likes and dislikes are acknowledged, they are more likely to not become distressed or engage in disruptive behaviors. Co-teachers who have a strong preference for risk taking and excitement may expect their partners to fend for themselves when they are in distress, then they may manipulate and create negative drama among the co-teaching team members, finally abandoning their partners. To keep them out of distress, co-teachers can help these people fulfill their psychological need for excitement by making deals with them, setting them up to be in the limelight, and asking them to promote the co-teaching agenda with the administration.

It should be emphasized that everyone moves in and out of distress many times a day. Knowing your own distress patterns can support you in getting your own psychological needs met. The bottom line is that when co-teachers perceive so-called disruptive or challenging behaviors as signals that they are in distress, helping them get their psychological needs met becomes a key to successful communication.

UNDERSTANDING THE DEVELOPMENTAL NATURE ■ OF CO-TEACHING RELATIONSHIPS

Most people learn to be competent in their group work as a direct result of actually working with other people. In addition, having the cognitive knowledge about the social psychology of how individuals behave when working as partners or groups can be helpful in understanding that co-teacher relationships go through various stages of development. Knowing that people in co-teaching relationships go through specific stages can help us choose to use specific interpersonal and communication skills that facilitate achievement of the goal and maintain a positive relationship.

Similar to the stages that members of groups experience, there are the four Fs that co-teachers pass through in the development of a co-teaching relationship: the forming stage, the functioning stage, the formulating stage, and the fermenting stage. Each stage can be experienced more successfully when co-teachers practice the collaboration skills associated with each stage. This is quite similar to how children feel when they first achieve a difficult task, such as climbing up and down stairs or riding a bicycle. They remember what it felt like to be unsure and incompetent before achieving mastery of the skill.

Many of the same feelings may be experienced when you begin to work as a member of a co-teaching team, even if you have worked as a co-teacher with others. When you are committed to an agreed-on goal and when you want to maintain positive relationships with your co-teachers (in case you ever have to work with them again!), however, it becomes particularly important to practice the specific interpersonal communication skills associated with each of the stages of group development. Because you and your co-teachers may take baby steps as you learn some of the skills, remember to give positive feedback on how well each other is doing. Some teams use these stages and skills as a checklist to measure their growth individually and as a team.

During the forming stage, the goal is to build a mutual and reciprocal relationship. The interpersonal skills that facilitate this goal include building trust, being on time, establishing goals, and setting norms (agreements) such as no put-downs and use of appropriate tone of voice to match co-teaching partners' communication styles.

During the functioning stage, co-teachers must come to an agreement about specifically how their co-teaching partnership will function. They decide how they will work together, specifying who will do what tasks and when. To facilitate this stage, communication and shared leadership skills are needed—clarifying or explaining one's views, coordinating tasks, paraphrasing other's views, and then checking for understanding of the decisions that have been made.

In the formulating stage, it is important to emphasize the task to be accomplished in the co-teacher relationship. During this stage, helpful collaboration skills that co-teachers should practice include decision making and creative problem solving. These skills refer to communication strategies such as stating the decision that needs to be made, thinking of new ways to include everyone in the decision, being willing to try something even though you aren't sure it will work, and being comfortable with taking risks.

The fermenting stage is when co-teacher team cohesiveness can reach its greatest potential. The skills of conflict management are important to facilitating the fermenting stage. Such skills include criticizing ideas not people, differentiating opinions, asking for more information to understand someone else's ideas, and using creative problem-solving techniques.

We believe that understanding these stages can improve the outcomes and enjoyment of the teams in which you participate. First of all, please understand that it's up to you! Only you can change your behaviors, and by modeling some of the skills required at each stage of development, you can help your co-teachers achieve better results and experience more enjoyment from the partnership. As shown in Table 12.1, the checklist of skills associated with each of the four stages of development illustrates the many different ways you can advance both goal achievement and maintenance of positive relationships with co-teaching team members. This checklist is also provided as a reproducible resource, Resource N, for teams to use in assessing and tracking their interpersonal development.

Second, you can enlist the support of your co-teachers by asking for feedback on how well you are communicating and how well you are using the skills associated with each stage of the co-teacher relationship. When receiving feedback, it is important to listen and keep an open mind as you hear what your

Table 12.1   Checklist of Skills for the Stages of Co-Teacher Development

Skills for the Forming Stage

____   Use co-teachers' preferred names

____   Use no put-downs

____   Come to co-teacher meetings on time, and stay for the entire time

____   Follow through on agreements (show I am trustworthy)

____   Acknowledge co-teachers for their follow-through

Skills for the Functioning Stage

____   State and restate the purpose of co-teaching

____   Set or call attention to the time limits

____   Suggest procedures for how to do the task effectively

____   Express support and acceptance verbally

____   Express support and acceptance nonverbally

____   Paraphrase and clarify

____   Energize co-teachers with humor, ideas, or enthusiasm

____   Describe feelings when appropriate

Skills for the Formulating Stage

____   Summarize what has been said

____   Seek accuracy by correcting or adding to the summary

____   Seek connections to other knowledge

____   Seek clever ways to remember ideas, facts, and decisions

____   Ask co-teachers to explain their reasoning

____   Ask co-teachers to plan aloud

Skills for the Fermenting Stage

____   Criticize ideas without criticizing people

____   Differentiate ideas when there is disagreement

____   Integrate different ideas into a single position

____   Probe by asking questions that lead to deeper understanding

____   Suggest new answers and ideas

____   Think of new ways to resolve differences of opinion

co-teachers are saying so that you can change your communication style or your actions to get the results you desire.

Third, you can practice, and encourage your co-teachers to practice, skills that you are not familiar with or comfortable in performing just yet. This takes a lot of courage; however, with a norm or expectation among co-teachers that feedback and corrective action are part of the relationship, practicing unfamiliar skills leads to increased success. To help guide your co-teaching partners, you might be interested in the definitions of various roles that help co-teachers go through the various stages of group development. Table 12.2 lists possible roles that co-teachers can practice to facilitate goal achievement. Table 12.3 lists the roles co-teachers can practice to maintain positive interpersonal relationships. Feel free to invent other roles, including those that are unique to the tasks your co-teachers need to achieve. Co-teachers can select two or three roles to practice during their planning time or while they communicate during their teaching time. For example, during the learning-stations lesson described in the elementary parallel teaching vignette (Chapter 5), Ms. Hernandez (the paraprofessional) was the timekeeper, Ms. Nugent (the speech and language therapist) was the recorder, and Ms. Gilpatrick (the classroom teacher) was the facilitator. Dave and Juan, the student co-teachers introduced in Chapter 9, reciprocally practiced two major roles: the relationship role of praiser and the task achievement role of checker.

Table 12.2   Roles That Facilitate Goal Achievement

Timekeeper

The timekeeper monitors the time, encourages co-teachers to stop at agreed-on times, and alerts co-teachers when it is approaching the end of the agreed-on time period. "We have five minutes left to finish."

Recorder

The recorder writes down the decisions made by the co-teachers and distributes copies to each present and absent co-teacher team member within one week's time.

Checker

The checker makes sure co-teachers understand discussion and decisions. "Can you explain how we arrived at this decision?"

Photocopier

The photocopier takes completed minutes from the recorder, copies them, and distributes them to absent and present co-teachers. Sometimes the photocopier makes copies of specific teaching/learning procedures so that all co-teachers can follow the same strategy.

"Yes, But . . ." Monitor

During brainstorming sessions, when all ideas are being recorded, the "yes, but . . ." monitor signals when judgmental or negative statements are made that might thwart the creative process and decrease the generation of ideas.

Others

To be added by you and your co-teachers.

Table 12.3   Roles That Maintain Positive Interpersonal Relationships

---

Facilitator

The facilitator encourages all co-teachers to participate and to carry out their roles. The facilitator summarizes outcomes of a discussion before moving on to a new topic and makes sure that co-teachers' needs are met by adding items as requested.

Praiser

The praiser lets co-teachers know when they are using collaborative skills that positively impact each other. The praiser is careful to make the praise sound and feel authentic and focused (e.g., "Thanks to [insert co-teacher's name] for keeping us focused on our tasks!") rather than general comments (e.g., "Good job!").

Prober

The prober makes sure all possibilities have been explored. "What else could we include?" "Are there any other ways we could do this?"

Jargon Buster

The jargon buster lets co-teachers know when they are using terms that not all those who are present may understand, such as acronyms, abbreviations, and so on. This is an especially important role when co-teachers include people from a specialty area that is not familiar to everyone. "Whoops—does everyone know what IEP means?"

Others

To be added by you and your co-teachers.

MANAGING CONFLICT ■

Johnson and Johnson (1991) are cooperative learning experts from the University of Minnesota who teach about the reality and value of conflict:

> Conflicts occur all the time. They are a natural, inevitable, potentially constructive, and normal part of school life. Students disagree over who to sit by at lunch, which game to play during recess, when to work and when to play, when to talk and when to listen, and who is going to pick the paper up off the floor. . . . Covert conflicts are ones where you and your classmates sit and fester about your perceived grievances. Covert conflicts have to be made overt and resolved. (p. 58)

In fact, the same is true of adults. Covert conflicts need to be made overt and resolved, or they will fester and destroy the potential for a positive co-teacher relationship. Conflict is a natural, ever-present part of co-teaching. Johnson and Johnson (1988) define conflicts in terms of actions that frequently prevent, block, or interfere with another person's attempts to achieve his or her goals. Knowing what kind of conflict you are having can help you select a conflict resolution strategy. Consider the following four types of conflict:

1. A controversy exists when a person's ideas or conclusions are incompatible with the ideas of another person, and an agreement must be reached.

2. A conceptual conflict occurs when a person has two incompatible ideas.

3. A conflict of interest exists when one person tries to achieve a goal and another person blocks it.

4. A developmental conflict occurs as part of normal social development, for example, when recurring incompatible actions occur between a child and an adult.

It can be helpful to understand the sources of conflict. As noted earlier, people thrive when their psychological needs are met. When there are limited resources, conflicts may arise when people become afraid that their needs will not be met. Schrumpf and Jansen (2002) suggest that some conflicts arise because of differing values and convictions. Concepts and beliefs about timeliness, equality, fairness, and honesty are culturally embedded. When these beliefs and concepts are clarified, co-teachers often can avoid conflicts among co-teaching partners.

There is a lot of research to support the notion that conflicts have value. For example, achievement, problem solving, positive social development, flexibility in the face of change, and the experience of fun—all can be improved when a conflict is constructive (Johnson and Johnson 1988). You know that a conflict is constructive when a problem is solved, when the relationship among those involved is strengthened, and when the people involved increase their ability to resolve conflicts in the future. Ensuring that a conflict is constructive requires co-teachers to practice the task and relationship skills for the fermenting stage described in Table 12.1: think of new ways to resolve differences of opinion, differentiate your ideas when there is disagreement, and integrate different ideas into a single position. A good example of constructive conflict occurred between Mr. Silva (the middle level science and math teacher) and Ms. Spaulding (the special educator) when they developed a creative way to use the Multiple Intelligences Pizza to teach Boyle's law (see Chapter 7). The co-teachers had to seek connections with MI theory to identify and then share their own MI strengths, and suggest new ways to present the ideas and then integrate their ideas into a single lesson plan.

■ TIPS FOR DEALING WITH CHALLENGING AND UNPRODUCTIVE BEHAVIOR

We agree that few of us are ideal co-teachers all of the time. Consequently, many people ask, "What do we do with co-teaching partners whose behavior is challenging or unproductive?" Some challenging behaviors that occur infrequently or in isolated situations can be ignored. Humor may provide another solution because it can be used to lightly call attention to the behavior. For example, Rich is a person who can talk on and on about any topic, often not allowing others to speak. One of his co-teachers often says with a smile, "Rich, I guess you are really excited about this topic. Let's check in with other teaching partners on our team to find out what they think." Another solution is to call attention to alternative desired behaviors. For example, Jacque frequently interrupts. During the regularly scheduled time to process, Ann notes how Jacque has waited for others to complete their statements to allow them to elaborate or piggyback on ideas, which results in even better ones. This encourages Jacque to do the same in subsequent meetings.

When a co-teacher's negative behavior becomes incessant and distracting, however, it may be necessary to confront the person directly. Confrontation is often uncomfortable for both the confronter and the confronted, yet it is necessary at times. If team members determine that the individual who is going to receive the negative feedback will respond positively, any team member may initiate the feedback process. If they believe the person will respond negatively, be embarrassed or angry, or that public feedback will escalate the person's behavior, a supervisor or one of the team members who has a positive relationship with the individual might offer the feedback in private. We have found it helpful to use a five-step procedure for confronting a person with regard to disruptive or challenging interactions:

1. Observe the person and the impact of his or her behavior on others.

2. Try to understand why the person may be persisting in the behavior.

3. Describe the behavior and its impact to the person by using nonjudgmental language (use "I" statements, not "you" statements).

4. Establish some rules for minimizing future undesired behavior and increasing alternative behaviors.

5. Turn the unfavorable behavior into a favorable one (e.g., assign an aggressor the role of devil's advocate for certain issues, ask the joker to open each meeting with a funny story, invite a dominator to take the role of encourager or equalizer, ask the person who often wanders off the topic to signal whenever anyone gets off track).

TIPS FOR AVOIDING POTENTIAL PROBLEMS ■

In our experience, when co-teachers practice the eight tips listed in Table 12.4, they can achieve more effective outcomes for their students, can feel happier about their work, and are more likely to work together in the future (Villa, Thousand, and Nevin 1999). Practicing these tips will help co-teachers be proactive and thus avoid many potential problems.

Know With Whom You Need to Co-Teach

Co-teaching partners need not be limited to other teachers. Your co-teachers can, and in many cases must, include students, parents, administrators, specialists, community members, and advocates. Consider these three guidelines for deciding who will be your co-teachers:

Table 12.4 Practical Tips to Avoid Potential Problems

1. Know with whom you need to co-teach.

2. Establish and clarify co-teaching goals to avoid hidden agendas.

3. Agree to use a common conceptual framework, language, and set of interpersonal skills.

4. Practice communication skills for successful co-teacher interactions—achieving the tasks and maintaining positive relationships.

5. Know how to facilitate a collaborative culture.

6. Recognize and respect differences in excellence and the multiple sources of motivation for co-teachers.

7. Expect to be responsible and to be held accountable.

8. Agree to reflective analysis of the co-teaching process, and celebrate often.

1. Include those whom decisions will affect.

2. Include those who have the needed expertise.

3. Include anyone who has an interest in participating.

To promote inventive and creative outside-the-box thinking and to capitalize on existing excitement and enthusiasm, think about working with people who may not be formally expected to participate with your co-teaching team.

Establish and Clarify Co-Teaching Goals to Avoid Hidden Agendas

A planned method of developing and articulating goals for the co-teachers decreases much of the anxiety of not knowing what is expected. Creating common goals also encourages positive interdependence. An essential component of goal setting is for each co-teacher to say what he or she needs from the other co-teachers. When such needs are not recognized, there is a real possibility that co-teachers may come to think of others' goals and needs as hidden agendas.

Agree to Use a Common Conceptual Framework, Language, and Set of Interpersonal Skills

More effective co-teaching outcomes occur when co-teachers use a common language to share meaning and avoid or demystify jargon. Participation in staff development and other training activities can support the development of a common conceptual framework. (See Chapter 10 for more details about staff development.)

Co-teachers can establish ground rules for how they will operate. For example, a ground rule might be that it is OK to ask questions when something is not understood. Per Table 12.3, one co-teacher could play the role of jargon buster, a person who asks others for clarification when terms are used that not everyone may understand.

Sometimes co-teachers agree to participate in inservice workshops or mentoring to acquire and master interpersonal and communication strategies and skills. Other co-teachers may agree to receive training in a particular problem-solving process to deal with conflict and then share the process with other co-teachers. Through such reciprocity, all members of the co-teaching team improve their skills.

Practice Communication Skills for Successful Co-Teacher Interactions

Co-teachers have an array of interpersonal skills (e.g., trust building, communication, creative problem solving, conflict resolution) to practice. Skills for helping co-teachers achieve their mutual goals and for maintaining relationships must be consciously practiced. Be sure that absent co-teachers receive the minutes or notes of meetings. Build in time to reflect on how well co-teachers are interacting, and then make adjustments as needed. Clarify lines of accountability by stating who will do what, setting deadlines, and building in celebrations for the small successes that occur every day.

Know How to Facilitate a Collaborative Culture

The education profession is well versed in the *lone arranger* way of doing business—one teacher is expected to teach a class of 30 students without support from or communication with others. The notion that the so-called self-contained classroom and the lone teacher can somehow meet the ever-increasing needs of a diverse student body is a myth. Only through sharing ideas, materials, resources, and expertise do teachers develop, survive, and thrive.

To facilitate the change to a collaborative culture, co-teachers must bring to consciousness their unconscious beliefs. An example of an unconscious belief is the following: "If I have to have a co-teacher to succeed, then I must be a less-than-adequate teacher." New traditions and celebrations that reflect the values of cooperation must replace old traditions. For example, instead of celebrating a teacher-of-the-year award, add a co-teacher team award. Include co-teaching and collaboration as expected roles in every job description.

Recognize and Respect Differences and Multiple Sources of Motivation

Co-teacher teams improve their effectiveness when the individuals improve. Make sure incentives are varied enough to meet individual preferences. Create flexible scheduling that encourages co-teachers to use their time to meet and plan as well as debrief and problem solve. Seek and use training opportunities for learning new ways to co-teach. Set up site visit opportunities to observe other co-teachers and interview them to find out their secrets of successful co-teaching.

Expect to Be Responsible and to Be Held Accountable

Effective co-teachers act responsibly. They follow through on what they agree to do. They show up for meetings on time. They consciously practice effective communication skills. They support and facilitate the participation of their co-teacher partners. They celebrate individual and team successes. They expect to be held accountable, and they hold their co-teachers accountable in return.

Agree to Reflective Analysis, and Celebrate Often

Create a tool to measure the changes you and your co-teacher partners experience as a result of your partnership. Consider Table 11.3, the Are We Really Co-Teachers? self-assessment, as one way to assess your development. Keep a journal of your feelings, thoughts, and observations. When co-teachers use some form of reflective analysis, they typically become more empowered to celebrate their current levels of co-teaching skills and to set goals for continued improvement. Yes, it takes time to learn the interpersonal and thinking skills needed for effective co-teaching, but the results are worth it. Celebrate often!

In the Epilogue that follows this chapter, Nancy Keller and Lia Cravedi-Cheng describe the development of their co-teaching relationship. They illustrate each of the eight tips for avoiding potential problems that are offered in Table 12.4. The tips are highlighted in set-aside boxes throughout their story.

Epilogue

Developing a Shared Voice Through Co-Teaching

Nancy Keller and Lia Cravedi-Cheng

Erin Jarry

■ NANCY'S VOICE

Several years of working as a middle level science teacher in an inclusive school district gave me the opportunity to experience how co-teaching with teachers from other content areas and with special educators can help children of varying abilities participate meaningfully in regular classrooms. I must confess that I was initially uneasy about the inclusion in my classroom of students with physical, academic, and social challenges. My teacher preparation program, although excellent at the time, did not include practical experiences in inclusive educational settings. Today my understanding of how we can educate all students together has broadened. I realize that my initial concerns about inclusive education had to do with the unknown and with not being able to visualize how it might work.

■ LIA'S VOICE

Before I began co-teaching with regular educators, I had worked for years as a special educator in pullout resource rooms and separate special education classrooms. Although I was uncomfortable with sorting students by perceived ability, teaching them in isolation, and then hoping they would be able to apply this learning in a new context, this was not an uncommon practice at the time. My contact with general educators was limited to saying "Hello" to each other as I pulled my students from their classes.

Co-teaching addressed my dilemmas and ended my social and professional isolation. Co-teaching with Nancy convinced both of us that when teachers have adequate support and the opportunity to share their respective expertise, a rich educational experience can be created that benefits all students.

■ OUR VOICE

What you will hear in the following pages is our shared voice, our description of how our co-teaching partnership evolved over the two years we taught together. We hope that what we learned will be helpful to you in your co-teaching endeavors. The school district in which we co-taught together was one that underwent a dramatic, decade-long transformation from a district in which students with special needs were placed in special classes or bussed outside of the district to a district in which all students were educated in general education classroom, with co-teaching as a predominant student support mechanism.

The first step in the district's transformation was to close the on-site special classes and discontinue the practice of sending students out of the district. Although all students were now on campus and included in most general education classes, the benefits of inclusive education were not being fully realized. Specifically, the dropout rate of students with disabilities was still high (30%), and their absenteeism was a chronic problem. We were convinced that a primary reason these students were reluctant to continue their education was that they did not feel as if they really were a part of the school community. They were still frequently separated from their classmates when pulled from their general education classes to receive academic coursework in a resource room. We were faced with a serious challenge: in what ways could we structure a learning environment in which these students would want to participate? We had to look no farther than our students and listen to what they were telling us: They wanted to learn alongside their friends, just like every other student wanted.

> **Tip 1** Know with whom you need to co-teach.

Now that we had embraced the concept of all students learning side by side, our administrator for special services decided that the general and special educators also needed to teach (and learn) side by side. He explained that with this co-teaching configuration, the differences in our general and special education teacher preparation would be an asset. For example, Nancy had been trained as a secondary science teacher with little focus placed on making accommodations for students with learning differences. Lia, on the other hand, possessed these very skills—the ones Nancy lacked. By combining teaching skills, we complemented one other.

Unlike some teaching teams, we did not enter into our co-teaching relationship by choice. It was an administrative decision. In fact, we had not previously worked with each other. We are here to tell you that this does not have to spell doom for a team. Given time to meet, a framework such as the one we describe here, and attention to the collaborative teaming process, teachers can form an effective teaching partnership. This is what occurred for us.

OUR FIRST YEAR—DEVELOPING TRUST ■

There are several important aspects to the way we worked together. We have since learned to describe them as the essential ingredients of the cooperative process: face-to-face interaction through planning time, positive interdependence, individual accountability, and monitoring and processing of our achievements.

Face-to-Face Planning Time

Before we could stand together in front of our students and represent ourselves as a viable teaching team, we had to establish a weekly planning time. Prior to the start of the school year, we agreed to set aside one prep period per week for this to occur. Given that we did not know each other very well, we knew that without this initial investment of time, our co-teaching would not be successful. Therefore, this became our sacred time, time that would not be interrupted by the typical demands that teachers face. Although it was just the two of us, we set an agenda, took minutes, and

> **Tip 2** Establish and clarify co-teaching goals to avoid hidden agendas.

> **Tip 4** Practice communication skills for successful co-teacher interactions.

> **Tip 5** Know how to facilitate a collaborative culture.

assigned tasks to be completed later (e.g., prepare worksheets, make copies, talk to a student, grade papers). Without investing adequate time to plan, we can almost guarantee that a co-teaching team will not reach its potential. Notes in the mailbox and planning on the run cannot build solid, trusting relationships.

Positive Interdependence

Setting Mutual Goals

Much of our weekly planning time was driven by the mission that we and our school district had adopted, namely, that all students were to receive instruction in the general education classroom. To accomplish this mission, Nancy wanted to learn how to differentiate curriculum and instruction. Lia wanted to ensure that all the students for whom she coordinated services would be successful in general education classrooms. In retrospect, we now see that establishing a common purpose and setting clear goals provided a meaningful context in which to work. Once determined, a mission can guide a team in decision making, prompting team members to ask, "Is what we are doing congruent with our mission?" For example, given our mission of maintaining students in the regular classroom, the choice to remove a student from that environment became a choice of last resort because such an action was not in sync with our mission.

> **Tip 2** Establish and clarify co-teaching goals to avoid hidden agendas.

In addition, our individual professional goals become a yardstick by which to measure our growth as teachers. Did Nancy learn how to differentiate curriculum and instruction? How successful was Lia at structuring for student success?

Defining Roles

Something that wasn't discussed during the year but that both of us assumed from the beginning was that Nancy would be responsible for delivering the content and Lia would play the supportive co-teacher role (see Chapter 4 for details about the supportive co-teaching approach). This assumption, although conventional (teacher and teacher assistant), provided the basis for dividing our labor. This meant that Nancy took on the tasks related to what would be taught and how (i.e., identify the content to be covered; set objectives and do the majority of lesson planning, teaching, and evaluating). Lia supported this instruction through her skilled classroom and student management, verbally and physically prompting students to focus on the instruction, checking for student understanding, and intervening when off-task behavior occurred. When defining roles, it is critical to consider what the students need as well as what expertise each co-teacher brings to a situation. Redefining roles requires the setting aside of egos. For Lia, being an assistant to another teacher may not have been a glamorous job, but it was exactly what the students needed in order to engage and learn.

Individual Accountability

Once our roles were defined, trust was further built by following through on our commitments. Lia promised Nancy that she would co-teach for a minimum of one period per day, four days per week. Nancy depended on Lia to be there; had Lia not been dependable, Nancy would not have trusted that what had been planned would be realized. Conversely, if Nancy did not clearly plan the objectives for the science lessons, Lia would have felt let down. She would not have known how to support the students in Nancy's classes. The glue to this co-teaching relationship was individual accountability. We recommend that co-teachers apply this glue liberally!

Monitoring and Processing of Accomplishments

In our first year working together, we kept our reflections and processing within the noncontroversial realm of how the students were doing. We avoided conversations regarding our performance as teachers. Although Nancy's goal was to improve skills in differentiation and instruction, she did not seek feedback from Lia in this area, fearing that she would be criticized instead of supported in Lia's evaluations. It wasn't until Lia suggested that we take a district-sponsored course together to focus on our co-teaching that Nancy felt she could trust Lia to offer feedback. Receiving feedback and reflection on one's own work can be a scary proposition. It takes trust, and that is what we developed, first and foremost, in our first year.

OUR SECOND YEAR—SUSTAINING TRUST ■

We were fortunate to be able to work together for a second year. Our school district is often fluid when it comes to scheduling and partnering personnel from year to year. When we requested that we remain partners, our administrators listened and granted us a second year to develop continuity as a team. We were deliberate about attending to the same collaborative ingredients (i.e., face-to-face planning time, positive interdependence, individual accountability, monitoring and processing of accomplishments) that had allowed us to succeed as a co-teaching team in our first year.

Face-to-Face Planning Time

Co-teaching teams that have been together for a while can easily be lulled into complacency about planning. After all, team members are familiar with each other, and a routine has been established. Much can be lost, however, if planning (in terms of instructional integrity and quality) is incidental. As in our first year, planning time remained key to our success.

A big challenge in our second year was to move beyond our routine—that is, to use the lessons learned from the previous year as a starting point for refinement and improvement. Because we believed the adage that two heads are

> **Tip 7** Expect to be responsible and to be held accountable.

> **Tip 8** Agree to reflective analysis of the co-teaching process, and celebrate often.

> **Tip 3** Agree to use a common conceptual framework, language, and set of interpersonal skills.

Tip 5 Know how to facilitate a collaborative culture.

better than one, we knew that adequate planning time needed to remain part of the routine, even if it sometimes seemed as if the lessons could write themselves and the classroom could run itself. We found it helpful to use a structured planning meeting format (much like the one in Table 11.2 of Chapter 11) to guide us when we met face-to-face. We found we made much more efficient use of the little planning time available to us when we had an agenda and time frames to keep us focused.

Positive Interdependence

In our second year, we established positive interdependence in new ways that resulted in an enhancement of our feeling that we were in this together. We revisited our goals, redefined our roles, and refined the monitoring of our progress so as to be more accountable for our individual and collective tasks.

Revisiting Goals

Although we were in our second year, we remained aware of our goal—ensuring that all students received instruction in general education—and continued to work toward it. In our first year, we had set broad goals, such as learning to differentiate instruction and adequately support students in general education classes. By our second year, we knew that there were several specific skills and strategies that we needed to master. We targeted the following as professional development areas: (1) positive discipline and behavior supports, (2) principles of effective instruction, and (3) the use of a universal design approach to planning that systematically considered our students' learning characteristics (this preceded the planning of content, instructional processes, and products of a lesson or unit; Udvari-Solner, Villa, and Thousand 2002). Participation in a district-sponsored course, which we took together, facilitated our professional goal setting. For us, this course was one concrete way that our school district supported us as a teaching team. In many ways, our studying and learning together enhanced our "all for one and one for all" ethic and encouraged us to revisit and redefine not only our goals but our co-teaching roles as well.

Redefining Roles

Just as our goals became more interdependent, so did our roles. In our first year, we defined our roles along the boundaries of our relative expertise—Lia was the special educator, and Nancy was the science teacher. During our second year, we both saw ourselves as teachers of children, not as different types of teachers for different types of children. This change of perspective significantly changed the roles we played when co-teaching. Now both of us were responsible for developing lesson objectives, evaluating student progress, conferencing with parents, managing student behavior, and covering the logistics (e.g., making copies, preparing worksheets, setting up labs). We jointly shared all of the responsibilities a regular classroom teacher would normally have. We learned about the importance of redefining roles throughout a co-teaching partnership so that we could evolve into what, by our second year, could truly be called a teaching team (see Chapter 7 for more details about the team-teaching approach to co-teaching).

Individual Accountability

Even in the second year, accountability continued to be the glue that held our relationship together. For example, each of us had come to expect that the other would follow through on her responsibilities, as demonstrated during the first year. At this point, it may have been easy for either of us to have occasionally neglected our commitments, thinking that the other could handle it or would understand. Given the skills we had acquired, either one of us probably could have handled it and likely would have understood, but the other person's accountability to our teaching team would have begun to erode. The challenge for established teaching teams is to not take each other for granted, but to maintain a high level of mutual support.

> **Tip 8** Agree to reflective analysis of the co-teaching process, and celebrate often.

Monitoring and Processing of Accomplishments

In our second year of working together, we continued to reflect on student performance, considering this a critical and safe topic. Because we had developed a high level of trust and because we now shared a common language of instruction gained from the course we took together, we were now able to discuss our own and each other's teaching methods as well. We became comfortable talking about our interpersonal actions and our progress as co-teachers. Although at times these discussions were difficult, they yielded tremendous results for us. We are both better teachers as a result of these open and honest discussions.

> **Tip 3** Agree to use a common conceptual framework, language, and set of interpersonal skills.

> **Tip 8** Agree to reflective analysis of the co-teaching process, and celebrate often.

FINAL REFLECTIONS ■

When school districts give general and special educators the opportunity to share their respective expertise by working as co-teachers, a rich and often remarkable educational experience for all students can emerge. In our two years as an evolving teaching team, we experienced for ourselves how students of all perceived abilities can learn and reach their potential together, in the same class, avoiding the stigma associated with being pulled out of the classroom for specialized instruction. Co-teachers benefit as well. Their social networks within the school community grow. They no longer experience teaching as the isolated profession, as they jointly experience the joy and fun of a student's success or a great co-taught lesson. Finally, co-teachers' perspectives evolve, as ours did, from a *yours-versus-mine* view of students, curriculum, and instruction to a *we-and-ours* view of everything about good schooling.

> **Tip 6** Recognize and respect differences and multiple sources of motivation.

Resources

Resource A.   Checklist of Sample Supplemental Supports, Aids, and Services

Directions:

When considering the need for personalized supports, aids, or services for a student, use this checklist to help identify which supports will be the least intrusive, only as special as necessary, and the most natural to the context of the classroom.

Environmental

___ Preferential seating

___ Planned seating

    ___ Bus __ Classroom __ Lunchroom __ Auditorium __ Other _____

___ Alter physical room arrangement (Specify: _____)

___ Use study carrels or quiet areas

___ Define area concretely (e.g., carpet squares, tape on floor, rug area)

___ Reduce/minimize distractions

    ___ Visual __ Spatial __ Auditory __ Movement

___ Teach positive rules for use of space

Pacing of Instruction

___ Extend time requirements

___ Vary activity often

___ Allow breaks

___ Omit assignments requiring copying in timed situations

___ Send additional copy of the text home for summer preview

___ Provide home set of materials for preview or review

Presentation of Subject Matter

___ Teach to the student's learning style/strength intelligences

    ___ Verbal/Linguistic __ Logical/Mathematical __ Visual/Spatial __ Naturalist

    ___ Bodily/Kinesthetic __ Musical __ Interpersonal __ Intrapersonal

    ___ Use active, experiential learning

    ___ Use specialized curriculum

    ___ Record class lectures and discussions to replay later

    ___ Use American Sign Language and/or total communication

    ___ Provide prewritten notes, an outline, or an organizer (e.g., mind map)

    ___ Provide copy of classmate's notes (e.g., use NCR paper, photocopy)

    ___ Use functional and meaningful application of academic skills

    ___ Present demonstrations and models

(Continued)

___ Use manipulatives and real objects in mathematics

___ Highlight critical information or main ideas

___ Preteach vocabulary

___ Make and use vocabulary files, or provide vocabulary lists

___ Reduce the language level of the reading assignment

___ Use facilitated communication

___ Use visual organizers/sequences

___ Use paired reading/writing

___ Reduce seat time in class or activities

___ Use diaries or learning logs

___ Reword/rephrase instructions and questions

___ Preview and review major concepts in primary language

Materials

___ Limit amount of material on a page

___ Record texts and other class materials

___ Use study guides and advanced organizers

___ Use supplementary materials

___ Provide note-taking assistance

___ Copy class notes

___ Scan tests and class notes into computer

___ Use large print

___ Use braille material

___ Use communication book or board

___ Provide assistive technology and software (e.g., Intelli-Talk)

Specialized Equipment or Procedure

___ Wheelchair	___ Walker
___ Standing board	___ Positioning
___ Computer	___ Computer software
___ Electronic typewriter	___ Video
___ Modified keyboard	___ Voice synthesizer
___ Switches	___ Augmentative communication device
___ Catheterization	___ Suctioning
___ Braces	___ Restroom equipment

___ Customized mealtime utensils, plates, cups, and other materials

Assignment Modification

___ Give directions in small, distinct steps (written/picture/verbal)

___ Use written backup for oral directions

___ Use pictures as supplement to oral directions

___ Lower difficulty level   ___ Raise difficulty level

___ Shorten assignments   ___ Reduce paper-and-pencil tasks

___ Read or record directions to the student(s)

___ Give extra cues or prompts

___ Allow student to record or type assignments

___ Adapt worksheets and packets

___ Use compensatory procedures by providing alternate assignments, when demands of class conflict with student capabilities

___ Ignore spelling errors/sloppy work ___ Ignore penmanship

___ Develop alternative rubrics

Self-Management/Follow-Through

___ Provide pictorial or written daily or weekly schedule

___ Provide student calendars

___ Check often for understanding/review

___ Request parent reinforcement

___ Have student repeat directions

___ Teach study skills

___ Use binders to organize material

___ Design/write/use long-term assignments timelines

___ Review and practice in real situations

___ Plan for generalization by teaching skill in several environments

Testing Adaptations

___ Provide oral instructions and/or read test questions

___ Use pictorial instructions/questions

___ Read test to student

___ Preview language of test questions

___ Ask questions that have applications in real setting

___ Administer test individually

___ Use short answer ___ Use multiple choice ___ Shorten length

___ Extend time frame ___ Use open-note/open-book tests

___ Modify format to reduce visual complexity or confusion

Resource A (Continued)

Social Interaction Support

___ Use natural peer supports and multiple, rotating peers

___ Use peer advocacy

___ Use cooperative group learning

___ Institute peer tutoring

___ Structure opportunities for social interaction (e.g., Circle of Friends)

___ Focus on social process rather than the end product

___ Structure shared experiences in school and extracurricular activities

___ Teach friendship, sharing, and negotiation skills to classmates

___ Teach social communication skills

      ___ Greetings __ Conversation __ Turn Taking __ Sharing

      ___ Negotiation __ Other:_____

Level of Staff Support (Consider *after* considering previous categories)

___ Consultation

___ Stop-in support (one to three times per week)

___ Part-time daily support

___ Team teaching (parallel, supportive, complementary, or co-teaching)

___ Daily in-class staff support

___ Total staff support (staff are in close proximity)

___ One-on-one assistance

___ Specialized personnel support (If indicated, identify time needed.)

Support	Time Needed
___ Instructional support assistant	
___ Health care assistant	
___ Behavior assistant	
___ Signing assistant	
___ Nursing	
___ Occupational therapy	
___ Physical therapy	
___ Speech and language therapist	
___ Augmentative communication specialist	
___ Transportation	
___ Counseling	
___ Adaptive physical education	
___ Transition planning	
___ Orientation/mobility	
___ Career counseling	

Resource B. Co-Teaching Daily Lesson Plan Format

Date: _____

Co-Teachers: _____
(Names)

Content Area(s): _____

Lesson Objectives:

Content Standards Addressed:

Underline the Co-Teaching Approach(es) Used:
Supportive   Parallel   Complementary   Team Teaching

What is the <u>room arrangement</u>? Will other spaces outside of the classroom be used? (Draw a picture of the room arrangement.)

What <u>materials</u> do the co-teachers need?

How is student <u>learning assessed</u> by co-teachers?

(Continued)

Resource B (Continued)

What specific supports, aids, or services do select <u>students</u> need? (See Resource A for suggestions.)

What does each co-teacher do before, during, and after the lesson?

Co-Teacher Name:			
What are the specific tasks that I do BEFORE the lesson?			
What are the specific tasks that I do DURING the lesson?			
What are the specific tasks that I do AFTER the lesson?			

Where, when, and how do co-teachers debrief and evaluate the outcomes of the lesson?

Resource C.   High School Supportive Co-Teaching Lesson Plan

Date: <u>Three-day lesson</u>

Co-Teachers: <u>Mr. Woo, H.S. Social Studies Teacher</u>
(Names)
<u>Mr. Viana, Special Educator</u>

Content Area(s): <u>U.S. History</u>

Lesson Objectives:

Academic objectives:

Working in groups of three with a variety of resource materials regarding the constitutional powers of the three branches of the U.S. federal government, members of each triad become "expert" in the powers of one of the three branches of government. (Days 1 and 2)

Given six scenarios regarding the constitutional powers of the three branches of government, members of triads comprising one expert for each of the three branches of government (a) share information learned in expert groups about each branch of government and (b) correctly decide on and agree to the responsibilities of each branch of government in each scenario (for a total of 18 decisions) for a minimum of 15 of 18 decisions (80% accuracy). (Day 3)

Social objective:

While working in two different cooperative groups of three (i.e., expert group, jigsaw group of experts), students demonstrate the small-group social skills of sharing information, active listening, equal participation, and reaching consensus as evidenced by anecdotal observational notes collected by the co-teachers. (Days 1, 2, and 3)

Content Standards Addressed:

Social Studies Standard 12.1.5: Describe the systems of separated and shared powers, the role of organized interests (Federalist Paper Number 10), checks and balances (Federalist Paper Number 51), the importance of an independent judiciary (Federalist Paper Number 78), enumerated powers, rule of law, federalism, and civilian control of the military.[1]

1. California Grade 12 Principles of American Democracy Standard 12.1.5. http://www.cde.ca.gov/be/st/ss/hstgrade12.asp

(Continued)

Resource C (Continued)

Underline the Co-Teaching Approach(es) Used:

<u>Supportive</u>   Parallel   Complementary   Team Teaching

What is the <u>room arrangement</u>? Will other spaces outside of the classroom be used?

Student desks are arranged facing each other in groups of three. Because of a strategic teacher decision regarding a particular student, one group has four members. Students also access the library media center for resources, as needed.

What <u>materials</u> do the co-teachers need?

U.S. History textbooks, news magazines, other related print materials, and videos; Internet access; a task instruction sheet for each expert group; a task instruction sheet for each jigsaw group.

How is student <u>learning</u> assessed by co-teachers?

Mr. Woo examines the 18 jigsaw team responses for correctness. Both co-teachers observe student groups and note examples of the use of the targeted small-group interpersonal skills identified above as social objectives.

What specific supports, aids, or services do <u>select students</u> need?

Certain students are strategically placed in groups with supportive peers and assigned roles that they can perform (e.g., assign time-keeper role to student who has difficulty performing secondary-level reading and writing tasks). One student is seated in a group of four rather than three in order to benefit from the academic modeling of an additional peer.

What does each co-teacher do before, during, and after the lesson?

Co-Teacher Name:	Mr. Woo, Social Studies Teacher	Mr. Viana, Special Educator
What are the specific tasks that I do BEFORE the lesson?	• Meet and plan • Clarify co-teaching responsibilities • Decide which co-teacher monitors which groups • Develop and copy a task list for the students	• Meet and plan • Clarify responsibilities • Divide class into three predetermined "expert" (i.e. legislative, executive, judicial branch) groups • Identify specific complementary roles within groups (especially for students who struggle with learning)
What are the specific tasks that I do DURING the lesson?	• Introduce the lesson, and explain the academic and social objectives • Explain the criteria for success, and emphasize that students have a common goal, individual roles, and are individually held accountable • Assign students to each of the three expert groups created by Mr. Viana • Assign group roles • Monitor time and student academic and social skill performance in the groups	• Adjust group membership if necessary (e.g., due to absences) • Pass out materials to groups • Monitor student academic and social skill performance in the groups
What are the specific tasks that I do AFTER the lesson?	• Reflect on that day's lesson, and make any necessary modifications or adjustments for the following day(s) • Read and score Day 3 jigsaw group responses	• Share any relevant observations with Mr. Woo to assist him in making any modifications

Where, when, and how do co-teachers debrief and evaluate the outcomes of the lesson?

We will meet each day for a couple of moments following that day's lesson to share observations about what worked well and what, if anything, needs to be changed for the next day. We will touch base briefly right before class each day to review any modifications to the plan developed by Mr. Woo and to clarify our responsibilities.

Resource D.   Elementary Parallel Co-Teaching Lesson Plan

Date: <u>One lesson period</u>   Co-Teachers: <u>Ms. Gilpatrick, classroom teacher Ms. Nugent, speech and</u>
                                                  (Names)
Content Area(s): <u>Language Arts</u>   <u>language therapist Ms. Hernandez, paraprofessional</u>

Lesson Objectives:

Working with classmates at four differentiated learning stations, students identify, create, and form sentences using compound words with instructor guidance and feedback.

Content Standards Addressed:

Reading/Word Identification: Uses structural cues to recognize words such as compounds, base words, and inflections.[2]

Underline the Co-Teaching Approach(es) Used:

Supportive   <u>Parallel</u>   Complementary   Team Teaching

What is the room arrangement? Will other spaces outside of the classroom be used?

There are four stations. Two stations are carpeted areas, a third is a kidney-shaped table with chairs, and the fourth is a bank of five computers.

What materials do the co-teachers need?

Eight sets of simple words written on large pieces of cardboard that can be combined to form compound words.

---

2. Texas English Language Arts and Reading Grade 1 Standard 8c. http://www.tea.state.tx.us/rules/tac/chapter110/ch110a.html#110.3

Materials for Station 1	Materials for Station 2	Materials for Station 3	Materials for Station 4
Four identical sets of simple words (i.e., three sets for pairs of students and one set for the teacher) written on flashcards that can be combined to form compound words Timer	Sets of three worksheets providing practice at creating compound words for each student Whiteboard Teacher data sheet on which to record level of support required by each student	Large whiteboard with markers Several Big Books 12 erasable markers Three marker erasers 150 eight-by-two-inch strips of paper (cut from regular paper)	Five computers with two student chairs at each computer

How is student learning assessed by co-teachers?

Station 1 (Ms. Hernandez)	Station 2 (Ms. Nugent)	Station 3 (Ms. Gilpatrick)	Station 4 (No co-teacher)
Engage in direct observation of student performance, and take notes regarding students who have difficulty, and share data with the classroom teacher	Collect data on each student's level of independence and need for adult or peer support, and share data with the classroom teacher	Engage in direct observation of student performance	Students work independently. Co-teacher examines computer printouts of sentences created by student pairs.

What specific supports, aids, or services do select students need?

The student with autism is strategically partnered with a classmate who is especially skilled at imitating instructors' modeling of tasks. Otherwise no specific supports are needed, given the intensity of teacher modeling, guided practice, and monitoring at each station.

(Continued)

What does each co-teacher do before, during, and after the lesson?

Co-Teacher Name:	Ms. Gilpatrick, classroom teacher	Ms. Nugent, speech and language therapist	Ms. Hernandez, paraprofessional
What are the specific tasks that I do BEFORE the lesson?	• Meet and preplan activities during regular weekly meeting	• Meet and preplan activities with Ms. Gilpatrick during regular weekly meeting • Meet with Ms. Hernandez during attendance to explain her station	• Brief on-the-spot at beginning of class during attendance regarding Station I, which she will lead
What are the specific tasks that I do DURING the lesson?	• Large group modeling of creation of compound words • Assign students to stations; explains independent task at Station 4 • Lead Station 3 • Signal time to switch stations • Be available to answer student questions at Station 4	• Large-group modeling of creation of compound words • Lead Station 2 • Complete data sheet regarding students' level of independence • Be available to answer student questions at Station 4	• Lead Station I • Available to answer student questions at Station 4
What are the specific tasks that I do AFTER the lesson?	• Examine student printouts from Station 4 • Review written data collected by Ms. Nugent • Consider Ms. Hernandez's observations and Ms. Nugent's data in planning next lesson	• Give Ms. Gilpatrick written data	• Verbally report observations to Ms. Gilpatrick

Where, when, and how do co-teachers debrief and evaluate the outcomes of the lesson?

Prior to the start of the next day's lesson, Ms. Gilpatrick shares with her co-teachers any adjustments to what they had planned, due to her review of student work and reports.

Resource E. Middle Level Complementary Co-Teaching Lesson Plan

---

Date: One class period

Co-Teachers: Ms. Kurtz, language arts teacher
(Names)
Ms. Olvina, paraprofessional

Content Area(s): Language Arts

Lesson Objectives:

Given adult and student modeling of antonyms, synonyms, and homonyms and access to hard-copy and online resources, students construct and identify pairs of antonyms, synonyms, and homonyms through partner and group activities and games (i.e., Charades, Go Fish) within the timeframes allocated by the teacher.

Content Standards Addressed:

Reading Grade 7 Vocabulary Standard: Explain relationships between and among words such as antonyms, synonyms, and homonyms.[3]

Underline the Co-Teaching Approach(es) Used:

Supportive   Parallel   Complementary   Team Teaching

What is the room arrangement? Will other spaces outside of the classroom be used?

Traditional row seating with desks rearranged when needed for partner and group activities

What materials do the co-teachers need?

Dictionaries, thesauruses, a kitchen timer, a stack of starter words for co-teachers to use with groups, a stack of lined paper for students to use, an overhead projector and transparencies, one or more computers with Internet access, five to six cans of 25 to 30 popsicle sticks with different words written on each stick

How is student learning assessed by co-teachers?

1. Sample and assess accuracy of select student's oral examples of antonyms, synonyms, and homonyms.
2. Review accuracy of pair-generated lists of antonyms, synonyms, and homonyms.
3. Observe and write notes about student performance during Charades and Go Fish games.

---

3. Extension of Maryland Reading Grade 7 Standard. http://mdk12.org/mspp/vsc/reading/bygrade/grade7.html

(Continued)

Resource E (Continued)

What specific supports, aids, or services do select students need?

While instructors monitor student performance during the pair activity, both carry around a set of starter words to offer to pairs who are having difficulty coming up with antonyms, synonyms, and homonyms.

What does each co-teacher do before, during, and after the lesson?

Co-Teacher Name:	Ms. Kurtz, language arts teacher	Ms. Olvina, paraprofessional
What are the specific tasks that I do BEFORE the lesson?	• Meet and plan the lesson with Ms. Olvina • Prepare materials for the lesson • Preassign students to pairs	• Meet and plan the lesson with Ms. Kurtz • Come prepared to act out charades of pairs of antonyms, synonyms, and homonyms
What are the specific tasks that I do DURING the lesson?	• Open lesson with examples of antonyms, synonyms, and homonyms • Select students to explain Charades and Go Fish • Solicit volunteers to model charade of antonym pair • Solicit volunteers to model charade of synonym pair • Solicit volunteers to model charade of homonym pair • Partner students for first activity, and explain the activity • Monitor students during first activity • Form quads from pairs, and explain second application activity (Go Fish) • Set timer for second activity • Monitor second activity • Debrief second activity by soliciting examples from students • Debrief by sharing additional examples on overhead while monitoring • Provide closure with a "flash" round review	• Model charades of antonym pair • Model charades of synonym pair • Model charade of homonym pair • Display overhead of student partnerships • Monitor students during first activity • Collect work product at end of first activity • Monitor second activity • Debrief by sharing additional examples on overhead while monitoring • Lead second "flash" round review, following Ms. Kurtz's model
What are the specific tasks that I do AFTER the lesson?	• If the lesson goes as planned, given that there are no permanent student products to examine, no follow-up tasks are planned or anticipated	• If the lesson goes as planned, given that there are no permanent student products to examine, no follow-up tasks are planned or anticipated

Where, when, and how do co-teachers debrief and evaluate the outcomes of the lesson?

After the lesson, we will set a time prior to the next day's lesson to meet to debrief and make any necessary adjustments.

Resource F.   Elementary Team-Teaching Co-Teaching Lesson Plan

Date: <u>One class meeting period</u>   Co-Teachers: <u>Ms. Gilpatrick, classroom teacher</u>

(Names)

<u>Ms. Nugent, speech and language therapist</u>

Content Area(s): <u>Reasoning</u>

Lesson Objectives:

Given co-teacher guidance in using the steps of the SODAS problem-solving process, students will practice generating options and settling on a solution for a common playground problem.

Content Standards Addressed:

Reasoning and Problem-Solving Standard: Students use reasoning strategies, knowledge, and common sense to solve complex problems related to all fields of knowledge.[4]

Underline the Co-Teaching Approach(es) Used:

Supportive   Parallel   Complementary   <u>Team Teaching</u>

What is the room arrangement? Will other spaces outside of the classroom be used?

Students are seated in a semicircle on the carpet facing their co-teachers, who use an overhead projector to display the SODAS steps and student responses on the wall.

What materials do the co-teachers need?

An overhead projector, overhead markers, transparencies of the SODAS format for recording student responses, and a box with a number of playground problem scenarios written on 3 × 5 index cards.

How is student learning assessed by co-teachers?

Co-teachers observe student engagement and participation at each step of the SODAS process.

What specific supports, aids, or services do select students need?

No additional supports, aids, or services are needed.

4. Vermont Reasoning and Problem Solving Standard 2.2. http://education.vermont.gov/new/pdfdoc/pubs/framework.pdf

(Continued)

What does each co-teacher do before, during, and after the lesson?

Co-Teacher Name:	Ms. Gilpatrick, classroom teacher	Ms. Nugent, speech and language therapist
What are the specific tasks that I do BEFORE the lesson?	• Meet beforehand to plan the weekly class meeting and agree on the problem-solving process	• Meet beforehand to plan the weekly class meeting and agree on the problem-solving process • Prepare playground problem scenarios for lesson and overhead transparency of SODAS problem-solving process
What are the specific tasks that I do DURING the lesson?	• Convene and clarify objective of the class meeting • Randomly select a problem from the problem-solving box • Call on student to identify the problem • Share responsibility for calling on students to identify options • Discuss with Ms. Nugent the disadvantages to Option I, and record the agreed-on disadvantages • Call on students to share disadvantages • Rotate roles of facilitator and recorder for remaining disadvantages • Model with Ms. Nugent a discussion of the advantages of Option I, and record the agreed-on advantages • Facilitate discussion of student-generated advantages • Tally student responses about worst disadvantages • Facilitate student discussion and identification of best advantages • Facilitate partner discussion and sharing of best solution(s) • Share an example of how she has used SODAS in her personal life	• Ask students to identify the problem • Record problem situation on the overhead • Ask students to identify options for solving the problem • Share responsibility for calling on students to identify options • Record student responses on the overhead • Discuss with Ms. Gilpatrick the disadvantages of Option I • Prompt students to discuss disadvantages of other options • Record student-generated disadvantages • Rotate roles of facilitator and recorder for remaining disadvantages • Model with Ms. Gilpatrick a discussion of the advantages of Option I • Record student-generated list of advantages for each option • Facilitate student discussion and identification of worst disadvantages • Tally student responses about best advantages • Tally students' best solution responses • Facilitate discussion about use of SODAS in school, home, and playground • Share an example of how she has used SODAS in her personal life, and tell students they will be using this process throughout the year
What are the specific tasks that I do After the lesson?	• Meet to debrief the class meeting	• Meet to debrief the class meeting

Where, when, and how do co-teachers debrief and evaluate the outcomes of the lesson?

Do a quick check-in during our common lunch period.

Resource G. Co-Teaching Lesson Featuring the Paraprofessional Role

---

Date: <u>Three consecutive days</u>   Co-Teachers: <u>Mr. Jeffries, fourth-grade classroom teacher</u>
                                                                      (Names)
                                                               <u>Ms. Katz, paraprofessional</u>

Content Area(s): <u>Language Arts</u>

Lesson Objectives:

Given lecture, guided practice, and numerous examples, students will develop their own stories with attention to character development and plot.

Content Standards Addressed:

Compare the use of literary elements within and among texts, including characters, setting, plot, theme, and point of view.[5]

Underline the Co-Teaching Approach(es) Used:

<u>Supportive</u>   <u>Parallel</u>   <u>Complementary</u>   Team Teaching

What is the room arrangement? Will other spaces outside of the classroom be used?

Students initially are seated in table arrangements of four. Following the opening of the lesson, students are assigned to one of three stations. Over the course of three days, all students rotate through all three stations.

What materials do the co-teachers need?

Co-teachers need a variety of books at different reading levels. They use computers, text-to-speech software, and Alpha Smart technology. Paper, colored markers, and paint are also collected.

How is student learning assessed by co-teachers?

Co-teachers assess student engagement, participation, knowledge, and products from each station. In addition, behavior checklists are used to assess behavior for Andreas and Wendy.

What specific supports, aids, or services do <u>select</u> students need?

No additional supports, aids, or services are needed.

---

5. Pennsylvania 5th-grade Academic Standards for Reading, Writing, Speaking, and Listening 1.3.5.A. http://www.pde.state.pa.us/k12/lib/k12/Reading.pdf

(Continued)

Resource G (Continued)

What does each co-teacher do before, during, and after the lesson?

Co-Teacher Name:	Mr. Jeffries, classroom teacher	Ms. Katz, paraprofessional
What are the specific tasks that I do BEFORE the lesson?	• Meet beforehand with Ms. Katz, Ms. Hoosokawa, the Title I teacher, the ESL teacher, and the gifted and talented consultant to select appropriate materials for diverse learners • Assign students to groups	• Meet beforehand with Mr. Jeffries, Ms. Hoosokawa, the Title I teacher, the ESL teacher, and the gifted and talented consultant to select appropriate materials for diverse learners • Assign students to groups
What are the specific tasks that I do DURING the lesson?	• Greet students as they enter • Open lesson with anticipatory set, minilecture, and reading • Prompt Wendy to solicit peer support before adult support • Day 1 and 2: Facilitate Station 1 (students all read the same book) • Day 3: Facilitate Station 3 (students write and illustrate their own stories) • Monitor Station 2 (independent station) • Check behavioral data and send home to Andreas's and Wendy's families	• Greet students as they enter • Add comments, ask questions, record, and illustrate while Mr. Jeffries leads discussion • Assign students to stations • Prompt Wendy to solicit peer support before adult support • Provide support to Andreas and Wendy, if needed • Day 1 and 2: Facilitate Station 3 (students write and illustrate their own stories) • Day 3: Facilitate Station 1 (students all read the same book) • Monitor Station 2 (independent station) • Record Andreas's and Wendy's behavioral data daily
What are the specific tasks that I do AFTER the lesson?	• Meet to debrief daily after the lessons • Select materials to include in student portfolios	• Meet to debrief daily after the lessons

Where, when, and how do co-teachers debrief and evaluate the outcomes of the lesson?

Mr. Jeffries and Ms. Katz meet to plan the next lesson sequence in a weekly 45-minute planning meeting.

Resource H.   Co-Teaching Lesson Featuring Students as Co-Teachers

Date: Daily 10-minute sessions   Co-Teachers: Elaine, third-grade classroom teacher; Laurie, special educator;
                                                          (Names)

Content Area(s): Third-grade math   Dave, third-grade student; Juan, third-grade student

Lesson Objectives:

Given six math facts per session (four known and two unknown or yet unmastered) and a 10-minute daily practice session with a peer tutor, students will participate in learning activities that match various learning styles (e.g., auditory, visual, kinesthetic) until mastery occurs.

Content Standards Addressed:

Arizona Mathematics Standard 1: Number Sense[6]—Students develop number sense and use numbers and number relationships to acquire basic facts, to solve a wide variety of real-world problems, and to determine the reasonableness of results. FOUNDA-TIONS (Grades 1–3) 1M-F3. Understand the meaning for and application of the operations of addition, subtraction, multiplication, and division.

Underline the Co-Teaching Approach(es) Used:
Supportive   <u>Parallel</u>   Complementary   Team Teaching

What is the room arrangement? Will other spaces outside of the classroom be used?

Students sit at their desks, or on the floor, so that they are face-to-face in order to show the math facts in such way that each student can see the fact without seeing the answer printed on the back. They need room to lay out the flashcards for activities such as Concentration, Jump Rope Number Facts (they chant the fact as they jump rope), and Math Facts Raps (they develop raps based on the particular facts they are acquiring).

What <u>materials</u> do the co-teachers need?

Student co-teachers need their own stack of math facts, a checklist to record the accuracy, a pencil, a graph to display the daily percent or number correct, an oven timer to set the 10-minute time frame, and directions printed on 3 × 5 cards for the learning activities.

How is student learning assessed by co-teachers?

Student co-teachers match their partner's response to the answer on the back of the math fact flashcard. They give immediate correction for errors and/or immediate praise for correct responses. They check off the selected learning activities that were practiced each day.

6. Arizona Mathematics Standards. http://ade.state.az.us/standards/math/Std1.pdf

(Continued)

What specific supports, aids, or services do select students need?

Select students (Dave and Juan) each have a learning contract that supports each of them to practice giving and receiving positive feedback (e.g., saying nice things, saying thank you).

What does each co-teacher do before, during, and after the lesson?

Co-Teacher Name:	Elaine, third-grade classroom teacher	Laurie, special educator	Dave, third-grade student	Juan, third-grade student
What are the specific tasks that I do BEFORE the lesson?	• Make sure the oven timers are working and available • For a part of the student roster, check to make sure the sets of math cards include four known and two unknown facts	• For the other part of the student roster, check to make sure the sets of math cards include four known and two unknown facts	• Collect and bring to the session his set of math cards and the daily checklist to record progress	• Collect and bring to the session his set of math cards and the daily checklist to record progress
What are the specific tasks that I do DURING the lesson?	• Conduct on-the-spot monitoring of student co-teacher pairs	• Conduct on-the-spot monitoring of student co-teacher pairs	• Show math flashcard to partner • Model correct answer for the partner • Encourage partner to imitate the model • Praise and go on to next math fact • Encourage variety of learning activities	• Show math flashcard to partner • Model correct answer for the partner • Encourage partner to imitate the model • Praise and go on to next math fact • Encourage variety of learning activities
What are the specific tasks that I do AFTER the lesson?	• Spot check accuracy of records and graphs and, for Dave and Juan, the quality of their exchanges	• Spot check accuracy of records and graphs and, for Dave and Juan, the quality of their exchanges	• Enter number or percent correct on graph • Celebrate successes	• Enter number or percent correct on graph • Celebrate successes

Where, when, and how do co-teachers debrief and evaluate the outcomes of the lesson?

There are brief conferences with specific reciprocal co-teacher partners on a rotating basis—at least once a week to review portfolio of math facts acquired, check on the tutorial exchanges, problem solve, and celebrate.

Resource I.   Levels of Student Support

- Classroom Companion—Student who assumes responsibility for supporting another student's participation in academic or elective classes. This may include helping with mobility to and from class, carrying or remembering materials, taking notes, assisting in task completion, facilitating communication, and being a role model for social/friendship interaction.

- Consultation—Support staff meet regularly with general education teacher to keep track of student progress, assess need for supplemental materials, problem solve, and maintain a positive and open communication. Students know that they can stop in or request assistance from support staff on a specific assignment or for general support.

- Stop-In Support—Support staff observe students on a regular or irregular basis to determine possible needs or to set up peer-support systems. They maintain open communication with the classroom teacher and the students.

- Part-Time Daily Support—Support staff provide support to students at a pre-determined time, on a rotating basis, or for specific assignments activities. Staff should maintain awareness of curriculum and assignments to encourage student productivity and tutorial or organizational support. Staff may also supply supplemental materials for classroom use.

- Team/Co-Teaching—Support staff assume half of the responsibility for teaching the curriculum, as prearranged by all involved staff members, who assume responsibility for the development of multilevel curriculum, appropriate strategies, grading the learning environment, and student arrangements.

- Daily In-Class Staff Support—Support staff assist all students by moving around the room, providing support as needed. Staff collaborate with general education teacher to develop and plan for specific support strategies and student needs of student. Staff may supervise or teach small groups within the class or based on a pullout model, as needed.

- Total Staff Support—Support staff remain seated in close proximity to students. Support staff also assume responsibility for developing or acquiring the strategies and materials that will support each student's success.

Resource J.   Administrator Actions to Promote Co-Teaching

Directions: Check off the items that have been attended to or accomplished.

____ Publicly articulate the rationale for co-teaching.

____ Redefine staff roles (i.e., in the job description of classroom teachers and support personnel) so that all are expected to participate in collaborative planning and teaching.

____ Assess the staff's need for collaboration (e.g., With whom do I need to collaborate to successfully adapt instruction? From which colleagues can I acquire skills through modeling and coaching?)

____ Create a master schedule that allows for collaboration (e.g., common planning and lunch periods).

____ Change the length of the workday or school year (e.g., provide teachers with 220-day instead of 185-day contracts, early dismissal of students).

____ Establish professional support groups to help staff learn about and begin to practice co-teaching.

____ Provide time for co-teachers to meet by relieving them from noninstructional duties that other staff who are not co-teaching are required to perform (e.g., bus duty, lunchroom supervision).

____ Provide training in collaborative planning (e.g., courses and workshops, mentoring and peer coaching systems, job shadowing, clinical supervision, pairing of new co-teaching teams with veteran co-teaching teams).

____ Educate school and community members about the accomplishments of collaborative planning and teaching teams.

____ Periodically provide additional time for co-teaching teams to meet (e.g., hire substitutes, use inservice time, provide release time).

____ Provide incentives for co-teaching (e.g., recognize co-teaching teams' accomplishments; offer additional training; provide release time for co-teaching teams to observe one another teaching, attend conferences, and make presentations about their accomplishments).

Resource K.   Action Plan Template

	Activities • Major activities • Chronological order • Preparation steps • Implementation steps	Success Measure "We will know we are successful if . . . • What is measured? • Who will measure? • When to measure?	Responsible Person(s)	Date	Outcomes
Build Consensus for a Vision of Co-Teaching					
Skill Development					
Incentives					
Resources					

Resource L.   Co-Teaching Planning Meeting Agenda Format

People Present	*Absentees*	*Others Who Need to Know*

Roles	*This Meeting*	*Next Meeting*
Timekeeper		
Recorder		
Other _____		

Agenda

Agenda Items		*Time Limit*
1. Review agenda and positive comments		5 minutes
2.		
3.		
4. Processing of task and relationships		5 minutes

Minutes of Outcomes

Action items	*Persons Responsible*	*By When?*
1. The way we will communicate outcomes to absent members and others		
2.		
3.		

Agenda Building for Next Meeting

Date: _____   Time: _____   Location: _____

Expected agenda items

1.

2.

3.

Resource M.   Self-Assessment: Are We Really Co-Teachers?

Directions: Check *Yes* or *No* to each of the following statements to determine your co-teaching score at this point in time.

Yes   No   *In our co-teaching partnership:*

____ ____   1. We decide which co-teaching approach we are going to use in a lesson based on the benefits to the students and the co-teachers.

____ ____   2. We share ideas, information, and materials.

____ ____   3. We identify the resources and talents of the co-teachers.

____ ____   4. We teach different groups of students at the same time.

____ ____   5. We are aware of what one another is doing even when we are not directly in one another's presence.

____ ____   6. We share responsibility for deciding what to teach.

____ ____   7. We agree on the curriculum standards that will be addressed in a lesson.

____ ____   8. We share responsibility for deciding how to teach.

____ ____   9. We share responsibility for deciding who teaches what part of a lesson.

____ ____   10. We are flexible and make changes as needed during a lesson.

____ ____   11. We identify student strengths and needs.

____ ____   12. We share responsibility for differentiating instruction.

____ ____   13. We include other people when their expertise or experience is needed.

____ ____   14. We share responsibility for how student learning is assessed.

____ ____   15. We can show that students are learning when we co-teach.

____ ____   16. We agree on discipline procedures and jointly carry them out.

____ ____   17. We give feedback to one another on what goes on in the classroom.

(Continued)

Resource M (Continued)

Yes	No	In our co-teaching partnership:
____	____	18. We make improvements in our lessons based on what happens.
____	____	19. We communicate freely our concerns.
____	____	20. We have a process for resolving our disagreements and use it when faced with problems and conflicts.
____	____	21. We celebrate the process of co-teaching and the outcomes and successes.
____	____	22. We have fun with the students and each other when we co-teach.
____	____	23. We have regularly scheduled times to meet and discuss our work.
____	____	24. We use our meeting time productively.
____	____	25. We can effectively co-teach even when we don't have time to plan.
____	____	26. We explain the benefits of co-teaching to the students and their families.
____	____	27. We model collaboration and teamwork for our students.
____	____	28. We are each viewed by our students as their teacher.
____	____	29. We include students in the co-teaching role.
____	____	30. We depend on one another to follow through on tasks and responsibilities.
____	____	31. We seek and enjoy additional training to make our co-teaching better.
____	____	32. We are mentors to others who want to co-teach.
____	____	33. We can use a variety of co-teaching approaches (i.e., supportive, parallel, complementary, team teaching)
____	____	34. We communicate our need for logistical support and resources to our administrators.

TOTAL   **YES:** _____   **NO:** _____

Resource N.   Checklist of Skills for the Stages of Co-Teacher Development

---

Skills for the Forming Stage

_____   Use co-teachers' preferred names

_____   Use no put-downs

_____   Come to co-teacher meetings on time, and stay for the entire time

_____   Follow through on agreements (show I am trustworthy)

_____   Acknowledge co-teachers for their follow-through

Skills for the Functioning Stage

_____   State and restate the purpose of co-teaching

_____   Set or call attention to the time limits

_____   Suggest procedures for how to do the task effectively

_____   Express support and acceptance verbally

_____   Express support and acceptance nonverbally

_____   Paraphrase and clarify

_____   Energize co-teachers with humor, ideas, or enthusiasm

_____   Describe feelings when appropriate

(Continued)

Resource N (Continued)

Skills for the Formulating Stage

_____ Summarize what has been said

_____ Seek accuracy by correcting or adding to the summary

_____ Seek connections to other knowledge

_____ Seek clever ways to remember ideas, facts, and decisions

_____ Ask co-teachers to explain their reasoning

_____ Ask co-teachers to plan aloud

Skills for the Fermenting Stage

_____ Criticize ideas without criticizing people

_____ Differentiate ideas when there is disagreement

_____ Integrate different ideas into a single position

_____ Probe by asking questions that lead to deeper understanding

_____ Suggest new answers and ideas

_____ Think of new ways to resolve differences of opinion

Glossary

active learning—This term refers to anything that involves students in doing things and thinking about the things they are doing. Active learning might include a spectrum of activities, from a modified lecture format to role playing, simulation, games, project work, cooperative problem solving, collaborative research, partner learning, service learning, and teaching others.

change agents—Change agents are those who direct reform efforts, such as a professional development director who guides inservice activities designed to help teachers learn how to co-teach effectively. G. E. Hall and Hord (2001) describe six dimensions of a job description for change agents that emerged from several studies of change agents in action: (1) developing, articulating, and communicating a shared vision of change; (2) planning and providing resources; (3) supporting teachers' professional learning and development; (4) checking on progress in the use of the innovation; (5) providing ongoing assistance during implementation; and (6) creating a school context supportive of the innovation.

complementary co-teaching—Complementary co-teaching is when co-teachers do something to enhance the instruction provided by the other co-teacher(s).

cooperative process—The cooperative process is an essential element of successful co-teaching and includes face-to-face interaction, positive interdependence, interpersonal skills, monitoring the progress of the co-teachers, and individual accountability.

co-teaching—Co-teaching is two or more people sharing responsibility for teaching some or all of the students assigned to a classroom. It involves the distribution of responsibility among people for planning, instruction, and evaluation for a classroom of students.

co-teaching lesson plan—A co-teaching lesson plan should include the essential elements of any good lesson plan, including the content objectives, the curriculum standard(s) addressed in the lesson, the materials needed by each partner, how student learning will be assessed, and any accommodations or modifications that might be needed for particular students. In addition, the lesson plan specifies which of the four types of co-teaching arrangements the team will use, exactly what each individual co-teacher will do (before, during, and after the lesson), how the classroom will be arranged so that each co-teacher has the space to deliver instruction, and whether instruction will be delivered by one or more co-teachers in another space outside of the classroom, such as the school library, for all or part of the lesson. Finally, the lesson plan explains where, when, and how co-teachers will debrief and evaluate the outcomes of the lesson. The lesson plan format should be set up in such a way that co-teachers can understand, implement, and use it to communicate their teaching actions to one another.

DI—DI is an acronym for *differentiated instruction,* which is defined as a way for teachers to recognize and react responsively to their students' varying background knowledge, readiness, languages, learning preferences, and interests (T. Hall 2002).

ELL—ELL is an acronym for *English Language Learner.* Teachers of students who are English language learners assist these students either through in-classroom supports or resource room supports. Instruction of students who are English language learners is sometimes referred to as English as a foreign language (EFL) or English for speakers of other languages (ESOL).

four approaches to co-teaching—supplementary co-teaching, parallel co-teaching, complementary co-teaching, and team teaching.

GATE—GATE is an acronym for *gifted and talented education,* services that are often provided in resource rooms, in separate schools, or by enhancing the general education curriculum.

IDEIA—IDEIA is an acronym for the *Individuals with Disabilities Education Improvement Act of 2004.* This federal mandate empowers educators to provide services and supports in the least restrictive environment for all students with disabilities in order to provide access to the general education curriculum.

multiple intelligences—The theory of multiple intelligences (Gardner 1983, 1997) poses the idea that there are at least eight (visual/spatial, musical, verbal/linguistic, logical/mathematical, interpersonal, intrapersonal, bodily/kinesthetic, and naturalist) rather than only one type of intelligence. Teachers who embrace this theory stop asking, "How smart is this student?" and instead search for answers to the question, "How is this student smart?"

NCLB—NCLB is the acronym for the *No Child Left Behind Act of 2001* (Pub. L. No. 107-110), a federal mandate for ensuring that schools and teachers are accountable for the academic progress of all students in public schools.

paraeducators—These are any school employees whose positions are either instructional in nature or who deliver other direct services to students and/or their parents and who work under the supervision of teachers or other professional staff who have the ultimate responsibility for the design, implementation, and evaluation of education and related services programs and student progress. Also known as aide, paraprofessional, educational aide, instructional aide, teacher aide, classroom assistant, or classroom aide.

parallel co-teaching—Parallel co-teaching is when two or more people work with groups of students in different sections of the classroom.

process communication model—The process communication model (PCM) is based on the premise that people have a unique personality structure consisting of six types, with the relative strength of each type varying from person to person. Co-teachers can enhance their communication when they practice the skills and strategies of the PCM, especially when interacting with those whose communication and personality preferences are quite different from their own (Kahler 1982; Pauley, Bradley, and Pauley 2002). PCM can create a more supportive and responsive classroom and working relationship with co-teachers who are the most difficult to reach.

RTI—RTI is an acronym for *Response to Intervention*, which allows professional educators to design and evaluate academic and behavioral interventions for students at increasing levels of intensity depending on the students' reactions to the intervention. RTI features the following elements: (1) high-quality classroom instruction, (2) research-based instruction, (3) classroom performance measures, (4) universal screening, (5) continuous progress monitoring, (6) research-based interventions, (7) progress monitoring during interventions, and (8) fidelity measures (Graner, Faggella-Luby, and Fritschmann 2005).

SODAS—SODAS is an acronym for steps in a problem-solving approach: *situation, options, disadvantages, advantages,* and *solution.*

speech and language therapists—Speech and language therapists often provide educational and therapeutic supports for students with special needs in communication and language.

stages of co-teacher development—Similar to the stages of group development, co-teachers should expect to experience and need different communication skills depending on whether they are just beginning (forming), deciding on how they'll work together (functioning), working through the problems they might face (formulating), or managing conflicts of ideas or procedures about what to emphasize or how to teach certain students (fermenting). The social interaction and communication skills they use at each of these stages will facilitate the development of their cohesiveness as a co-teaching team.

supportive co-teaching—Supportive co-teaching is when one teacher takes the lead instructional role and the other(s) rotate among the students providing support.

teaching—If you consult any dictionary, you will find multiple meanings that the English language attributes to the word *teaching*. For example, to teach is to impart knowledge or skills, to give instruction, to cause to learn by experience or example, to advocate or preach. On the other hand, to instruct or to tutor or to train to educate implies methodological knowledge in addition to content knowledge.

team teaching—Team teaching is when two or more people do what the traditional teacher has always done—plan, teach, assess, and assume responsibility for all of the students in the classroom.

Zone of Proximal Development—The Zone of Proximal Development (ZPD) refers to an individual child's potential level of learning if helped by a teacher or peer. A ZPD is defined as a particular range of ability with and without assistance from a teacher or a more capable peer (Vygotsky 1987). To scaffold students effectively within their ZPDs, a teacher should also have an awareness of the various roles students and teachers assume throughout the co-teaching process. The teacher or peer models behavior for the student, the student imitates the teacher's or peer's behavior, the teacher or peer fades out instruction, and the student practices reciprocal teaching (scaffolding others) until the skill is mastered. Vygotsky emphasizes that what children can do with the assistance of others is an even better indicator of their mental development.

References

PART I: INTRODUCTION TO CO-TEACHING ■

Chapter 1: What Is Co-Teaching?

Brandt, R. 1987. On cooperation in schools: A conversation with David and Roger Johnson. *Educational Leadership* 45(3): 14–19.

Fishbaugh, M. S. E. 1997. *Models of collaboration.* Needham Heights, MA: Allyn & Bacon.

Friend, M., and L. Cook. 2002. *Interactions: Collaboration skills for school professionals.* 4th ed. Needham Heights, MA: Allyn & Bacon.

Hourcade, J., and J. Bauwens. 2002. *Cooperative teaching: Re-building and sharing the schoolhouse.* Austin, TX: PRO-ED.

Idol, L., A. Nevin, and P. Paolucci-Whitcomb. 1999. *Collaborative consultation.* 3rd ed. Austin, TX: PRO-ED.

Johnson, D. W., and R. T. Johnson. 1999. *Learning together and alone: Cooperative, competitive, and individualistic learning.* 5th ed. Needham Heights, MA: Allyn & Bacon.

Skrtic, T. 1991. *Behind special education: A critical analysis of professional culture and school organization.* Denver, CO: Love.

Villa, R., and J. Thousand. 2004. *Creating an inclusive school.* 2nd ed. Alexandria, VA: Association for Supervision and Curriculum Development.

Chapter 2: Why Co-Teach?
What History, Law, and Research Say

Arguelles, M. E., M. T. Hughes, and J. S. Schumm. 2000. Co-teaching: A different approach to co-teaching. *Principal* 79(4): 48, 50–51.

Bahamonde, C., and M. Friend. 1999. Teaching English language learners: A proposal for effective service delivery through collaboration and co-teaching. *Journal of Educational and Psychological Consultation* 10(1): 1–9.

Bauwens, J., J. J. Hourcade, and M. Friend. 1989. Cooperative teaching: A model for general and special education integration. *Remedial and Special Education* 10(2): 17–22.

Blackorby, J., M. Wagner, R. Camero, E. Davies, P. Levine, L. Newman, C. Marder, and C. Sumi. 2005. *Engagement, academics, social adjustments, and independence.* Palo Alto, CA: SRI.

Caywood, K. D., and S. I. Fordyce. 2006. Facilitation of language skills via co-teaching model to integrate children with autism. Paper presented at the annual conference of the Teacher Education Division of the Council for Exceptional Children, San Diego, CA.

Compton, M. V., A. Stratton, A. Maier, C. Meyers, H. Scott, and T. Tomlinson. 1998. It takes two: Co-teaching for deaf and hard of hearing students in rural schools. In *Coming together: Preparing for rural special education in the twenty-first century,* ed. D. Montgomery, 204–9. (ERIC Document Reproduction Service No. ED417901)

Cramer, E. D., and A. I. Nevin. 2006. A mixed methodology analysis of co-teacher assessments: Implications for teacher education. *Teacher Education and Special Education 30*(1): 261–274.

Cramer, E., A. Nevin, L. Salazar, and K. Landa. 2006. Co-teaching in an urban, multicultural setting: Research report. *Florida Educational Leadership 7*(1): 43–50.

Dieker, L. 1998. Rationale for co-teaching. *Social Studies Review 37*(2): 62–65.

Duke, D., B. Showers, and M. Imber. 1980. Teachers and shared decision-making: The costs and benefits of involvement. *Educational Administration Quarterly* 16: 93–106.

Garrigan, C. M., and J. S. Thousand. 2005. The effects of co-teaching on student achievement in the reading domain. *New Hampshire Journal of Education* 8: 56–60.

Glasser, W. 1999. *Choice theory: A new psychology of personal freedom.* New York: Perennial.

Hourcade, J., and J. Bauwens. 2002. *Cooperative teaching: Re-building and sharing the schoolhouse.* Austin, TX: PRO-ED.

Johnson, D. W., and F. F. Johnson. 1997. *Joining together: Group theory and skills.* 6th ed. Needham Heights, MA: Allyn & Bacon.

Luckner, J. 1999. An examination of two co-teaching classrooms. *American Annals of the Deaf 144*(1): 24–34.

Magiera, K., C. Smith, N. Zigmond, and K. Gebauer. 2005. Benefits of co-teaching in secondary mathematics classes. *Teaching Exceptional Children 37*(3): 20–24.

Mahoney, M. 1997. Small victories in an inclusive classroom. *Educational Leadership 54*(7): 59–62.

Miller, A., W. Valasky, and P. Molloy. 1998. Learning together: The evolution of an inclusive class. *Active Learner: A Foxfire Journal for Teachers 3*(2): 14–16.

Nevin, A., J. Thousand, P. Paolucci-Whitcomb, and R. Villa. 1990. Collaborative consultation: Empowering public school personnel to provide heterogeneous schooling for all. *Journal of Educational and Psychological Consultation 1*(1): 41–67.

Pugach, M., and L. Johnson. 1995. Unlocking expertise among classroom teachers through structured dialogue: Extending research on peer collaboration. *Exceptional Children 62*(2): 101–10.

Rice, D., and N. Zigmond. 2000. Co-teaching in secondary schools: Teacher reports of developments in Australian and American classrooms. *Learning Disabilities Research and Practice* 15: 190–97.

Salazar, L., and A. Nevin. 2005. Co-teachers in an urban multicultural school. *Florida Educational Leadership* 5(2): 15–20.

Santamaria, L., and J. Thousand. 2004. Collaboration, co-teaching, and differentiated instruction: A process-oriented approach to whole schooling. *International Journal of Whole Schooling* 1(1): 13–27.

Schwab Learning. 2003. Collaboratively speaking: A study on effective ways to teach children with learning differences in the general education classroom. *The Special EDge* 16(3): 1–4.

Skrtic, T. 1987. The national inquiry into the future of education for students with special needs. *Counterpoint* 4(7): 6.

Thousand, J., A. Nevin, and W. Fox. 1987. Inservice training to support education of learners with severe handicaps in their local schools. *Teacher Education and Special Education* 10(1): 4–14.

Thousand, J., R. Villa, and A. Nevin. 2007. Collaborative teaching: Critique of the scientific evidence. In *Handbook of special education research,* ed. L. Florian, 417–28. London: Sage.

Thousand, J., R. Villa, A. Nevin, and P. Paolucci-Whitcomb. 1995. A rationale and vision for collaborative consultation. In *Controversial issues confronting special education: Divergent perspectives.* 2nd ed., ed. W. Stainback and S. Stainback, 223–32. Baltimore: Paul H. Brookes.

Trent, S. 1998. False starts and other dilemmas of a secondary general education collaborative teacher: A case study. *Journal of Learning Disabilities* 31: 503–13.

U.S. Department of Education. 2006. *Twenty-sixth annual report to Congress on the implementation of the Individuals with Disabilities Education Act.* Washington, DC: United States Department of Education.

———. 2007. Fact sheet series 2005—closing the achievement gap fact sheet.

Vaughn, S., B. Elbaum, J. Schumm, and M. Hughes. 1998. Social outcomes for students with and without learning disabilities in inclusive classrooms. *Journal of Learning Disabilities* 31: 428–36.

Villa, R., and J. Thousand. 2004. *Creating an inclusive school.* 2nd ed. Alexandria, VA: Association for Supervision and Curriculum Development.

Villa, R. A., J. S. Thousand, A. I. Nevin, and A. Liston. 2005. Successful inclusion practices in middle and secondary schools. *American Secondary Education Journal* 33(3): 33–50.

Villa, R., J. Thousand, A. Nevin, and C. Malgeri. 1996. Instilling collaboration for inclusive schooling as a way of doing business in public education. *Remedial and Special Education* 17: 169–81.

Walther-Thomas, C. 1997. Co-teaching experiences: The benefits and problems that teachers and principals report over time. *Journal of Learning Disabilities* 30: 395–407.

Welch, M. 2000. Descriptive analysis of team teaching in two elementary classrooms: A formative experimental approach. *Remedial and Special Education* 21: 366–76.

Zigmond, N. 2004. Research findings paint dark picture of co-teaching. *Inclusive Education Programs* 11(9): 1–3, 6.

Chapter 3: The Day-to-Day Workings of Co-Teaching Teams

Friend, M. 2008. *Co-teach! A manual for creating and sustaining effective classroom partnerships in inclusive schools.* Greensboro, NC: Marilyn Friend.

National Center for Educational Restructuring and Inclusion. 1995. *National study on inclusive education.* New York: City University of New York.

■ PART II: THE FOUR APPROACHES TO CO-TEACHING

Chapter 4: The Supportive Co-Teaching Approach

Doyle, M. B. 2002. *The paraprofessional's guide to inclusive education: Working as a team.* 2nd ed. Baltimore: Paul H. Brookes.

Villa, R., and J. Thousand. 2002. One divided by two or more: Redefining the role of a cooperative education team. In *Creativity and collaborative learning: The practical guide to empowering students, teachers, and families.* 2nd ed., ed. J. S. Thousand, R. A. Villa, and A. I. Nevin, 303–24. Baltimore: Paul H. Brookes.

Chapter 5: The Parallel Co-Teaching Approach

Carson, R. 2002. *Silent spring.* 40th anniv. ed. Boston: Houghton Mifflin.

Marzano, R., D. Pickering, and J. Pollock. 2001. *Classroom instruction that works: Research-based strategies for increasing student achievement.* Alexandria, VA: Association for Supervision and Curriculum Development.

Chapter 7: The Team Teaching Co-Teaching Approach

Armstrong, T. 2000. *Multiple intelligences in the classroom.* 2nd ed. Alexandria, VA: Association for Supervision and Curriculum Development.

Hazel, J., J. Schumaker, J. Sherman, and J. Sheldon. 1995. *ASSET: A social skills program for adolescents.* Champaign, IL: Research Press.

Marzano, R., D. Pickering, and J. Pollock. 2001. *Classroom instruction that works: Research-based strategies for increasing student achievement.* Alexandria, VA: Association for Supervision and Curriculum Development.

Vygotsky, L. 1987. *The collected works of L. S. Vygotsky.* Trans. R. W. Rieber and A. S. Carton. New York: Plenum Press. (Orig. pub. 1934, 1960).

■ PART III: CHANGING ROLES AND RESPONSIBILITIES

Chapter 8: The Role of Paraprofessionals in Co-Teaching

Ashbaker, B., and J. Morgan. 2005. *Paraprofessionals in the classroom.* Boston: Allyn & Bacon.

Bueno Center for Multicultural Education. 1997. *7 modules for para-educators in culturally and linguistically diverse classrooms.* Boulder: University of Colorado, Bilingual Special Education Training of Trainers Institute.

Downing, J., D. Ryndak, and D. Clark. 2000. Paraeducators in inclusive classrooms. *Remedial and Special Education* 21: 171–81.

Doyle, M. B. 2002. *The paraprofessional's guide to inclusive education: Working as a team.* 2nd ed. Baltimore: Paul H. Brookes.

Etscheidt, S. 2005. Paraprofessional services for students with disabilities: A legal analysis of issues. *Research and Practice for Persons With Severe Disabilities* 30: 60–80.

French, N. K. 2002. *Managing paraeducators in your school: How to hire, train, and supervise non-certified staff.* Thousand Oaks, CA: Corwin Press.

Gerlach, K. 2006. *Let's team up: A checklist for para-educators, teachers, and principals.* Reprint. Washington, DC: National Education Association.

Giangreco, M., C. Smith, and E. Pinckney. 2006. Addressing the paraprofessional dilemma in an inclusive classroom: A program description. *Research and Practice for Persons With Severe Disabilities* 31(3): 215–29.

Littleton, D. M. 1998. Preparing professionals as teachers for the urban classroom: A university/school collaborative model. *Action in Teacher Education* 19(4), 149–58.

Marks, S., C. Schrader, and M. Levine. 1999. Para-educator experiences in inclusive settings: Helping, hovering, or holding their own? *Exceptional Children* 65: 315–28.

Morgan, J., and B. Ahsbaker. 2001. Work more effectively with your paraeducator. *Intervention in School and Clinic* 36: 230–31.

Morgan, R., D. Forbush, and D. Avis. 2001. *Enhancing skills of para-educators: A video-assisted program.* 2nd ed. Logan: Utah State University, Technology, Research, and Instruction in Special Education.

Mueller, P. 2002. The paraeducator paradox. *Exceptional Parent* 32(9): 64–67.

Mueller, P., and F. Murphy. 2001. Determining when a student requires para-educator support. *Teaching Exceptional Children* 33(6): 22–27.

National Center for Education Statistics. 2000. Education statistics: Elementary and secondary schools and staffing survey: Non-professional staff in the schools and staffing survey (SASS) and common core of data (CCD). Working Paper 2000-13. Washington, DC: U.S. Department of Education, Office of Education Research.

Nevin, A., E. Cramer, J. Voigt, and L. Salazar. 2007. Instructional modifications, adaptations, and accommodations of co-teachers who loop: A case study. Paper presented at the American Educational Research Association, Special Education Research Special Interest Group, Chicago.

Perez, J., and J. Murdock. 1999. Investigating the effects of a paraprofessional teaching sharing behaviors to young children with special needs in an inclusive kindergarten classroom. Dissertation, University of New Orleans. *Dissertation Abstracts International*, AAT9900965, DAI-A 59/08: 2928.

Pickett, A. L., and K. Gerlach, eds. 1997. *Supervising para-educators in school settings: A team approach.* Austin, TX: PRO-ED.

———. 2003. *Supervising para-educators in school settings: A team approach.* 2nd ed. Austin, TX: PRO-ED.

Piletic, C., R. Davis, and A. Aschemeier. 2005. Paraeducators in physical education. *Journal of Physical Education Recreation and Dance* 76(5): 47–55.

Radaszewski-Byrne, M. 1997. Issues in the development of guidelines for the preparation and use of speech-language paraprofessionals and their Sl supervisors working in education settings. *Journal of Children's Communication Development 18*(1): 5–21.

Riggs, C., and P. Mueller. 2001. Employment and utilization of para-educators in inclusive settings. *Journal of Special Education 35*(1): 54–62.

Rogan, P., and M. Held. 1999. Paraprofessionals in job coach roles. *Journal of the Association for Persons with Severe Handicaps* 19: 32–42.

Rueda, R., and P. Monzo. 2002. Apprenticeship for teaching: Professional development issues surrounding the collaborative relationship between teachers and para-educators. *Teaching and Teacher Education* 18: 503–21.

Salazar, L., and A. Nevin. 2005. Co-teachers in an urban multicultural school. *Florida Educational Leadership 5*(2): 15–20.

Villa, R., and J. Thousand. 2005. *Creating an inclusive school.* 2nd ed. Alexandria, VA: Association for Supervision and Curriculum Development.

Wenger, K. J., T. Lubbes, M. Lazo, I. Azcarraga, S. Sharp, and G. Ernst-Slavit. 2004. Hidden teachers, invisible students: Lessons learned from exemplary bilingual paraprofessionals in secondary schools. *Teacher Education Quarterly 31*(1): 89–111.

Young, B. 1997. An examination of paraprofessional involvement in supporting inclusion of students with autism. *Focus on Autism and Other Developmental Disabilities 12*(1): 31–38, 48.

Chapter 9: The Role of Students as Co-Teachers

Chisholm, I. 1995. Computer use in a multicultural classroom. *Journal of Research on Computing in Education* 28: 162–74.

Conn-Powers, C. 2002. Upper elementary mathematics for a student with gifts and talents. In *Creativity and collaborative learning: The practical guide to empowering students, teachers, and families.* 2nd ed., ed. J. Thousand, R. Villa, and A. Nevin, 333–39. Baltimore: Paul H. Brookes.

Countryman, L., and M. Schroeder. 1996. When students lead parent–teacher conferences. *Educational Leadership 53*(7): 64–68.

Echevarria, J., and A. Graves. 1998. *Sheltered content instruction: Teaching English language learners with diverse abilities.* New York: Allyn & Bacon.

Faltis, C. 1993. Critical issues in the use of sheltered content teaching in high school bilingual programs. *Peabody Journal of Education* 69: 136–51.

Fuchs, D., L. Fuchs, P. Mathes, and E. Martinez. 2002. Preliminary evidence on the social standing of students with learning disabilities in PALS and non-PALS classrooms. *Learning Disabilities Research and Practice* 17: 205–15.

Fuchs, D., L. Fuchs, A. Thompson, S. Al Otaiba, K. Nyman, N. Yang, and E. Svenson. 2000. *Strengthening kindergartners' reading readiness in Title 1 and non-Title 1 schools.* Paper presented at the Pacific Coast Research Conference, La Jolla, CA.

Garcia, E. 2002. Using instructional conversations for content area learning. In *Student cultural diversity: Understanding and meeting the challenge.* 3rd ed., 392–93. New York: Houghton Mifflin.

————. 2005. *Teaching and learning in two languages.* New York: Teachers College Press.

Genesee, F., K. Lindholm-Leary, W. Saunders, and D. Christian. 2002. *Language learning and academic achievement: Executive summary.* Santa Cruz, CA: Center for Research on Education, Diversity, and Excellence. http://crede.berkeley .edu/research/crede/synthesis/llaa/llaa_exsum.html

Gersten, R., and S. Baker. 2000. What we know about effective instructional practices for English-language learners. *Exceptional Children* 66: 454–70.

Graves, A. W., R. Gersten, and D. Haager. 2004. Literacy instruction in multiple-language first-grade classrooms: Linking student outcomes to observed instructional practice. *Learning Disabilities Research & Practice* 19: 262–72.

Harris, T. 1994. Christine's inclusion: An example of peers supporting one another. In *Creativity and collaboration: A practical guide for students and teachers to implement cooperative group and partner learning, creative problem solving and social support systems.* 2nd ed., ed. R. Villa, J. Thousand, and A. Nevin, 293–301. Baltimore: Paul H. Brookes.

Hunter, M. 1988. *Motivation theory for teachers.* El Segundo, CA: Theory Into Practice.

Hunter, M. 1994. *Enhancing teaching.* New York: Macmillan College.

Hunter, R., and M. Hunter. 2006. *Madeline Hunter's mastery teaching: Increasing instructional effectiveness in elementary and secondary schools.* Thousand Oaks, CA: Corwin Press.

Johnson, D. W., and R. T. Johnson. 1989. *Cooperation and competition: Theory and research.* Edina, MN: Interaction Book Company.

————. 2000. Cooperative learning, values, and culturally plural classrooms. In *Classroom issues: Practice, pedagogy, and curriculum,* vol. 3, ed. M. Leicester, S. Modgill, and C. Modgill, 15–29. London: Falmer Press.

————. 2002. Ensuring diversity is positive: Cooperative community, constructive conflict, and civic values. In *Creativity and collaborative learning: The practical guide to empowering students, teachers, and families.* 2nd ed., ed. J. Thousand, R. Villa, and A. Nevin, 197–208. Baltimore: Paul H. Brookes.

Johnson, D., R. Johnson, and E. Holubec. 1998. *Circles of learning: Cooperation in the classroom.* 6th ed. Edina, MN: Interaction Book Company.

Kluth, P., R. Diaz-Greenberg, J. Thousand, and A. Nevin. 2002. Teaching for liberation: Promising practices from critical pedagogy. In *Creativity and collaborative learning: The practical guide to empowering students, teachers, and families.* 2nd ed., ed. J. Thousand, R. Villa, and A. Nevin, 71–84. Baltimore: Paul H. Brookes.

Kourea, L., G. Cartledge, and S. Musti-Rao. 2007. Improving the reading skills of urban elementary students through total class peer tutoring. *Remedial and Special Education* 28: 95–107.

LaPlant, L., and N. Zane. 2002. Partner learning systems. In *Creativity and collaborative learning: The practical guide to empowering students, teachers, and families.* 2nd ed., ed. J. Thousand, R. Villa, and A. Nevin, 271–83. Baltimore: Paul H. Brookes.

Palinscar, A., and A. Brown. 1984. Reciprocal teaching of comprehension: Fostering and monitoring activities. *Cognition and Instruction* 1: 117–75.

Villa, R., and J. Thousand. 2004. *Creating inclusive schools.* 2nd ed. Alexandria, VA: Association for Supervision and Curriculum Development.

Walter, T. 1998. *Amazing English!* New York: Addison-Wesley.

■ PART IV: ADMINISTRATIVE SUPPORT AND PROFESSIONAL DEVELOPMENT

Chapter 10: Training and Logistical Administrative Support for Co-Teaching

Bauwens, J., and P. Mueller. 2000. Maximizing the mindware of human resources. In *Restructuring for caring and effective education: Piecing the puzzle together,* ed. R. Villa and J. Thousand, 328–59. Baltimore: Paul H. Brookes.

Cook, L. 2004. *Co-teaching: Principles, practices, and pragmatics.* Paper presented at the New Mexico Public Education Department Quarterly Special Education Meeting, Albuquerque.

Cramer, E., A. Nevin, J. Thousand, and A. Liston. 2006. Co-teaching in Urban School districts to meet the needs of all teachers and learners: Implications for teacher education reform. Paper presented at the annual meeting of the American Association of Colleges for Teacher Education, San Diego. (ERIC Document Reproduction Service No. ED491651)

Friend, M. 1996. *The power of two: Making a difference through co-teaching.* VHS. Port Chester, NY: National Professional Resources.

Hall, G. E., and S. M. Hord. 2001. *Implementing change: Patterns, principles, and potholes.* Needham Heights, MA: Allyn & Bacon.

Johnson, D. W., and R. Johnson. 1999. *Learning together and alone: Cooperative, competitive, and individualistic learning.* Needham Heights, MA: Allyn & Bacon.

McLaughlin, M. V. 1991. The Rand change agent study: 10 years later. In *Education policy implementation,* ed. A. R. Odden, 143–56. Albany: State University of New York Press.

Roy, P. 2005, February. A fresh look at follow-up. http://www.nsdc.org/library/publications/results/res2-05roy.cfm

Thousand, J., and R. Villa. 2000. Collaborative teams: A powerful tool in school restructuring. In *Restructuring for caring and effective education: Piecing the puzzle together,* ed. R. Villa and J. Thousand, 254–91. Baltimore: Paul H. Brookes.

Thousand, J. S., R. A. Villa, and A. I. Nevin. 2006. What special education administrators need to know about co-teaching. *In CASE* 43(6): 2–3, 5.

———. 2007a. *Differentiating instruction: Collaborative planning and teaching for universally designed learning.* Thousand Oaks, CA: Corwin Press.

———. 2007b. *Differentiating instruction: Collaboratively planning and teaching for universally designed learning: A multimedia kit for professional development.* Thousand Oaks, CA: Corwin Press.

Tomlinson, C. 1999. *The differentiated classroom: Responding to the needs of all learners.* Alexandria, VA. Association for Supervision and Curriculum Development.

Udvari-Solner, A., R. Villa, and J. Thousand. 2002. Access to the general education curriculum for all: The universal design process. In *Creativity and collaborative learning: The practical guide to empowering students, teachers, and families.* 2nd ed., ed. J. Thousand, R. Villa, and A. Nevin, 85–103. Baltimore: Paul H. Brookes.

Villa, R. 2002a. *Collaborative planning: Transforming theory into practice.* VHS. Port Chester, NY: National Professional Resources.

———. 2002b. *Collaborative teaching: The co-teaching model.* VHS. Port Chester, NY: National Professional Resources.

Villa, R., and J. Thousand. 2004. *Creating an inclusive school.* 2nd ed. Alexandria, VA: Association for Supervision and Curriculum Development.

Villa, R., J. Thousand, and A. Nevin. 2008. *Facilitator's guide to* A guide to co-teaching: Practical tips for facilitating student learning: *A multimedia kit for professional development.* Thousand Oaks, CA: Corwin Press.

Chapter 11: Meshing Planning With Co-Teaching

Raywid, M. A. 1993. Finding time for collaboration. *Educational Leadership 51*(1): 30–34.

Thousand, J., A. Liston, and A. Nevin. 2006. Differentiating instruction in inclusive classrooms: Myth or reality? (A lesson plan and process for using principles of universal design). Paper presented at the annual conference of Teacher Education Division, Council for Exceptional Children, San Diego, CA. (ERIC Document Reproduction Service No. ED493953.)

Thousand, J., and R. Villa. 2000. Collaborative teams: A powerful tool in school restructuring. In *Restructuring for caring and effective education: Piecing the puzzle together,* ed. R. Villa and J. Thousand, 254–91. Baltimore: Paul H. Brookes.

Chapter 12: From Surviving to Thriving: Tips for Getting Along With Your Co-Teachers

Bradley, D., J. Pauley, and J. Pauley. 2006. *Effective classroom management: Six keys to success.* Lanham, MD: Rowman & Littlefield.

Glasser, W. 1999. *Choice theory: A new psychology of personal freedom.* New York: Perennial.

Johnson, D., and R. Johnson. 1988. *Advanced cooperative learning.* Edina, MN: Interaction Book Company.

———. 1991. *Teaching children to be peacemakers.* Edina, MN: Interaction Book Company.

Kahler, T. 1982. *Process communication model: A contemporary model for organizational development.* Little Rock, AR: Kahler Communications.

Keefe, E. B., V. M. Moore, and F. R. Duff. 2004. The four "knows" of collaborative teaching. *Teaching Exceptional Children 36*(5): 36–42.

Pauley, J., D. Bradley, and J. Pauley. 2002. *Here's how to reach me: Matching instruction to personality types in your classroom.* Baltimore: Paul H. Brookes.

Schrumpf, F., and G. Jansen. 2002. The role of students in resolving conflicts. In *Creativity and collaborative learning: The practical guide to empowering students, teachers, and families.* 2nd ed., ed. R. Villa, J. Thousand, and A. Nevin, 283–302. Baltimore: Paul H. Brookes.

Villa, R., J. Thousand, and A. Nevin. 1999. Eight habits of highly effective collaborators. *Missouri Educational Leadership 9*(2): 25–29.

■ EPILOGUE

Udvari-Solner, A., R. Villa, and J. Thousand. 2002. Access to the general education curriculum for all: The universal design process. In *Creativity and collaborative learning: The practical guide to empowering students, teachers, and families.* 2nd ed., ed. J. Thousand, R. Villa, and A. Nevin, 85–103. Baltimore: Paul H. Brookes.

■ GLOSSARY

Gardner, H. 1983. *Frames of mind: The theory of multiple intelligences.* New York: Basic Books.

———. 1997. Are there additional intelligences? The case of naturalistic, spiritual, and existential intelligences. In *Education, information, and transformation,* ed. J. Kane, 135–52. Upper Saddle River, NJ: Prentice Hall.

Graner, P., M. Faggella-Luby, and N. Fritschmann. 2005. An overview of responsiveness to intervention: What practitioners ought to know. *Topics in Language Disorders,* 25: 93–105.

Hall, G. E., and S. M. Hord. 2001. *Implementing change: Patterns, principles, and potholes.* Needham Heights, MA: Allyn & Bacon.

Hall, T. 2002. *Differentiated instruction.* http://www.cast.org/publications/ncac/ncac_diffinstruc.html

Kahler, T. 1982. *Process communication model: A contemporary model for organizational development.* Little Rock, AR: Kahler Communications.

Pauley, J., D. Bradley, and J. Pauley. 2002. *Here's how to reach me: Matching instruction to personality types in your classroom.* Baltimore: Paul H. Brookes.

Vygotsky, L. 1987. *The collected works of L. S. Vygotsky.* Trans. R. W. Rieber and A. S. Carton. New York: Plenum Press. (Orig. pub. 1934, 1960).

Index

CORWIN
PRESS

The Corwin Press logo—a raven striding across an open book—represents the union of courage and learning. Corwin Press is committed to improving education for all learners by publishing books and other professional development resources for those serving the field of PreK–12 education. By providing practical, hands-on materials, Corwin Press continues to carry out the promise of its motto: **"Helping Educators Do Their Work Better."**

The worldwide mission of The Council for Exceptional Children is to improve educational outcomes for individuals with exceptionalities.

CEC, a non-profit association, accomplishes its mission, which is carried out in support of special education professionals and others working on behalf of individuals with exceptionalities, by advocating for appropriate governmental policies, by setting professional standards, by providing continuing professional development, by advocating for newly and historically underserved individuals with exceptionalities, and by helping professionals achieve the conditions and resources necessary for effective professional practice.